The Razor's Edge

Bob Dylan
and the
Never Ending Tour

by

Andrew Muir

Helter
Skelter

publishing

First published in 2001 by Helter Skelter Publishing
4 Denmark Street, London WC2H 8LL

First edition
Text copyright Andrew Muir © 2001
The moral right of the author has been asserted
Photographs copyright see picture credits page

Design by Bold; Typesetting by Caroline Walker
Printed by The Bath Presss

Every effort has been made to contact the copyright holders of the photographs in this book, but one or two were unreachable. The publishers would be grateful if those concerned would contact Helter Skelter Publishing.

A CIP record for this book is available from the British Library

ISBN 1-900924-13-7

The Razor's Edge

Bob Dylan
and the
Never Ending Tour

by

Andrew Muir

Helter Skelter Publishing, London

To Pia

"The lamp of my soul...."

Contents

Introduction

This book concerns itself with what Bob Dylan originally dubbed, and his fans still call, the Never Ending Tour (or N.E.T.), which began on 7th June 1988 at the Concord Pavilion, Concord, California and is still going strong as I type this in the year 2000: over 1,200 shows in the last 13 years.

My aim is to put the vast and unwieldy N.E.T. into some kind of perspective: to examine its importance in the context of Dylan's overall career; and to chronicle the comparisons and contrasts between each individual leg of the tour. But this book isn't just about the N.E.T. as a lengthy episode in the life of Bob Dylan. The Never Ending Tour has also become a phenomenon in my life – the life of a fan who has travelled to a substantial number of these shows over the years and who has listened to tapes (or watched video footage) of many of the others. These unofficial recordings have been obtained over the years via fan networks, initially on C-90 tape and now more often on CD-Rs or as MP3s. Now I check my e-mail inbox for songs each morning, for any live debuts of a song.

To be specific, I want to tell you about my N.E.T. – the fan's experience of a tour that has already lasted more than a decade, and which has affected its followers as deeply as the artist who ostensibly stands at the centre of the proceedings. That experience has been both a cherished and an exhilarating one, though admittedly not without a degree of obsession that borders on the unbalanced. However, this is not simply a fan's memoir; I do intend to bring some critical analysis, objectivity and balance to my account, though these are not always qualities that I can guarantee to take to the shows themselves!

The sheer scale of the N.E.T., which stretches over an era that inevitably has brought major changes in one's own life, is overwhelming. It is amusing to imagine what a fan would have felt in 1988 had he been told that Dylan would tour continually for at least the next thirteen years; and then that he would be playing mainly with a small back-up band in relatively intimate settings as well as the occasional arena and stadium tour.[1] No fan would have believed it, far less that Dylan would play countless wonderful, unexpected songs, and undertake residencies at favoured venues where the set-lists would change so drastically from one night to the next that sometimes barely one song would be repeated at consecutive shows.

Yet, that is exactly what did happen, and here is one fan's story of how it unfolded for him.

Prologue

Any study of Dylan's career prior to the N.E.T. would demand a huge book in itself, and I do not plan to repeat that well-documented story. Since the N.E.T. began at what was widely regarded as a commercially and artistically low point in his career, however, it may be worth pointing out – using the broadest of brushstrokes – just what Dylan had already given to the world, before I pick up his story in the late 1980s.

Dylan's early years could be characterised as a journey from Woody Guthrie-clone to The Prince of Protest. Emerging from the early 60s Greenwich Village music scene, he quickly became the acknowledged master of the protest song, wielding an enormous influence on the Civil Rights movement with songs that denounced racism, war-mongering, poverty and injustice. Acoustic anthems and legendary ballads such as "Blowin' In The Wind", "Masters Of War", "Oxford Town", The Times They Are A-Changin'", and "The Lonesome Death Of Hattie Carroll" – to name but a very few – not only profoundly affected millions of listeners, but also arguably became part of the history of the times.

At the same time Dylan was producing some of his most affecting love songs, including "Girl From The North Country", "Don't Think Twice, It's All Right", "One Too Many Mornings", "Boots Of Spanish Leather" and "Tomorrow Is A Long Time".

These early years alone would have been enough to make Dylan a legend, but in 1964 he upped the ante by moving from Folk Idol to Rock Demi-God, producing over the course of little more than two years a string of visionary social critiques, intense profiles of the psychological minefields of relationships and more truly rapturous love songs. Oh yes – along the way, he also changed the world of popular song forever. At this time, Dylan seemed to be a veritable fountain of poetic insight. The many highlights from this period of inspiration form a breathtaking oeuvre that includes "Chimes Of Freedom", "It Ain't Me, Babe", "Maggie's Farm", "Love Minus Zero/No Limit", "Mr. Tambourine Man", "Gates Of Eden", "It's Alright, Ma (I'm Only Bleeding)", "It's All Over Now, Baby Blue", "Like A Rolling Stone", "Ballad Of A Thin Man", "Queen Jane Approximately", "Desolation Row", "Visions Of Johanna", "I Want You", "Stuck Inside Of Mobile With The Memphis Blues Again", "Just Like A Woman" and "Sad-Eyed Lady Of The Lowlands".

Dylan's plunge into the maelstrom of his "electric" tour of 1966 was followed by media reports of a motorcycle crash and a subsequent retreat from the madness into rural life and a search for a simpler truth. The first fruits of this quest, *The Basement Tapes* and *John Wesley Harding*, can stand proudly alongside anything in his canon. The focus may have changed but, at first, anyway, the fecundity and profundity were unchecked. Key songs from 1967 include "Tears Of Rage", "I Shall Be Released", "You Ain't Going Nowhere", "This Wheel's On Fire", "Quinn, The Eskimo (The Mighty Quinn)", "I Dreamed I Saw St. Augustine", "All Along The Watchtower", "I Pity The Poor Immigrant" and "I'll Be Your Baby Tonight". The last-named signified a move from rural retreat into a period of creativity-diminishing contentment.

Although the next album, *Nashville Skyline*, had its moments, ("I Threw It All Away", "Lay Lady Lay", "Tell Me That It Isn't True", "Tonight, I'll Be Staying Here With You"), it was essentially a slight offering compared to its predecessors. Nevertheless, for the counter-culture's undisputed leader to emerge with an album of "redneck" country music was extremely brave – and provocative. Dylan's courage was rewarded when the hit single "Lay Lady Lay" helped make *Nashville Skyline* Dylan's best selling – if least compelling – album to date.

Still, with much of the rock world following Dylan "back to the garden" (to borrow Joni Mitchell's phrase), like the eponymous "hero" of "John Wesley Harding", he could reasonably be said during the mid-60s to "never [have been] known to make a foolish move". Decades later, these are still the years for which Dylan is lauded: honoured at award ceremonies, feted by film stars, politicians, presidents and cultural gurus as one of the great artistic geniuses of the 20th Century.

The huge influence – on musicians, on society, on history – of Dylan's songs from this period is something that he has had to live with ever since, and it would be fair to say that he has not found that an easy task. The man had opened millions of eyes to the inequalities of the day: he not only told them what to see but also, in the words of David Bowie's "Song For Bob Dylan", "sat behind a million eyes and told them how they saw".[2] Indeed, he had assumed a central place in the lives of an entire generation. Such a level of responsibility was an intolerable burden, and one Dylan has tried to shake off ever since that 1966 motorcycle accident.

As the album market continued to expand at the turn of the decade, Dylan's reputation and mystique did likewise, making 1970's *Self Portrait* another big seller. It was also a huge disappointment; being a portrait of a self that nobody wanted to know, far less acknowledge as Bob Dylan. The "I am not the person you think I am" battle was apparently going to run and run.

Patchy success followed with 1970's *New Morning* and the subsequent, and rather lovely, *Pat Garrett and Billy The Kid* soundtrack album, which did yield one of Dylan's biggest and most enduring hits, "Knockin' On Heaven's Door". Nonetheless, the period 1968-1973 seemed a barren desert when compared to the ocean of brilliance of 1962-1967.

Fortunately, the mid-70s brought about a re-awakening. Nineteen seventy-four's *Planet Waves* album, a hastily-produced mix of the banal and the brilliant, reunited Dylan with his old sparring partners from 1966-67, The Band,

and their resulting "comeback tour" of stadiums, capitalising on the return of the supposed 60's idol[3], was a huge commercial – if qualified artistic – success.

The genuine "return" of Dylan's mercurial genius came in 1975 with the release of *Blood On The Tracks*, a record that not only lived up to his previous achievements but that proudly stood as the single greatest album he had produced. On the road, too, his creativity returned in spades, with 1975 and 1976 witnessing Dylan deliver two of his finest ever tours. Nineteen seventy-six also saw the release of his chart-topping *Desire* album – a fine work, though it did not match the overall brilliance of its predecessor.

For all the acclaim garnered by *Blood* and *Desire*, Dylan's popularity in the States was beginning to diminish by 1976. His four-hour epic arthouse movie, *Renaldo and Clara*, was ripped to shreds by the press. Worse, Dylan's next studio album, *Street Legal*, was by far his least successful release of the decade in the US.

However, beyond American shores it was a completely different story. When in 1978 Dylan embarked on his first world tour since 1966, enormous media attention, magnificent shows and legions of delirious fans kept Dylan very much in the international spotlight and *Street Legal* topped the charts in many countries. In the UK, the album's first single, "Baby Stop Crying", even made the Top 20 – and was played on *Top Of The Pops*. *Renaldo and Clara* also received a somewhat more sympathetic press in Europe (especially France), though it was still, more often than not, heavily panned, and overseas too it was a financial flop. Dylan also had other matters on his mind. A messy divorce from his wife, Sara, was turning his life upside down.

In perhaps the biggest shock of a shock-filled career, after Dylan lost Sara, he found Jesus....

Chapter One

Live Aid and Beyond

Street Legal's poor US sales notwithstanding, Dylan was still very much regarded as rock's main man in 1978. He had, after all, survived punk – along with perhaps only Neil Young from the old guard. The UK's hugely influential *New Musical Express* may have switched to a predominately punk-based content, but it still lauded Dylan's shows and excitedly revealed the mutual admiration that he and The Clash felt for each other's work.

In this context, Dylan's highly publicised conversion to Christianity in 1979 dealt a hammer blow to his worldwide following. Dylan had taught his fans to think for themselves and reject false leaders. It would have been difficult for them to cope with Dylan espousing any kind of authoritarian belief system; it was downright unthinkable for most of them to accept Dylan's chosen religious path. It wasn't just that Dylan had become a born-again Christian[4], but that his conversion seemed to have taken him in a disturbing direction, where authoritarianism – "Well, it may be the devil or it may be the Lord/ But you're gonna have to serve somebody" ("Gotta Serve Somebody") – was to be found alongside racism –

"Sheikhs walking around like kings, wearing fancy jewels and nose rings/ Deciding America's future from Amsterdam and Paris" ("Slow Train").

Even more disturbing statements could be heard in Dylan's "preaching" at concerts where homophobia[5] was accompanied by paranoid "political" ranting[6] and pure out-to-lunch wackiness:

"....god of this world, prince of the power of the sin. That's the devil and he's infiltrated into e-v-e-r-y thing. Medicine, science, you name it, he's there.

"You know we read in the newspapers every day how bad the world is getting. The situation in Iran, the students rebelling, you know, even over here they're rebelling. They don't let the Iranians sneak into the whorehouses. But that don't matter much because we know this world will be destroyed.

"Well, let ... me tell you now: the devil owns this world: he's called the god of this world.

"Every time God comes against a nation, first of all he comes against their economy. If that doesn't work, He comes against their ecology... He did it with Egypt. He did it with Persia. He did it with Babylon. He did it with the whole Middle East. It's desert now. It used to be flourishing gardens. Alright. If that doesn't work He just brings up another nation against them. So one of these three things has got to work. Now Jesus Christ is that solid rock. He's supposed to come two times. He came once already – He's coming back again. You gotta be prepared for this. No matter what you read in the newspapers, that's all deceit. The real truth is that He's coming back already. You just watch your newspapers, you're gonna see – maybe two years, maybe three years, five years from now, you just wait and see."

So said Dylan on April 20th, 1980 at Toronto.

John Lennon is perhaps the only other rock writer-performer to have enjoyed as iconic, and iconoclastic, a status as Dylan. While discussing Bob's Christian song "Gotta Serve Somebody",[7] the former Beatle publicly avowed that Dylan should be allowed to do and say what he wanted. "...Whatever reason he's doing it...it's a personal reason for him and he needs to do it," Lennon maintained. "I'm not distressed by the fact that Dylan is doing what Dylan wants to do ... If that's what he wants to do, he has to do that now, you know, let him do it... "[8]

Ironically, Lennon added: "But I must say I was surprised ... when old Bobby Boy did go that way. You know, very surprised. I'm sure I wasn't the only one ... because all I ever hear whenever I hear him ... is: '*Don't follow leaders/ Watch your parking meters*' [sic]."

Lennon's off-the-cuff remark echoed the widespread shock engendered when Dylan seemed either oblivious to – or felt himself above? – the irony that he, of all people, was denying others the freedom to think for themselves. Even as he was preaching:

"I told you that 'The Times They Are A Changin'' 20 years ago, and I don't believe I've ever lied to you.... Never told you to vote for nobody; never told you to follow nobody." – he was singing: "*You're gonna have to serve somebody*."

Perhaps unsurprisingly given Dylan's fervent commitment to his new faith, the "Christian tours" found him performing at an astonishing level, vocally and musically. Only the very best of his mid-sixties and mid-seventies shows can match the passion, subtlety and mesmeric vocal and musical power of those performances. The message may have been unpalatable, but few who have heard the shows with open ears have been anything less than enthralled by their presentation.

By the time of his 1981 tours of Europe and America, Dylan was mixing old songs and new songs rather than sticking to the "Christian ones". It was a year of many great vocal performances, and wonderful playing by a talented band. I saw the shows in London at Earls Court and was appalled that the seats were empty till the moment Bob was due to take the stage. This casual attitude was a graphic illustration of the audience's shocking drop in attention since his previous Earls Court shows back in 1978, when the hall had been packed long before Dylan appeared. Still, at least he could still sell out large venues back then.

The shows themselves were fine; in particular the newer songs shone. "In the Summertime" was gorgeous while "I Believe In You" was literally spine-tingling; but there were also notable performances of older material like "Simple Twist of Fate" and "Girl From The North Country".

"In the Summertime" hailed from *Shot of Love*, an album released to poor reviews and even poorer sales. Its follow-up, *Infidels*, and associated videos and TV appearances improved matters somewhat. (Though goodness knows how much more of a positive impact *Infidels* would have made, had the finished album included the best tracks from the sessions.) Although *Infidels* was initially panned by *Rolling Stone*, the magazine, like other commentators, subsequently deemed it a "return to form". Dylan was back – "the 60s man was singing protest songs for the 80s"; and all that kind of nonsense. Dylan built on this resurgence of critical acclaim by giving a great performance on the *Late Night With David Letterman* TV show in March 1984. He then played a tour of European stadiums, co-billed with Santana. The shows had a somewhat mixed reception amongst fans, but certainly sold well and garnered a fair share of media attention.

Still, these were small victories. Undeniably, as the decade reached its midpoint, Dylan's career badly needed a shot in the arm. Instead, Dylan nearly shot it dead.

From Philadelphia to Concord

1985's massive Live Aid charity rock concert, in aid of African famine relief, drew a worldwide audience estimated at anywhere up to two billion. When guitar icon Eric Clapton was asked who he thought should close the event, he opined that Dylan was the only possible choice. In fact he seemed astonished the question should even be asked. Certainly Dylan's career achievements dwarfed those of any rock act still performing, but it was equally clear that his lofty reputation had little to do with his work in the 1980s. Still, here was a chance for Dylan to re-assert both his primacy and contemporary relevance.

It is arguably admirable that, as we will see, he chose not to exploit this fund-raising event as a way of rejuvenating his career. The album charts, on both sides of the Atlantic, would soon be full of records by people who had impressed at Live Aid, with the *Greatest Hits* of hypocritical Sun City patrons Queen the most conspicuous. Dylan albums would not be joining them, for Bob ended the successful day-long spectacular on a sour, deflating note.

I watched the event on television, along with most of the people on the planet. There were one or two performers on the bill that I still admired – Elvis Costello, for example – and a few other senior acts I was curious to see. However, I watched the Global Jukebox, as it became known, first and foremost as a Bob fan – for me, Live Aid was another concert that Dylan would be headlining and I spent the entire day geared up in anticipation of his appearance. For sure, reservations notwithstanding, I was aware that the fundraiser was palpably a good and extraordinary thing, but I was more excited by the promise of Dylan's performance than by what was being done for Ethiopia, and throughout the event, I kept my ears pinned back for any mention or cover of his Bobness. A completely over-the-top, impassioned, soul version of "Forever Young" further whetted my appetite for the man himself, despite it being many hours before he was due to appear.

Finally, at 3:39am UK time, Dylan was given a magnificent introduction by Jack Nicholson – which turned out to be the best part of Dylan's "set". "Some artists' work speaks for itself," Nicholson began. "Some artists' work speaks for its generation. It is my deep, personal pleasure to present to you one of America's great voices of freedom. It can only be one man – the transcendent BOB DYLAN...."

A rather puffy, soon to be sweaty, Dylan emerged onto the stage, looked around and then addressed the audience: "Let me introduce some people who just came along tonight, Keith Richards and Ron Wood – I don't know where they are."

Wood and Richards appeared a few moments later, both looking and acting as though they had just been interrupted in the middle of a backstage party – it all looked very spontaneous but, in fact, Dylan had invited them to join him well before the day of the show.

The whole planet was watching; but unfortunately our boys didn't seem to be on it. Keef and Ronnie were certainly appropriate guests – especially given Mick Jagger's preceding piece of showmanship with Tina Turner – but the problem was that they were on acoustic guitars and – especially in Keith's case – didn't seem to realise it. Nor did they seem to have any idea which songs they were playing. Wood was concentrating so hard on smoking his cigarette that he completely ignored his guitar until well into the first song. While Richards did not shun his instrument quite so blatantly, it was not entirely clear what he was doing with it.

Still, initially things looked fairly hopeful. When Dylan began singing "Ballad of Hollis Brown" his voice was clear and strong and the line, "*Is there anyone who knows, is there anyone who cares?*", got a cheer from some attentive folk in the audience. Unfortunately, some terrible feedback immediately unsettled Dylan. He just about managed to hold it together, but the song fizzled out pretty weakly.

Dylan followed this inauspicious version of a well-chosen song with a startlingly inappropriate little speech. He initially explained that he "thought that was a fitting song for this important occasion....". However, it soon became clear that he had something more on his mind. "I'd just like to say," he continued, "I hope that some of the money that's raised for the people in Africa, maybe they could take just a little bit of it, maybe one or two million maybe, and use it say to pay the, uh, the mortgages in some of the farms, mmm, that the farmers here owe to the banks."

Given the situation, I found – and still find – the comments indefensible. There are two main points people make when they attempt to justify Dylan's bizarre speech. The first is that Dylan was bucking the trend by speaking out about something important on a day of self-satisfied superstar smugness and cynical careerism; and the second that he was only bravely standing up for the truth in the old saying "charity begins at home".

On the first point, far be it from me to be against Dylan bucking a trend – and yes, there were undeniably cynical elements to the day. Seeing Queen, who had broken the Western boycott of apartheid-ridden Sun City, boosting their career while getting credit for helping starving Africans, made one even keener than usual to discover what a true individual like Bob Dylan would make of the whole event. However, the cynicism of some performers should not be allowed to colour one's judgement of the entire event.

"The purpose of Live Aid was to raise money," event organiser Bob Geldof maintained. "If a band sold a million records, it meant more people would watch than if they sold a thousand. If more people contributed, more people lived. If I have a choice between Steel Pulse or Wham! on this show, I'll take Wham!"

To fully appreciate the appalling impact of Dylan's speech, it is essential to see it in the exact context of the night. Just before 3.30am, a shattered, ill-looking Geldof appeared on UK television to thank those who had pledged donations, and to implore the viewers to donate further. He also made a final plea against the insanity and inhumanity of mass starvation in the Third World during an era of Western prosperity, railing against the ignorance and indifference of Western political leaders.

"...Again I pose the question that I've yet to receive an answer to," he raged, "Why, if we sit on food surplus stocks, why are there people dying? Why don't they simply open the gates to these silos and send it to those people?"

Asked how he pulled the event off, Geldof retorted, "You have to find a cause that is above moral or political argument – everybody agrees 130 million people dying is wrong...."

With eyes nearly closing with fatigue Geldof made one last plea to the audience to open their wallets. The camera then switched to the studio presenter. "You are looking absolutely shattered," he told Geldof. "Quite obviously it has been a very long day for you.... Well, sit back and enjoy this, because at JFK Stadium in the Philadelphia we can now go to Bob Dylan and the finale."

Moments later, the bleary-eyed Europeans who had stayed up for the great finale heard Dylan ask for money to be taken away from the starving African children, whose cause Geldof had so passionately put forward, to be used to pay mortgage loans to rich American banks. Regardless of Dylan's motives, this was a slap in the face to all that was good about the day. Also, it is hard to determine how daring Dylan actually was: his words were greeted by a large cheer from the American crowd – though it is impossible to tell if this was because, impervious to the starvation of the faceless black African masses, the well-heeled, mostly white Philadelphia crowd agreed with him, or because they were simply ready to cheer anything Dylan said.

Furthermore, Dylan just came across as petty and mean; there was certainly no offer of any of his own millions to help kick the "one or two million off". Which brings me to the second point – that "charity begins at home". Even if one agrees with Dylan on this count, this was hardly the time or the place. Why not wait a week and hold a press conference acknowledging Live Aid's success and suggesting a similar fundraiser for American farmers? Hell, even the next day wouldn't have seemed so crass – but to make this point at the climax to the whole Live Aid day was to me shameful. To directly equate the plight of struggling Western farmers[9] with that of starving babies with distended stomachs, disease-ridden bodies, and faces covered in flies they were too weak to brush off; desperate for any water or food at all far less medical aid was... well, the last words on this issue should go to Geldof himself, who accused Bob of "a complete lack of understanding of the issues raised by Live Aid...". Clearly riled, Geldof continued: "Live Aid was about people losing their lives. There is a radical difference between losing your livelihood and losing your life. It did instigate Farm Aid, which was a good thing in itself, but it was a crass, stupid, and nationalistic thing to say."[10]

Having made his little speech, Dylan went into his second song, "When The Ship Comes In". It sounded OK at the beginning, if a little thin. However, by now the level of intrusive background noise was so loud that it must have seemed like retribution for his outburst. Dylan, who later used the word "sabotaged" when talking about it, occasionally glanced at Keith Richards, who remained obliviously in happy, smiling, rock guitarist mode.

Soon Dylan started to sweat: the strain was beginning to tell. The song became increasingly tuneless and Dylan's attempt at a harmonica break had to be curtailed. Presumably by now almost unable to hear himself, he screeched towards the song's conclusion; shouting the lyrics and vainly trying to put the right emphasis on the right word. A wry grimace and self-deprecating smile after "conquered" let us know he probably had a good idea how this sounded. Ron and Keith tried to buddy-buddy him on stage and lift his spirits, but things were going very badly. The song ended to muted cheering. Dylan asked the crowd if the sound was OK, and then asked how much time he had left. To be honest, you felt he was hoping there wasn't much.

Then it was into "Blowin' In the Wind" – pretty apt considering another hugely obvious answer was blowin' around the whole world – with Dylan's voice cracking in the second line. He recovered sufficiently to give it a fair reading.

Dylan then introduced a Keith Richards solo. The camera caught Dylan turning his face to Ron and looking to the sky. It was a clear gesture that Dylan had no idea what Keith would do, and Ron seemed to feel the same. To be fair to Keith, the solo was probably completely unplanned and a cover for Dylan to do something about a problem he had with his own guitar. Dylan's guitar then broke down completely and he had to take Ron's. Keith ended his solo before the instrument swap was completed and Dylan did really well to keep singing as he tried to strap on his replacement guitar. Ron got a guitar from a roadie a verse later but it seemed, to put it mildly, to be a stranger to him. I am not sure it had a single string properly tuned.

The whole thing ended with a "thank you". Lionel Richie came on and cuddled them all and the curtains opened to reveal nearly all of the day's participants gathered for a massed finale. Bob initially remained near the front of the stage, playing a few guitar licks, then – somewhat comically – he ran off to the side like a small schoolboy rushing to meet his pals. He nudged Richie in the back on his way past – presumably to let him know he would not be singing his line in "We Are the World".

There are many excuses for Dylan's performance; not least, the situation on stage was chaotic at best. Perhaps, though, proper preparation would have helped. The circulating tapes of rehearsals – other than being a more unlikely discovery than the Loch Ness Monster – show the boys had been enjoying themselves, but the quality of the rehearsal performances[11] was so bad that Ron Wood speculated on how terrible it would be if Dylan were to mess things up on the night in front of so many people. Ironically, he and Richards reassured themselves that this would not happen.

Perhaps, also, less partying before the event would have helped; but to be fair to Dylan, lack of preparation and indulgence in pre-concert "refreshments" have, both before and since, led to some sparkling performances. Certainly, at the start Dylan's voice sounded unaffected by any backstage revels.

When questioned about the shambles, Rod Stewart commented that they should have let Bob Dylan go on stage alone: "He's the best in the world at that". Unfortunately, it was Dylan's decision to have two Stones with him. And, to some degree at least, it was Dylan's fault that they had no idea what they were supposed to be doing on the stage.

To make things worse, Dylan looked awful. His bloated and sweaty frame was such a depressing contrast to the wiry, ultra-cool Dylan of previous years. He seemed a sad, bitter and marginalised figure at an event that he should have totally dominated.

His appearance, performance and embarrassing words brought him to an all-time low. Quite an achievement given an audience of somewhere between one and two billion on a plate.

***

So, by the summer of 1985, Dylan had managed to lose any ground he had reclaimed with *Infidels* and his career had reached its nadir. He had to start turning things around.

Dylan followed Live Aid's global showcase with a low-key performance at a poetry festival in Moscow. His next gig was at the Memorial Stadium, Champagne, Illinois – at the first Farm Aid show, inspired by his ill-judged remarks at Live Aid (organiser Debra Winger heard Dylan's comments and thought, "Yes, I agree with that"!). This gave him a chance to redeem himself in front of a vast audience.

Farm Aid united another all-star cast and enjoyed, if not a global audience to begin with, a huge American one. This time, though, the Dylan fan did not need to worry; the contrast with Live Aid was marked. Dylan was alert and clearly enjoying the experience. He was backed by the accomplished and professional Tom Petty and the Heartbreakers, and four black female back-up singers (known as the Queens of Rhythm).

In the US at least, Dylan's Live Aid debacle had not alienated any of the audience. There was an enormous ovation when his name was announced. He was still a huge name, if no longer the automatic headliner, and was introduced as a "superstar" by American TV. Gone was the puffy-looking Dylan: in fact, earring aside, he looked great, with his trademark hair and profile, leather jacket, and jeans tucked into motorbike boots.

He opened with "Clean Cut Kid", a song I have no enthusiasm for, its irony being about as subtle as that of "John Brown", but it was a good number for Bob and the Heartbreakers to rip into with gusto. The televised segment then began as Dylan launched into "Shake", one of a number of fun old rock 'n'rollers the band had rehearsed. Complete with suitable guitar hero poses and Dylan trading licks with Petty, it was very well received.

Next was the rather mawkish "I'll Remember You", but it still sounded wonderful (as, indeed, it has done at various times on the Never Ending Tour). Dylan managed to bring out the song's intimacy – which was no small feat in such a setting – and also appeared to be brimming with confidence, another contrast with his Live Aid persona. There was more intimacy, too, in his glances at his co-singer, Madelyn Quebec. When Dylan sings this song well he transcends its saccharine platitudes and turns it into something quite moving.

By the time Dylan got to "Trust Yourself", he had been joined by a crowd of musicians, including Willie Nelson, and was clearly having fun. This was a new song, a live debut indeed (as was "I'll Remember You"), and he usually performs his newest songs with special, extra presence.

Towards the song's conclusion, Dylan approached the front of the stage and stared out at the crowd while rocking out on his guitar. It was as if he was looking to see if they were still his audience. He appeared confident that they were. The contrast with Live Aid could not have been sharper.

"Lucky Old Sun" was fabulous – worth all the rest of the set put together – a great treat for the crowd though not, alas, for the TV audience as, like "Clean Cut Kid", it was omitted from the broadcast. Its contrast of earthly toil and heavenly ease was also ironically appropriate for an event in aid of those who were being denied the chance to toil on their farms.

Dylan finished his set with a good rocking ensemble performance of a song that demanded to be played at Farm Aid: "Maggie's Farm".

Dylan's set at Farm Aid was pretty damn good. If "Lucky Old Sun" plus any two of the other tracks could have been transplanted to Live Aid, Dylan's set there would have been a triumph rather than an abject failure – as long as he had stuck to performing and dropped his between-song patter.

Another glaring contrast between Farm Aid and Live Aid is the evidence we have of the rehearsals for the two events. There is a circulating video of the Farm Aid rehearsal sessions which gives a magnificent glimpse into Dylan at work. In these rehearsals he is extremely focused and looks absolutely great!

As far as the event itself was concerned, though, and, even in its truncated televised form, Dylan's set helped re-establish some credibility. This collaboration with Tom Petty and the Heartbreakers continued for two very different tours in 1986 and 1987. The 1986 double-headers encompassed New Zealand, Australia, Japan and then Dylan's first US tour since 1981.

This US leg of the tour was described by *Rolling Stone* as "the hottest ticket of the summer". The tour as a whole was immortalised in the video *Hard To Handle*, filmed at Sydney on 24th and 25th March. However, the tour is not looked upon kindly by most Dylan fans, who consider the shows too similar to each other: not enough variation in the song selection or execution. Yes, you got it: Live Aid was too sloppy and the 1986 tour was, well, too professional[12]! The tapes of the US tour capture some good, hard-hitting rock'n'roll, fun for the audience on the night, but like the 1974 tour, these are not tapes one returns to often. It is all relative, of course; this tour would probably seem full of variation and surprise compared to many touring performers who actually do play the same songs in the same way and the same order night after night. Despite the overall similarity of the set lists, there were in fact variations and introductions of fresh songs throughout the tour; especially, and significantly for the N.E.T., in the cover versions.

"Shake" was the first of a succession of delightful – and often obscure – covers from the back pages of R&B, rock 'n' roll and other vintage sources. "Lucky Old Sun" was also reprised to fabulous effect, and special mention has to be made of two other great covers – "Lonesome Town" (by Baker Knight, but made famous by Ricky Nelson) and Ry Cooder, John Hiatt and Jim Dickinson's "Across The Borderline". The latter performed by Dylan takes on the whole range and power of great American literature, and it is hard to remember that it is not a Dylan original.

Delightful covers aside, the sets were a high-energy romp spanning songs from throughout his career. Alhough leaning heavily on the "greatest hits", Dylan also showcased his recent album, *Empire Burlesque*. One should also not overlook Dylan's pointed performance of "In The Garden" from *Saved* as a centrepiece of the sets, prefaced with remarks about how Jesus was still his "hero".

The change in Dylan's appearance from the previous year was startling. "Dylan on stage in 1986 looked muscular and healthy," Paul Williams comments, "a relaxed, confident performer who had prepared carefully for this tour, this set of shows. It is as if a year earlier he watched footage of himself at Live Aid and resolved to do whatever he had to, to regain his power and dignity."

Dylan's new look appeared to have been deliberately chosen to banish the image of that Live Aid footage but it involved curiously non-Dylan-like attire. Apart from his predilection for an absurd earring, the wearing of leather vests and the macho bare-arm posturing seemed much more of a sub-Bruce Springsteen-stereotypical-rawk'n'roll-look than a Dylan one.

The 1986 trek was a very high-profile tour; backing band Tom Petty and the Heartbreakers were huge album sellers in their own right and on something of a commercial roll. In fact, one interviewer quizzed Petty about opening for someone who sold so few records in comparison with himself. Petty wondered aloud how it could be any other way, finding the idea of Dylan opening for someone else ludicrous. One wonders whether Petty would feel the same way these days, when Dylan has at various times opened for The Rolling Stones, Van Morrison, Joni Mitchell, Santana and The Grateful Dead.

So how would Dylan follow this big "event of the year" tour that introduced him to the huge fan base of a multi-platinum selling group? Well, why not go for the biggest fan base of any touring band? Which is what he did by teaming up with The Grateful Dead, the legendary 60s survivors who continued, year in and year out, to draw the biggest concert audiences in the USA.

In fact, Dylan's live adventure with the Grateful Dead would have very unfortunate results. He played in front of huge audiences, but the vast majority of them were there to see the Dead. The opening show on July 4th 1987 found Dylan looking much older and frailer than in the previous year, wearing a too-obviously-casual-to-be-accidentally-thrown-together outfit as if to please the Deadheads. He hunched over the microphone as though in pain, and the light (it was an outdoor show) seemed to bother him greatly. The group and Dylan played as though they had never met, far less spent time rehearsing – which, it later transpired, they most certainly had. Dylan's voice was reduced to a thin rasp as he proceeded to slaughter most of his set. He sounded for all the world like an under-rehearsed Dylan impersonator. Unfortunately, this poor display was not greatly improved upon during this curious little mini-tour of stadiums. But if the performances were, at best, erratic, the selection of songs was simply stunning.

Songs that Dylan fans would never have predicted came tumbling out – songs never before played live, or in the case of "Chimes of Freedom" not for almost a quarter of a century. (I mention "Chimes of Freedom" particularly, because if there was one redeeming feature of these shows, it was to be found in the sublime versions of this great song.) To hear Bob perform "Queen Jane Approximately", "The Ballad Of Frankie Lee And Judas Priest", "John Brown", "Joey", and "The Wicked Messenger" was simply extraordinary. I have to give Jerry Garcia and his cohorts great credit for galvanising Dylan to rediscover old gems from his back pages – especially songs that they themselves were wont to cover.[13]

Dylan himself was later to specifically credit The Dead with giving him back the idea of what touring was all about.

"I'd kind of reached the end of the line," he told *Newsweek*'s David Gates ten years later. Whatever I'd started out to do, it wasn't that. I was going to pack it in. Onstage, Dylan struggled to perform his old songs. "You know, like how do I sing this? It just sounds funny," he told Gates, before giving the journalist an all-too-convincing imitation of panic: "I – I can't remember what it means, does it mean – is it just a bunch of words? Maybe it's like what all these people say, just a bunch of surrealistic nonsense." During the tour with The Dead, Garcia encouraged him to try again. "He'd say, 'Come on, man, you know, this is the way it goes, let's play it, it goes like this.' And I'd say, 'Man, he's right, you know? How's he gettin' there and I can't get there?' And I had to go through a lot of red tape in my mind to get back there."

Exactly how he was going to "get there", struck Dylan when he brought the Heartbreakers across the Atlantic for what was billed as the "Temples In Flames" tour, though not without a struggle. Things had to get worse before they could get better. What a contrast this was to the Dylan/Heartbreakers shows of 1986. The greatest hits were still present but were often mangled and contemptuously tossed aside in wildly unpredictable set-lists. I am not against either of these developments in themselves; the latter makes it great for those who go to more than one show, and substituting a more "obscure" title in place of another big crowd-pleasing finale of "Like A Rolling Stone" is fine by me. Nor am I against the fact – which seemed to upset so many reviewers and attendees – that Dylan never spoke to the audience. However, Dylan did seem wilfully sullen on this tour. He dressed bizarrely badly and looked dreadful, or at least insofar as one could see him on the barely-lit stages. It was hard to comprehend the disparity between his current sorry appearance and the re-energised rocker of the US Heartbreakers tour.

"He came on stage... contorted in a Keef Richard's slouch," Gavin Martin wrote of 1987's Wembley Arena Dylan, "with semi-biker gear and what looked like a dead rodent on his head. His strained, strangled wretch of a voice seemed to fit his appearance."

Dylan did look utterly wasted. Seeing him this way I felt he was pushing himself to an early grave. Without wanting to invade Dylan's privacy, such incontrovertible evidence of drug use is impossible to ignore – especially in relation to its effect on his stage performance. In fact, as with the whole of rock's history, Dylan's career was heavily influenced by drug (including alcohol) usage. And around this time he was not hiding it. In the great BBC Omnibus interview (recorded 18th October 1986) he sniffs away and even makes a point of going out to "re-energise" himself. A security guard at Birmingham's NEC reported that he saw Dylan, just prior to the show, alone in a room, snorting from a "mountain of cocaine" that was larger than the guard had ever seen before, including, even, the entire stash of a notoriously indulgent Heavy Metal group. While that story is, naturally, hearsay, it appeared to be corroborated by Dylan's appearance that night.

In Dylan's legendary 1966 tour the use of drugs seemed overwhelmingly present on every track, yet his control was total and exquisite – from the dopey haze of the gorgeous acoustic sets to the speed-fuelled rush of the second half – night after night, country after country. When it works for Dylan it seems to work unimaginably well, but whatever uppers and downers one indulges in, the outcome can be hard to predict. What can be said with a degree of certainty is that the older one gets the harder it must be for the body to recover, especially during gruelling tours. "It's a goddamn impossible way of life", Robbie Robertson said of touring in the Band's farewell concert film *The Last Waltz*. Dylan in Europe in 1987 and 1991 seemed a physical embodiment of that statement.

There is, though, something to be said for this "scorched earth" policy toward touring. (Well, not in 1991, but more of that later.) The "Temples In Flames" tour also produced performances of beauty, often of songs that one had had no expectation of ever hearing in concert, let alone in such intensely felt, close-to-the-edge performances. Nonetheless, at the time the general impression amongst (many) Dylan fans and (most) reviewers was that Dylan was losing the plot altogether. Looking ill and sporting bizarre, ill-chosen headgear he skulked in the shadows throughout incredibly short sets, wherein he distorted his best melodies in a strangulated vocal parody of himself more hurtful than any malicious satirist has ever managed. Later, once they started listening to the tapes, most Dylan fans would discover that rare jewels and fabulous performances lay within. Mostly, though, only negativity remained amongst onlookers as Dylan's last pre-N.E.T. tour wound its way to a close.

It was amidst this backdrop, and on an uninspiring windy and foggy evening at an outdoor show at Locarno, Switzerland, that Dylan had an epiphany as he stepped up to the microphone.

"It's almost like I heard it as a voice," Dylan told *Newsweek*'s David Gates. "It wasn't like it was even me thinking it. I'm determined to stand, whether God will deliver me or not. And all of a sudden everything just exploded. It exploded every which way. And I noticed that all the people out there – I was used to them looking at the girl singers, they were good-looking girls, you know? And like I say, I had them up there so I wouldn't feel so bad. But when that happened, nobody was looking at the girls anymore. They were looking at the main mike. After that is when I sort of knew: I've got to go out and play these songs. That's just what I must do. "

As 1988's tour kicked off, all Dylan's 1980s touring paraphernalia – huge stadiums, big name groups, backing singers etc. – were to be swept away. The new shows would mark a whole new approach, or, rather, a return to an earlier format. Dylan was ready for the Never Ending Tour. His fans had no idea what was about to hit them.

The Fan's Never Ending Tour

Despite what historians might argue, I need to stress that, from the fan's perspective, the Never Ending Tour itself is not a single, monolithic entity. No two people witness a show with the same dispassionate objectivity. Even more pertinently, no-one aside from Dylan has attended every show on the Never Ending Tour. As a result, we dedicated fans each carry our own version of the Never Ending Tour around with us, based not only on memories of the shows we attended, but also (mainly) on our after-the-fact exposure to recordings on cassettes, DATs, mini-disks, CDs and CD-Rs, and from audience and profes-sional video footage. This leaves us at the mercy of our distorted memories, the quality of our recordings and our particular moods and circumstances when listening to them.

One of the Dylan "voices of authority" that I most respect – a really careful listener – received two tapes from me in February 1994. I thought I had sent him the 7th and 9th of February. In those days I was getting tapes direct from the Japan shows and copying and forwarding them to as many friends and as quickly as possible. It was the routine of "listen as you tape, label, package, post" that obsessive fans perform so often. So my error in sending the tape of the 7th twice to the same person, one labelled correctly, one as the 9th, is perhaps understandable.

What is also understandable – if initially surprising – is that the recipient of these tapes did not like the show labelled as the 7th at all, but thought the "9th" was a big improvement. On the next listen he realised it was the same tape and compared the two to find if there was an alteration in the recording quality – but there was not. The difference had been in his personal circumstances. When first listening, he was pressed for time, and tried to make the most of his one listen by studiously concentrating on every moment of the tape. The tape did not repay this level of concentration. Also, crucially, it was the first tape he had heard from this leg of the tour (the first of the year at that) and he had expectations that were not met. By the time he got the next tape, a couple of days later, his expectations were considerably lower and he had less time pressure. He was listening further away from the sound source (this can be remarkably beneficial in non-professionally made concert tapes, unless one has the very best sources) and so forth. And he liked it – the same tape he hadn't liked two days earlier. When you remember the highly subjective way in which we listen to music in private, this is perfectly understandable, and it is a major reason why the N.E.T. is so much easier to talk about in general terms (various legs of the tour, for example) than particular shows.

Other personal circumstances also come into play. I have tapes that resonate with what I was doing when I first heard them, and I have "favourite shows", because they were the only ones that I had in good enough quality to play on my walkman as I travelled to and from work Other people I know have favourite "car tapes". And these are people who have the vast bulk of more than 1,200 shows on tape, who dedicate time to listening to these tapes; a more casual listener may have only a few tapes from a given year, with the result that their feel for that whole year will be based on those. Given Dylan's variable performances from night to night on the N.E.T., the possibilities for misinterpreting the "artistic worth" of a given year are immense. Someone listening to three shows from Europe 1991 and three shows from the fall tour of the USA that same year might almost believe they are listening to two different people, or at the very least the same person from two years far apart in his career.

The same difficulties in discussing individual shows are exacerbated by one's personal attendance. What mood were you in? How was your personal life going at the time? Were you clear-headed, or in party mood? Was it the first show you'd seen in years, or that particular year, or that month or week, or was it one of eight shows you were seeing in a row? Did you have a great seat/standing position? Could you see Dylan's face clearly? Did you have an annoying person near you, in front of you – or did you have a nice enough person in front of you but the bugger was a foot taller than you? On and on this litany could go, and the likelihood of some kind of personal, travel or emotional problem is exacerbated by the very intensity that diehard fans bring to the shows. In their excited state functioning properly can be a task too far. Oh, and we haven't even mentioned Dylan's "mood" yet!

The first N.E.T. concert I attended was Glasgow 1989. Now, the Glasgow '89 show I can listen to on a cassette in my room in the year 2000 is not the same event at all. For a start, I am eleven years older: my life and my perceptions have changed. To put that in perspective, eleven years *before* Glasgow, I saw Dylan live for the first time at Earls Court, London. I wonder what my 19-year-old self would have made of the Glasgow '89 show, or of some of the latest shows that I hurry to listen to.

This is not to decry the Never Ending Tour as an inevitable decline – it is far from that. But even the most fanatical of Dylan fans must admit that he is only human, and age brings an inevitable waning of powers – vocal cords, stamina, concentration levels all deteriorate. In the sixties Dylan was in his 20s, in the seventies his 30s. He was also, in the middle of both those decades, at performing heights that the word Olympian fails to do justice to – and his band of musicians were shit-hot too, constantly pushing him to further achievements. He is approaching sixty now, so any comparison is unfair. And yet, and yet... the fan who goes to the Never Ending Tour is also the fan who still collects tapes and videos of those earlier years. While for Dylan it seems that he must ignore his legendary past in order to keep working, for the fan Dylan's past is always present.

One also has to embrace the consequences of Dylan continuing to play over 100 shows per year. A variation in quality is an inevitable side-effect of N.E.T.'s annual slog, night after night, city after city. Thinking otherwise will spark vain comparisons to times when a younger Dylan was consistently performing with that intensity, menace, concentration – that sheer damn presence – that set his concerts apart from anything else you could experience. That's not to say that the N.E.T. does not at times afford us Dylan in all his raging glory, but it does not – indeed, *could* not – at each of 100 or so shows every year.

That's why, despite all its limitations and distortions, the recorded medium offers a better chance of a balanced judgement of this Never Ending Tour phenomenon than attendance at a few of the shows. If I picked my favourite 50 Dylan shows of all time, I would have attended none of them; if I picked my favourite ten Never Ending Tour dates, I would have attended none of those either. If I were only to write about the shows I have attended, this would give neither a feel for their place in the unfolding story of the N.E.T., nor how they came to be heard by me and the effect they had on me. The shows I attended were just one facet amongst many in my experience of these extraordinary events; I was also listening to tapes, watching videos, sharing stories with friends, avidly following setlist changes in far off countries I could never visit and so on. The entirety of this N.E.T. experience is the subject of this book.

Nonetheless, for the fan there will always be a particular thrill about a live show. The special connection that you feel when you are in the same hall as the singer – that bond is what the Never Ending Tour is all about. So the shows I attended, as well as the tapes I love and esteem, form the basis of my Never Ending Tour. What follows is one fan's experience of this utterly unpredictable, constantly changing and regularly inspiring period in the career of an artist who has been attracting exactly those adjectives from the press and public for almost forty years.

Chapter Two: 1988

The People Themselves Will Tell You
When To Stop Touring

"I really don't have any place to put my feet up. We want to play because we want to play. Why tour? It's just that you get accustomed to it over the years. The people themselves will tell you when to stop touring."

Bob Dylan, August 5th 1988[14]

I cannot recall exactly who told me, but early in the summer of 1988 I became aware that Dylan had started a new tour with a small band, was playing some hard-hitting, rock-driven shows and was looking far healthier than in 1987. I also knew that Neil Young had guested on guitar for a number of shows and that Dylan was tending to play theatres rather than arenas. It all sounded very exciting. As I was not part of the world of Dylan fandom at the time, I had to settle for what few scraps of information were given out by the regular music press or what I garnered from my cousin Andy. This only heightened my anticipation, so it was with great expectation that I awaited the tapes Andy would forward to me. Unsurprisingly, the first ones I received were from the opening shows. So let us go back in time to Concord, to where it all began.

FIRST N.E.T. SHOW: Concord June 7 1988
Concord Pavilion, Concord, California
1   Subterranean Homesick Blues
2   Absolutely Sweet Marie
3   Masters Of War
4   You're A Big Girl Now
5   Gotta Serve Somebody
6   In The Garden
7   Man Of Constant Sorrow (Acoustic)
8   The Lakes Of Pontchartrain (Acoustic)
9   Boots Of Spanish Leather (Acoustic)
10   Driftin' Too Far From Shore
11   Gates Of Eden

12   Like A Rolling Stone
        *

13   Maggie's Farm

After the years of big bands, string sections, horns and female backing singers, it must have been quite a shock to see Dylan take the stage flanked only by a three-piece band: Chris Parker on drums, G.E. Smith on lead guitar and Kenny Aaronson on bass. They looked and sounded like a band of rock and roll gangsters from the wrong side of the tracks. Neil Young was there too, though his presence was barely audible.

The opening show started with a shock as a fairly throaty Dylan sped through his first ever live performance of "Subterranean Homesick Blues", which proved so successful an opener that it remained in the starting slot throughout 1988. It was followed by an even greater live debut in "Absolutely Sweet Marie" – a point often overlooked by commentators in their excitement over "Subterranean". It was a great, aggressive rendition, with Dylan's voice exploding into action as though he had been waiting to get back to this stripped-down rocker with as much longing as his audience.

Next, guitars riffing like machine guns propelled Dylan into an ominous "Masters Of War". By now his voice had shed all vestiges of rustiness and the subsequent "You're a Big Girl Now" had strong, clear vocals. Also, after the blistering opening three-song salvo, there was a bit of space as Dylan squeezed tremendous emotion from phrases like "*back in the rain*". There were many more great versions of this song to come in 1988 – Dylan even re-wrote a verse as the shows progressed. This was hardly remarked upon at the time, as re-writing a song from *Blood On The Tracks* for live performance was not unusual in those days; it certainly would cause more than a ripple in fan circles today.

Dylan's first address to a N.E.T. audience followed: "All right, thank you; we got Neil Young here playing tonight". Then he swung into "Gotta Serve Somebody", a song that allowed him the pleasure of playing around with rhyming couplets without changing the import of the chorus. Despite the kick-ass treatment it had a refreshing jauntiness too, with Dylan enjoying changing the emphasis and playing with the song: "*Serve somebody... oh yes... ohhh... serve somebody.*"

A dramatic, declamatory "In The Garden" was next, just in case anyone had missed the previous song's Christian message. As a song, this just shades the early finger-pointing of "Who Killed Davey Moore?" in subtlety, the browbeating, rhetorical questioning having the same bludgeoning effect. Here, however, Dylan was into the song – it was, after all, the centrepiece of his '86 shows – and he performed it in a challenging, ranting style to close the first electric set. (This spot in the N.E.T. set lists is usually occupied by a theatrically key song.)

The surprises did not stop in the acoustic set, which opened with "Man Of Constant Sorrow", a traditional song that Dylan had covered on his debut album so many years before. This alternate version was just beautiful, a great arrangement with expressive vocals. It was a worthy beginning to the extraordinary procession of traditional songs that Dylan would cover over the years of the N.E.T.. Night after night, year after year, they have supplied the high points. So fully does Dylan inhabit these traditional numbers that they often sound more like Dylan songs than some he has penned himself – especially in some later years, when he would often toss off his own most familiar material with no feeling of being engaged in the songs at all.

Back at Concord '88, he was about to play another: "The Lakes Of Pontchartrain", a magnificent, timeless song of unfulfilled love. (*"I asked her if she would marry me, she said that never could be/For she had got a lover, and he was far off at sea "*).

In Dylan's hands, both here and many times since, you live the story with and through him. Indeed unfulfilled love is a theme that shot through the contemporary *Down in The Groove* album in songs such as "Ninety Miles An Hour (Down A Dead End Street)": *"You're not free to come along with me/ And you know I could never be your own"*.

The new record seemed, at this moment, to be present in spirit, though I'm sure that was of little comfort to the record company executives who would have preferred to hear Dylan sing actual tracks from *Down In the Groove*. Then again, fans who bought that criminally short LP would have preferred the inclusion on the record of a few more traditional songs like "The Lakes Of Pontchartrain".

Finally, with one of his own "traditional" sounding songs – an appealing version of "Boots Of Spanish Leather" – Dylan brought the riveting acoustic set to an end.

Somewhere along the way the audience may have noticed they had no opportunity to give the customary rousing acclaim to Dylan's harmonica-playing. In yet another surprise, Bob didn't play harmonica on the 1988 tour at all.

The second electric set opened with another debut, "Drifting Too Far From Shore". It was too much to expect this feeble work to follow comfortably in the footsteps of the marvellous songs just played. Nonetheless, the first live outing of a new-ish Dylan song was exciting in itself, even if it was played as though it was the "Julius And Ethel" out-take from *Infidels*. The song itself is so weak that it was held over from the impoverished *Empire Burlesque* album and released on the near catastrophic successor, *Knocked Out Loaded*. It shows. It may, or may not, be relevant that it also formed the B-side of Dylan's current single. The A-side was the soon-to-be unveiled in concert – and as yet still being played, alas – "Silvio". This single was released in June 1988, coinciding with the beginning of the tour. (And they wonder why the halls were rarely sold out!)

Another surprise followed in an electric version of the usually acoustic "Gates Of Eden"- slow, but punchy and dramatic. The guitar parts had obviously been worked on, and formed a compelling backdrop against which Dylan recited his tale like an old-time harbinger of Deep Truth.

"Like A Rolling Stone" was the crowd-pleasing closer; Dylan was clearly enjoying himself too. (I'd love to know what made him give that open throated laugh as he sang *"secrets to conceal "*.) The audience's rapture was further increased by a foot-stomping encore of "Maggie's Farm", preceded by Dylan thanking, with marvellous intonation, "You people for being so nice".

And that was that, 13 songs, approximately 70 minutes of prime Dylan, classic rock 'n'roll with an acoustic set from folk heaven, a hugely enthusiastic crowd and a patently-in-high-spirits Dylan. What more could you want? Well, quite a lot more if you were writing for the San Francisco newspapers. With a history of antipathy towards Dylan, they launched yet another offensive.

The Examiner's Philip Elwood, in an article entitled "Dylan Show Sinks Like A Lolling Stone", gleefully crowed that the Concord Pavilion was "barely half full", that Dylan "mumbled" and that nearly all the songs were "both unrecognisable and unintelligibly sung", while "Dylan's vocals were so poorly defined and so lacking in melody that most were at a loss to catch any lyric thread or phrase".

Now I have been to shows where Mr Elwood's comments would have been hard to rebuff. However, even though my original tape is rather lo-fi[15], I can tell you he is mis-reporting here. Most songs were played at a fast pace but the vocals were clearly intelligible.

Mr Elwood may have been right that Neil Young's guitar was "kept so low his playing was seldom clearly defined", but, you know, who cares? I would not go as far as the famous British fan Lambchop (who will reappear regularly throughout this history), who amusingly, if unsupportably, remarked that "worrying about the band when you go to see Dylan is like making a fuss about the chandeliers in your favourite restaurant".[16] However, Neil was just a guest dropping in, his prominence or lack thereof was of no great matter.

Joel Selvin of *The Chronicle* also accused Dylan of "mumbling" and even unfavourably compared the rendition of "Like A Rolling Stone" to a live version by John Cougar Mellencamp! "(Dylan) failed utterly to appear as if he cared in the slightest about what he was doing," Selvin continued. "Dylan managed to perform the set in relative darkness.... There were ragged endings, a sloppy mix and a tentative, uncertain ensemble sound.... There were no particular highlights or dramatic moments[17], just a flat, uninspired, almost rote recitation of inconsequential selections."

Selvin also complained that Dylan stuck to "an undistinguished lot of songs drawn from throughout his career". Considering that all the way through 1988 and ever since Dylan has relied heavily on a mere handful of his albums, this is "criticism" that should be praise! Needless to say, Dylan often gets castigated for doing the opposite. When asked in an interview why he played all the old "hits", Dylan replied that when he tried to play new songs people didn't like it. With comments such as "He boasts one of the deepest repertoires of great songs anybody could claim but roundly ignored the cornerstones, other than the obligatory 'Like A Rolling Stone'...", this journalist might be one of those responsible for Dylan's frequent reliance on old material, when the crowd (mainly now people who have seen him before), contrary to Dylan's stated perception, want something new. Dylan was also criticised for the brevity of his Concord set – an extremely odd reaction when you consider the superlative quality of those 70 minutes.

Dylan's next stop was at Sacramento. After an opening show that was wonderful for the fans, but rocky in terms of attendance and press reaction, the tour was about to nearly run aground. If Concord was not a long set, the Sacramento show – twelve songs and no encore, clocking in at under one hour – was to be by far the shortest of the tour.

The story is that Dylan was in a foul mood and stormed off without encores as he was disappointed by the size of the crowd (less than half the 12,000 capacity.) Also, who knows, maybe he'd seen the *SF Examiner* and *Chronicle* reviews. He may say that he ignores reviews but there's been many a bitter retort from him to negative press comments over the years, and he was to answer one of the newspapers' jibes just a couple of shows later. Certainly the show was so much shorter than any other gig in the tour that you feel Dylan must have been disturbed by something, but writing the whole show off as a disaster simply cannot be supported by the taped evidence. By the end of the set Dylan may well have been upset but there seems no indication that he was at the beginning.[18]

The first thing to mention about the Sacramento show is that only two songs – the opener and closer – were repeated from the first night, repaying fans who went to consecutive shows.

SECOND N.E.T. SHOW: Sacramento June 9 1988
Cal Expo Ampitheatre, Sacramento, California

1	Subterranean Homesick Blues
2	It's All Over Now, Baby Blue
3	The Man In Me
4	Stuck Inside Of Mobile With The Memphis Blues Again
5	I Shall Be Released
6	Ballad Of A Thin Man
7	Baby, Let Me Follow You Down (Acoustic)
8	Two Soldiers (Acoustic)
9	Girl From The North Country (Acoustic)
10	Had A Dream About You, Baby
11	Just Like A Woman
12	Maggie's Farm

A typically great 1988 performance of "Subterranean Homesick Blues" was followed by a surprise electric set slot for "It's All Over Now Baby, Blue". A brave choice this, especially before his voice had warmed up, but it was a fine performance – though there are elements of what Mick Ronson termed Dylan's "Yogi Bear"[19] voice. "The Man In Me" was another surprise choice and another fine delivery. With the story surrounding the show, I was prepared for a Verona 1984-type shambles[20] but I did not hear that. Then a scorching "Stuck Inside of Mobile With The Memphis Blues Again" got the biggest cheer of the night so far, and was followed by "I Shall Be Released" and "Ballad Of A Thin Man" – both featuring strong vocals.

Even though the songs changed so much between the opening nights you can see that Dylan had a fixed set structure in his mind. As at Concord, the acoustic set opened with a song covered by Dylan at the beginning of his career, then there was a traditional folk song and finally an old favourite from the early days. Then, again as at Concord, Dylan opened the second electric set with a new song (or "obscure song", as the press would call them, leading to Dylan's remark after playing "I'll Remember You" at the fourth show of the tour, at Mountain View, California: "I don't think that's an obscure song. Do you think that's an obscure song? I don't think so!").

Concord	Sacramento
7. Man Of Constant Sorrow (Traditional)	7. Baby, Let Me Follow You Down (Eric Von Schmidt)
8. The Lakes Of Pontchartrain (Traditional)	8. Two Soldiers (Traditional)
9. Boots Of Spanish Leather	9. Girl Of The North Country
10. Driftin' Too Far From Shore	10. Had A Dream About You, Baby

"Baby, Let Me Follow You Down" – a song that saw sterling service in 1966 and at the Band's farewell concert, *The Last Waltz* – appeared in the same slot as "Man Of Constant Sorrow", another cover song that appeared on Dylan's first LP. It was great to hear it again – and the audience responded enthusiastically.

"The Lakes of Pontchartrain" was replaced by a cover of another traditional folk song, "Two Soldiers". Dylan was maybe straining his voice, a little uneasy at having to hit some difficult notes, and yet... this was far from a poor performance. On receiving the tape I already knew of the furore surrounding the gig. I am re-listening to it now, searching as I did then, for things that sound wrong. If you start to look for something you can convince yourself you have found it, yet there was great applause at the song's end, and there has been no sign to me yet that Dylan is in his reported "sulk", "foul mood" or "rage".[21]

Certainly, the noise the crowds made throughout Dylan's beautifully crafted and executed acoustic set would give him just cause for being angry. But this happens every night and either he doesn't hear it or he rises above it. Why should Sacramento have been different? "Girl From The North Country" is more than passable, though nothing special and, like a number of other songs ("Simple Twist Of Fate", for example), it usually is a stand-out when Dylan is on form. You can hear – on my original tape – somebody shouting: "Everybody back! Everybody back!" followed by an excited melee and much cheering. Perhaps there was a stage rush, but this usually delights rather than irritates Dylan. Nonetheless, it was from this point onwards that the show began to deteriorate.

The electric set opened with yet another debut, and for a new Dylan song at that, from *Down In The Groove*. Unfortunately, it was the sub-standard "Had A Dream About You, Baby", but at least on stage Dylan and the audience could have some fun with it. Not surprisingly, given that the song dates from the ill-advised and ill-fated 1986 *Hearts of Fire* movie, Dylan sounded more like he did in 1986 than 1988. I cannot in all honesty tell if there is a problem with Dylan singing this song or not, as it is just a thrash. I can say, though, that it sounds as if the more "distant" Dylan of 1986 was now present in the old favourite that followed, "Just Like A Woman".

Some of the early part of the show's freshness and vitality had been lost; nonetheless, Dylan does not seem to me to have been merely going through the motions – and the crowd certainly seemed to be loving it. When the predictable choice of "Maggie's Farm" closed the second electric set, there was still no sign that Dylan was annoyed. Granted, he was galloping through the set, but then he did so throughout the 1988 tour. Granted also, he sounded nowhere near as strong at the end of the show as he did at the beginning – but, again, this is hardly a surprise. We were only on the second night of a new tour, and his voice and energy levels might just have been flagging before he got back into the touring routine.

Whatever the problem was, Dylan left after twelve songs and did not return. The set was only one song shorter than at Concord, but the unannounced, abrupt ending and the psychological effect of the show being under an hour made it seem far shorter. Encores were expected, at the very least. Some in the audience no doubt hoped that Dylan's departure signalled only a mid-show break, with the second half still to come. Their disappointment soon turned to anger and the night ended in acrimony that further inflamed the bad feeling toward Dylan in the local press. A vicious circle was in danger of dragging down the tour that had started so well at Concord.

After the dust had settled on Sacramento, renowned concert promoter Bill Graham is alleged to have informed Dylan that this would not do; that Bob would have to make a greater effort to please his audience or he'd lose it altogether. The result? Dylan pulled up his socks and delivered a brilliant 17-song, 90+-minute set at Berkeley and went on to complete a glorious tour. This is the received wisdom – yet it just does not sound like Dylan: a naughty schoolboy, who, when rebuked, turns into a star pupil? In addition, Berkeley is often blessed with special shows, and opening concerts are often greatly at variance with what follows on Dylan tours (the first four shows contained about half the songs played in the whole tour). Whether the alleged warning from Bill Graham changed Bob Dylan's plans for the tour, or whether Dylan just had an off night at Sacramento – for whatever reason – we will probably never know for sure.

Still, after Berkeley's 17-song feast (including many songs that were not played in the first two shows, "Rank Strangers To Me" among them), the set lists/structure settled down to a fairly consistent pattern of 15 or 16 songs per night (though there were a large number of 14s and 17s too), rising on special occasions and peaking with a 21-song set at Upper Darby, Pennsylvania on October 13th, as Dylan warmed up for the concluding dates that had been added at New York's Radio City Music Hall in response to the rave notices posted as the tour progressed.

Generally speaking there were six or seven electric songs, followed by three or four acoustic numbers (on which G.E. Smith accompanied Dylan). Dylan would then return for another three or four electric numbers and round it all off with a one- or two-song encore. Surprises continued throughout the 71-date tour, with some 87 different songs being played.

Contrary to the poor turnouts early in the tour, the Radio City residency was a complete sell-out; and, in the middle of those shows, *The Traveling Wilburys, Volume One* was released to further praise and impressive sales.[22]

Throughout 1988, I continued to receive tapes of the tour, and it soon became evident that a key facet of the shows was the way in which Dylan was – yet again – defying attempts to pigeonhole him. Though they were dominated by the greatest hits from his prince of protest and sixties rock god phases, the mixture of songs played included country, rockabilly, gospel, Tin Pan Alley and traditional folk. I remember various shows that I carried around on my Walkman; the one from George on August 20th, for example, where there is a comment from the audience after "Highway 61 Revisited" – "It's much better than I thought it would be" – which could stand as a verdict on the whole tour. I remember from that show, too, the pile-driving rhythm and the glorious "*eee*" endings in "Absolutely Sweet Marie", and listening intently to the way he enthusiastically pronounced the words to fit a new stop-start rhythm in "You're A Big Girl Now". But there were so many other gems from other shows that people started making and trading compilation tapes. These tapes included great performances like the rarely played but exquisite "I Dreamed I Saw St. Augustine" from *John Wesley Harding*. It is almost as if Dylan had deliberately plucked out a song from his own back catalogue which – although rarely played live – will surely survive for as many hundreds of years as the treasures from the trove of traditional songs that he was performing with such care and intensity.

There was even a great "Joey", a modern tale told as a fable, oft attempted live, but seldom with lyrics remembered. My favourite concert version comes from this tour. Then there was "My Back Pages", which he took and gave a good shaking to, aptly renewing it. Byrds-like celebratory guitars chimed while Dylan's voice veered from anxiety to a laughing, dismissive tone on "*ripped down all hate*". As the performance progressed, the song regained its original, confident declamation. The driving beat of the tight band suited this perfectly, Dylan's trademark pinched voice notwithstanding.

There were great one-off outings, too, for "License To Kill", "One More Cup Of Coffee", and "Tomorrow Is A Long Time". He also gave us, though you'd be forgiven for thinking this was not the musical setting for it, a one-off performance of "Visions Of Johanna". When he played "Ballad Of Hollis Brown" – at Alpine Valley on June 18th (another "Walkman" favourite, incidentally) – it was interpreted as an oblique sign of support for local farmers then enduring a drought. Since it was the sole performance in the year this seems a reasonable assumption – though quite why its next appearances would be at Helsinki, Dublin and London (in 1989) would be harder to figure.[23] "Song To Woody" made it four songs from Dylan's debut album, and there were a few outings for "The Ballad Of Frankie Lee And Judas Priest", for which I guess we have to credit the Grateful Dead. Even "Bob Dylan's 115th Dream" was unexpectedly debuted in one of the Upper Darby "warm-up" gigs for the Radio City Music Hall residency. It was a year of surprises and of great shows.

Most of all, though, I remember marvelling at the wonderful cover versions. They sprang up all over the place, in show after show, compilation tape after compilation tape. Some were played but once, some a few times and others became commonplace. But it was the breadth of sources that was most amazing: from "Across The Borderline" to "Give My Love To Rose"; "Eileen Aroon" to "Pretty Peggy-O"; "Waggoner's Lad" to "Wild Mountain Thyme" and "I'm In The Mood For Love" to "Trail Of The Buffalo".

Of these, the first to strike home were the traditional songs. As far back as 1966, Dylan had hinted at how important these songs were to him:

"Traditional music is based on hexagrams. It comes about from legends, bibles, plagues, and it revolves around vegetables and death... All these songs about roses growing out of people's brains and lovers who are really geese and swans that turn into angels...I mean you'd think that the traditional-music people could gather from their songs that mystery is a fact, a traditional fact. I could give you a descriptive detail of what they do to me, but some people would probably think my imagination had gone mad." [24]

The N.E.T. has been honoured, each and every year, by Dylan singing traditional songs and giving us every "descriptive detail" his immense interpretative powers can imbue them with.

"Barbara Allen" – played in a variety of ways – was a regular standout. I swear that on some nights the way he sang the last word of "*Oh yes, oh yes, I'm very sick, and I shall not be better*" was worth the admission alone. And the same could be said for any version of "Lakes Of Pontchartrain" or "Eileen Aroon" – which provided yet further evidence of how incomparable a communicator Dylan is. Here, in later life, he could not manage the vocal brilliance of his staggering early '60s rendition of the traditional "Moonshiner Blues"; but, remaining within his diminished vocal range, he still managed a breathtaking delivery.

The brilliance of the song – with a melody, lyric and conceit that seems as old as expression itself – is given full and deserved embodiment in Dylan's delivery. The following lines, when sung by Dylan, surpass even Robert Browning's great poetic attempt at capturing the same feeling in "Love Among The Ruins".

"Youth will in time decay,
Eileen Aroon
Beauty must fade away
Eileen Aroon
Castles are sacked in the war
Chieftains are scattered far
Truth is a fixéd star
Eileen Aroon."

The deliberate emphasis on the éd ending of fixéd was only one of many "goosebump" moments.

And all this from a man they say can't sing. You want to ask such detractors to define "singing", for whatever they mean by the word can only be a limited sub-branch of what we hear.

We are not just listening to a singer, accomplished or otherwise, re-telling a tale and pushing the buttons of our emotional responses. Here we are involved in the story, in myth. We are dragged, perhaps even reluctantly, towards what Dylan went on in the 1966 *Playboy* interview to call traditional music, "the one true, valid death you can feel today off a record player".

Dylan could also cover modern songs to similar dramatic effect. The pick of these was Leonard Cohen's "Hallelujah" – unveiled in Montreal on July 8th, presumably as a tribute to the Canadian poet – which sounded like a brand new Dylan masterpiece. I first heard the song when Cohen closed a fine show in Helsinki with it three years earlier; listening to Dylan perform the notable song was like hearing it for the first time. Cohen was reportedly delighted at the tribute, but he would have been ecstatic if he had heard what a majestic version it was. (Dylan played it one more time, and in a very different but equally effective style, on the last of three splendid nights at the Greek Theatre, on August 4th.)

***

The tour "ended" on September 24th in New Orleans, but this was not quite the finish. As previously mentioned, popular demand had led to four further nights being added at Radio City Music Hall in New York. These shows quickly became a focus for the press and fans alike. The former, previously misguided critics of the tour, now praised Dylan to the skies; the latter, trying to read the runes of relatively unchanging set-lists, talked of a live album being released from the shows. All this is rather ironic as the shows themselves – though fine – were far from being the best (or even up to the average standard) of the year.

Certainly, press coverage of Dylan has always been extremely erratic, but to be fair to the journalists, Dylan's N.E.T. shows are bound to be challenging for music critics uninitiated in his current art of performing. If a writer prepared for a Dylan show by playing Bob's "Greatest Hits" or his latest album, the scribe would be lucky to recognise any of the former – until the song was well underway – in the case of the latter he might be lucky to hear any tracks from it at all. Furthermore, sometimes journalists' most uneducated criticisms are valid; it is just that, at times on the N.E.T., inspired re-invention can seem much the same to the layman as massacring a classic song. Dylan's performing art during the N.E.T. is not beyond reproach, but much of the ill-founded criticism he has garnered[25] can get wearing. Still, it works the other way too: when somebody is "hot", good reviews beget more good reviews – merited or otherwise. As the Radio City Music Hall shows became hot news, so the good reviews multiplied.

As for the fans, they were pleased with the attention and praise Dylan was receiving, but also rather miffed that the shows which generated all this press euphoria were attended by those attracted solely by this month's "hot ticket". This was in stark contrast to the previous months' shows, where die-hard fans witnessed Dylan in top vocal form with a rapidly changing set-list. Also, by the time he got to Radio City Music Hall, Dylan's voice was under pressure from the year's touring and a cold which settled in during the residency. This is not to say that the Radio City shows were poor, but they became – due to the wide circulation of PA quality tapes of the closing show, allied to the media buzz – falsely representative of the whole year. Still, at least they were more typical than the February 1989 release of the shambolic *Dylan and the Dead* live album (from the 1987 shows), which might have been sub-titled "the very worst songs from a very poor tour".

LAST N.E.T. SHOW of 1988: New York, 19th October 1988
Radio City Music Hall, New York, New York

1	Subterranean Homesick Blues
2	I'll Remember You
3	John Brown
4	Stuck Inside Of Mobile With The Memphis Blues Again
5	Simple Twist Of Fate
6	Bob Dylan's 115th Dream
7	Highway 61 Revisited
8	Gates Of Eden (Acoustic)
9	With God On Our Side (Acoustic)
10	One Too Many Mornings (Acoustic)
11	Barbara Allen (Acoustic)
12	Silvio
13	In The Garden
14	Like A Rolling Stone
	*
15	Waggoner's Lad (Acoustic)
16	The Lonesome Death Of Hattie Carroll (Acoustic)
17	Knockin' On Heaven's Door (Acoustic/Electric)
18	All Along The Watchtower
19	Maggie's Farm

As mentioned above, by now Dylan's voice was showing some wear and tear, but he started this last show in strong form: ripping through "Subterranean Homesick Blues", before calming things down with "I'll Remember You", a slight song redeemed by a few well-chosen couplets and Dylan's powers of delivery. The subsequent "John Brown", while laudable for its sentiments, remains one of my least favourite songs in Dylan's entire catalogue; but he performed it splendidly. In fact, this was about as good as you could ever expect to hear it.

A fine "Simple Twist of Fate" was the next treat, but Dylan's voice was starting to go in places and the song came to a hesitant, oddly stumbling end. One of the surprises of the tour had been saved for the October shows, with the first ever live version of "Bob Dylan's 115th Dream" at Upper Darby on 13th

October. I don't think there was any fan who could have envisaged this long, comic monologue being pulled from his back pages; but Dylan clearly enjoyed tackling it. You could hear the relish in his voice particularly when he sang the words "my way" near the song's conclusion.

"Gates of Eden" was back to the acoustic set, while Dylan's old protest classic "With God On Our Side" now included a verse on Vietnam, which had been added by the Neville Brothers in their version. It was strange in 1988 to hear Dylan, the definitive '60s protest-singer, for the first time ever, sing lyrics explicitly about the Vietnam war. Strange too that he was singing someone else's words in one of his own songs, though the new verse brought a huge cheer from the audience.

If you wanted two songs to round off an acoustic set and were allowed to pick one Dylan original and one traditional, you would be hard pressed to beat the 19th October pairing of "One Too Many Mornings" and "Barbara Allen".

"Silvio" opened the second electric set, Dylan having decided to "promote" his current single and album by playing this regularly from 21st June onwards. The 1988 version was certainly better than the bloated, falsely theatrical renditions he has inflicted on us since, though even here it still sounded like a Dylan parody.

"In the Garden" was preceded by a great little speech, the impish Dylan of yore well evident as he managed to be charming while giving a pointed barb to those (like me) who are not as keen on this song as its author is.

"Thank you, I was really honoured last year when the Amnesty tour chose a Bob Dylan song as a theme song. A song called 'Chimes Of Freedom'. This year, to my great surprise, they chose another Bob Dylan song. Actually that one was this year. 'I Shall Be Released' was the song they chose last year. Anyway I guess they're gonna have another Amnesty tour next year. I think the theme song they're gonna use is another Bob Dylan song called 'Jokerman'. But I'm trying to get them to change their minds. Trying to get 'em to use this one."

With that he swung into a fine, clear rendition; a bit less actively aggressive than the one at Sacramento, but in the same basic style.

Having made his point Dylan gave the crowd the rousing, "Like A Rolling Stone". However, by the time he got to "secrets to conceal" his voice had been reduced to a growl, and sounded completely shot. He left the stage when the song finished.

Somehow Dylan's vocal powers recovered sufficiently for him to pull out a half-acoustic/half-electric five-song encore – a feat accomplished by making the third song of the five, "Knocking on Heaven's Door", start acoustic but switch to electric midway through.

The encores opened with a wondrous, traditional lament to the woman's lot, "The Waggoner's Lad", sung with such empathy it is hard to believe he is the same man who in life, interview and song has often seemed far from understanding the female perspective.

All that is forgotten whenever Dylan sings the opening lines:

"Hard is the fortune of all womankind
It's always controlled, it's always confined
Controlled by her parents until she's a wife
Then a slave to her husband for the rest of her life. "

Following the yearning pleading in this heartbreaking traditional song, Dylan's voice becomes stronger and deeper for one of his own masterly songs about injustice and the hard lot of womankind, the breathtaking, humbling, "The Lonesome Death of Hattie Carroll".

That remarkable pairing was succeeded, without pause, by the half acoustic/half electric "Knockin' On Heaven's Door".

The evening, the residency and the 1988 tour then closed with the double-barrelled electric blast of "All Along The Watchtower" and "Maggie's Farm".[26]

After the disappointment of the *Down In The Groove* album, Dylan fans had been boosted by Bob's blistering June-onwards live performances. What would make 1989 perfect would be for the tour to continue and Dylan to release an album of impressive original songs.

Chapter Three: 1989

The Songs Themselves Do The Talking

"It's not stand-up comedy or a stage play – it breaks up my concentration to have to think of things to say or to respond to the crowd. The songs themselves do the talking."

Bob Dylan, 1989 [27]

The 1989 tour, just like the 1988 one, started amidst controversy and recriminations, but I was still not yet part of the Dylan fan world and did not know much about it until later in the year. My Dylan year really began with my first N.E.T. show at Glasgow, which was his 6th show of 1989.

In 1989 I had very little cash available for Bob-trekking. I certainly couldn't afford to take leave to see Bob, particularly as at the very time he was touring the UK, I was due to run a computer training course in Eastbourne on the southern coast of England – where I got overtime for working evenings – just about as far from Glasgow as one could get without leaving the UK.

Enter my boss, one Mr. Paul Stevenson, who kindly agreed to fill in my evening duties. I did a morning shift and then headed for the train to Gatwick Airport to catch a flight to Glasgow and – get a load of this – meet my parents and a cousin to go to the show with.

My parents, like most parents of obsessive Dylan fans, I guess, were long-suffering – though I am certain they were more open to Mr. Dylan's charms than most who had endured his voice permeating every corner of their house for years on end. Their healthy approach to parenting – it seemed almost revolutionary at the time – was to take an interest in what their teenage offspring were "into". And as we all know, if Dylan is approached with an open mind, he will captivate it, if it is at all worth captivating. In fact, before this concert both my parents had become "fans" to an extent themselves; what with my father using "John Wesley Harding" in a lecture he was giving on poetry and my mum averring a number of "favourite" songs including "Just Like A Woman".[28]

Still, it had never occurred to my parents to go and see Dylan themselves, although this may have been partly because he had not toured their country since 1966. Anyway, they expressed a convincing display of delight when I suggested they go. Also in attendance would be my cousin, Andy, who was once described as my "Frankenstein creation" because of the convenient way he got into Dylan and started collecting tapes with fanatical completism just as I loped off to Europe to do a bit of bumming around and, perforce, stop collecting them myself.

So you can see why this concert, Dylan's first in my homeland for 23 years, was so very special. OK, there were more UK dates to follow for me but this was a bit different. Besides, I hadn't seen a Dylan show since October '87.

***

June 6th 1989 found me in Eastbourne in a state of some excitement. I was so keyed up when I left at lunchtime that I forgot to leave Paul any documentation for the evening session I was supposed to be taking. Even if I had realised my oversight would I have cared? After all I was on my way to see Bob...

...Or was I? Because the kind of panic-inducing crisis that seems to occur so often to fans on their way to see Dylan was waiting for me at Eastbourne station. Oblivious to the fact that the station was almost deserted, in the holiday spirit already, I happily strode straight up to the designated platform only to be confronted by a big metal barrier whereupon hung a sign that said "Train to London cancelled".

While I was on a comfortable enough schedule given the proviso that I had made this (now cancelled) train, the next one would not guarantee that I caught the plane. This was presuming the next one would run. I had already decided, with the inherent dread fatalism of a panicking fan, that it would probably be cancelled too. In fact, I was in the icy cold grip of a creeping realisation that I might not make it at all.

I was quickly reduced to a gibbering wreck and reeled about the station moaning, unable to deal with the reality of my situation. And then I spotted a woman reacting to the sign on the platform with horror. I had never seen anyone so distressed at missing a train. "*Taxi*", we both intoned simultaneously – "we could share a taxi". And so we did. It came to £100 or so – thus nullifying the whole point of me being in Eastbourne – but what the hell? We still had a chance of making our plane(s). I did make mine – and got to Glasgow in time to meet my family before the concert, seeing old friends from years before as we went in – and I have every reason to believe that my fellow taxi traveller caught her flight too. I hope so.

The Glasgow show took place in the Scottish Exhibition Centre, a hangar-like place built for exhibitions of ideal homes and yachts, copper kettles for fake mahogany kitchen ranges or whatever – the kind of absurd events thronged by people who think that following Dylan around is a sign that one "needs to get a life." It was a cavernous, acoustically awful mess of a place that I would only consider visiting in order to see Bob.

So bad, in fact, was the venue's sound that it became a case of "the worst tape player will later be best". There is only a small area in the hall where the acoustics are not completely ruined and none of the experienced tapers with expensive equipment happened to be seated there, so the best tapes of this event actually came from cheap recorders that just happened to be in the right place. As, by pure luck, happily, were we – though I only realised this later.

"Subterranean Homesick Blues" was the first song. Though predictable, it was a great opener for this band and – as has become increasingly important as the years have passed – allowed Dylan's vocals to warm up. Not having to listen too carefully to a surprise song choice also permitted me to soak in every image of Bob that my Dylan-starved-for-nearly-two-years retinas could absorb. Oh, and we could hear every word as Dylan attacked the song with gusto, throwing in the odd bit of inspired intonation.

The second song, "Congratulations", was as unexpected as the opener was predictable, but it was equally enthusiastically received. Well, this was Glasgow, after all: if the audience there love you, they really love you; if they don't, well, it's safest to go to Edinburgh. Dylan sang in a deep growl of disenchantment; and played some neat harp, too.

"Stuck Inside Of Mobile With The Memphis Blues Again" followed. I still cannot type that sentence without an overwhelming sense of joy that it wasn't "All Along The Watchtower". At times like this, hindsight is paramount. The subsequent experience of show after show, year after year, featuring "All Along The Watchtower" as the set's third song has driven myself and many other Dylan followers into a peculiarly intense state regarding the possibility of the third song being something else. But, that was all still to come. As it stands, "Memphis Blues Again" is a song I've now tired of nearly as much in live performance as "Watchtower", but back then this was magnificent and still sounds so now.

Next came a driving "Ballad Of A Thin Man" which emphasised how much stronger Dylan's voice was compared to 1987's frequent bouts of frailty. Most live versions of this song are much more declamatory than the original: offhand and even shouted. However, there was still a clarity and force in this take. His vocals had fully warmed up and this was well sung, with the spirit of the original still intact. I loved the way his voice descended into the "*You've been with the professors*" line.

Yet another of Bob's mid-sixties classics, "Just Like A Woman", followed. There was no way the 1989 Glasgow performance of it could have the warmth, depth, control and wit of the 1966 incarnations (or, for that matter, the beautiful 1981 versions) but still, it was damn fine... Dylan was clearly alive to the song, still exploring its (endless?) possibilities, and producing all kinds of interesting stresses.

The first electric set closed with a hard-rocking, guitar-driven "All Along The Watchtower" pushing the crowd to further heights of passion.

The acoustic set opened with the traditional Scottish ballad, "Barbara Allen". It had featured in nearly half the 1988 shows, so there was good reason to hope for it – but with a paranoid fan's dread, I had feared it would be dropped. Now it was magical to be back in my hometown with my family, who were hearing Dylan sing a ballad they had known long before they had heard of the Minnesota Minstrel who brought us together that night.

The Glasgow Herald not only reviewed the show, but even included a wonderful editorial extolling Dylan's unique ability to "transcend the transitory". At the same time they claimed that, despite Dylan not saying a word to the audience (just why does that irk so many people?), he acknowledged them by playing this song. Given the song's regulaur presence in the 1988 shows and its occurrence in Dublin two nights earlier, *The Herald*'s comment is factually inaccurate, but it did feel as if Dylan was singing this song specifically for us; a Scottish ballad for a Scottish audience.[29]

The opening chords of "Mr. Tambourine Man" brought huge applause, practically drowning out the first words, till Dylan's strong, confident vocals came sailing through the quickly quietening hubbub. Dylan was now in complete control of the crowd, the night, his vocals, the band... the whole damn shebang. We were indeed "ready to go anywhere", following this musician as he followed that Tambourine Man.

The audience tried to show its appreciation with a determined effort to sing along on "It Ain't Me, Babe", though this was easier said than done. There was a huge guitar build-up as the groundswell of crowd approval rose; then Dylan pulled back and "tricked" the crowd before singing "melt back into the night".

Like all Dylan's classics that I have heard too often, my memory of "It Ain't Me, Babe" suffers from subsequent over-exposure. But it was just so well performed in Glasgow. Take the "*die for you and more*" line, for example; I cannot remember when I last heard it sung like this.

"Silvio" kicked off the second electric set. I have no memory of actively disliking it, but back then I had about a decade's more tolerance for the song than I have now!

"I Shall Be Released" was next, another "greatest hit" – at least a hit in a Dylanesque way (famous, but no hit single – not properly released). To my mind there are only two versions which really get to the heart of this song: the original Big Pink sessions take, criminally omitted from *The Basement Tapes*; and the extraordinary, one-off adaptation Bob unveiled for the Martin Luther King Birthday celebration show in 1986. This version was just OK, though with a lovely finale.

Then it was time for the crowd to go nuts to "Like A Rolling Stone". I think I still had the "this is the special song that going to Dylan's shows is all about" attitude then. The whole "Royal Albert Hall" legend, the intrinsic value of the song itself and its pivotal role in Dylan's career made it so special. Even Bobby ain't stopping a Glasgow crowd singing along to this one, especially as by now a large portion of the crowd had surged to the front of the stage to party in front of him. Sing along they did, with many a "*YO-AH*", "*HEY- HEAAAYH*" and "*gaun yersel Boabby*" thrown in.

Suddenly we were into the encores. The night had simply flown by. "The Times They Are A-Changin'" quietened things down to an extent, with Dylan playing it simultaneously as a crowd-rousing anthem and an attempt to discourage a sing-along. Eventually, Dylan wrestled "The Times" back from the audience, rediscovering the song beneath the anthem. From there he launched into "Knockin' On Heaven's Door", a great choice of song at this stage, elastic enough to encompass everything from meaningful communication to catchy pop, and, in this arrangement, to serve as both an acoustic and electric rock treat. Dylan sounded – unsurprisingly – a bit strained in the opening verses. However, just when I thought he'd given us all he could, he got a second (third? fourth?) wind and pulled off a fine verse and a second harmonica solo before launching into a blistering rendition of the show's closer, "Maggie's Farm" – of which a long term Dylan disdainer wrote, in a grudgingly enthusiastic review in *The Herald*: "During Maggie's Farm I swear I heard a government topple".[30] The same reporter summed up the whole evening as "an experience much more intense than I had bargained for and one I'll always be glad I felt." Ian Woodward, in his splendid diary of all things Dylan, *The Wicked Messenger*, was equally enthusiastic: "There was an energy and urgency in these shows we haven't seen for a long time", he enthused.

"Energy and urgency" indeed! I don't know if Dylan was exhausted afterwards, but I sure was. The adrenaline boost of seeing Bob kept me awake until it was time to rise at dawn to try to reach Eastbourne by 9am. I arrived at 8:58, grabbed a coffee and began to tell the class all about the show.

I didn't read most reviews until later, though at some point that evening I caught a fine notice in *The Guardian*,[31] whose critic Bob Flynn was clearly bowled over. "What we got was the happy shock of Dylan not only playing the best of his extraordinary song book," Flynn gushed, "but playing it with the glorious intensity of that star-burning ruthless youth... We were expecting an old man to be wheeled into the arc lights, we were faced with this extraordinary vision of a withered priest somehow plugging himself back into his unique, mystic jukebox of hits."

But I couldn't really enjoy reading Mr. Flynn's fine writing as I really should have been in Birmingham that night when "Congratulations" was played again, this time in the encores. Still there was always Wembley Arena to look forward to the next day!

Sure enough, I was bowled over by Wembley too – with the first rush of seeing Dylan over, I probably concentrated harder on the actual performances. Remembering back now, the clearest song in my mind was a spectacular, edge-of-despair rendition of "Ballad of Hollis Brown". Then, fittingly enough, another from the same album, "The Lonesome Death of Hattie Carroll". There was no "Congratulations" here; instead the "surprise" number two slot was taken by "When Did You Leave Heaven".

The heavyweight music press was full of praise for the Wembley show. "Oh yes: this was a rejuvenated Dylan," *Melody Maker*'s Allan Jones concluded, "the master in all his raging glory. Unforgettable, unsurpassable."

NME's Gavin Martin enthused: "Tonight all the images of Dylan fused into the crucible of his raw genius.... Poet, seer, mystic, iconic rocker, ravaged salvationist, virulent misanthrope – such descriptions are paltry. The meaning of the songs weren't simply buried in nostalgia or in the lyrics, it was in the way he played with inflections and the sounds of the words, the way he changes the timbre of his voice to exact the most from the frazzling guitar cauldron or the weird, disfigured acoustic interludes... tonight he proved that on form he was still unimpeachable, miles ahead of pretenders both young and old."

Coda

The Monday morning after the Wembley show finds me back on my way to Eastbourne, tired and laden down with luggage. I collapse on to the London tube, put down my bags and cases and switch on my Walkman to listen to the Glasgow show. Out of the corner of my eye, I spot someone next carriage up, also wearing a Walkman. This bloke has long hair, an eccentric hat, a wolf-like grin and an alarmingly intense stare. He looks like a nutter and the music in his Walkman appears to be driving him mad. His arm is beating the empty air,[32] while his right leg simultaneously pounds the floor. I assume he is listening to heavy metal!

In these situations, you simultaneously wish to distance yourself from attracting the nutter's attention but are so drawn by their eccentric behaviour and appearance that you cannot look away. My "excuse" for staring was that I needed to confirm my earlier thoughts regarding his choice of listening. I glanced across to sneak a look at his T-shirt... and, yes, you've guessed it, it was a Dylan T-shirt ("Temples In Flames", if I recall correctly).

The inevitable result of not resisting the temptation to look at a nutter is that said nutter immediately homes in on you. He caught my eye as it left *his* T-shirt and he appeared to notice that the Walkman-listening eccentric in the next carriage to him, *i.e.* me, was wearing a Dylan T-shirt too. He immediately came over to talk. Within about 33 seconds he had announced that the tape in his Walkman was not only more recent than mine from Glasgow (true – by all of a day!) but also, without hearing mine, he absolutely guaranteed that his was better quality. We swapped tapes for a moment to test his theory, which was quickly proved.

We gibbered Bob at high speed for the next couple of stops; he informed me that he had been on his way to give this Birmingham tape to *Melody Maker*'s Allan Jones, but would now leave it with me, as he clearly thought someone with such a dated tape in his Walkman was in need of charity. With a scribble of his phone number he was off, taking the tube in the opposite direction to return home and dub another copy for Mr. Jones.

This was my first encounter with the man they call Lambchop.

***

That was my N.E.T. year as far as live shows went; but for Dylan these concerts came after the European tour had got off to a shaky start, and there were months of touring to follow afterwards.

At Glasgow and Wembley I'd heard plenty of stories about the start of the 1989 leg of the tour: like the previous year, controversy had dogged the opening concerts. The tour kicked off on the 27th May with a ragged show at Christinehof Slott, Andrarum, in Sweden, that nonetheless had its moments, like a splendid "Gates of Eden". Dylan seemed very unhappy and his peculiar get-up of windcheater, cap, and hood pulled up over the cap meant that not only did the Swedes get a surly non-communicative Dylan but a mostly hidden one to boot. Covered up though Dylan was, he still clove to the darkness on stage, revealing as little of himself as possible. A similar bizarre appearance and erratic performance the next night at Stockholm was at least partly redeemed by an adventurous set list that included "My True La-La", "Eileen Aroon" and "When Did You Leave Heaven".

The Swedish press were taken aback. "Bob Dylan doesn't smile...the mouth grimaces in a grotesque manner at times but his eyes never smile. Somehow, he might as well be in pain," said one. The tabloid *Kvallposten* had a photo of the strangely garbed Dylan on its front page under the banner headline: "SKANDAL" (no translation needed!) and deemed the show "pure catastrophe"! "Dylan appeared stand-offish both on and off the stage," the article continued. "He ignored the audience as well as the many journalists who attended. *Kvallposten* can reveal that Dylan earned nearly 1.5 million Swedish kronor for the scandalous performance."

Other reports were fairer; one even stressed that "Differently from so many other performers Bob Dylan doesn't go on auto-pilot when he performs. His mood, how he feels, always becomes apparent – whether good or bad." Nonetheless, all the Swedish journalists were either baffled or outraged, or both, by the short sets and by Dylan's appearance – hidden in hood, cap and darkness.

This did not sound like the man I had seen at Glasgow, and it was the next show in Helsinki, Finland, that proved the turning point on his road to the stunning performances later in the year. That night was also when a contrast between the European tours of 1989 and 1987 began to emerge – a theme that would run throughout that summer.

My own feelings on 1987 are very mixed – there were plenty of high points, but I find it an incredibly erratic tour. While the peaks are mountainously high, so the low points are buried way below what you expect from someone of Dylan's stature.

I had lived in Helsinki in 1985-1986 so, typically, Dylan popped up there for his first ever visit the very next year, on 23rd September 1987! The anticipation amongst my Finnish friends for Dylan's first show in their country was acute. Their expectations were dashed, and they came out bitterly complaining that Dylan looked and sounded appalling, and didn't seem to care. Dylan had played for approximately one hour and looked and acted as though he had the worst hangover of his life. Looking 25 years older than he had in 1986, he contemptuously mangled the melodies and spat out the lyrics to his audience's favourite songs.

And yet, and yet... one man's "mangled melody" is another man's "artistic bravery". "Spat out lyrics", for some, mark a "stunning re-creation, evoking new emotions from tired old words". I defy anyone to say that Helsinki will ever again hear anything of the quality of 1987's sublime "Simple Twist Of Fate", the brooding yet hopeful "Senor", and the moving "It 's All Over Now, Baby Blue" – to say nothing of a magnificent, first encore, "Desolation Row", and a set-list that mixed the familiar 60s songs with less well-known material like "Dead Man, Dead Man" and "Gotta Serve Somebody".

At that first Helsinki show in 1987, as with most performances from that year's inconsistent but often mesmeric European tour, there was golden wheat to be found among the chaff. However, the "presentation" of the show – not least Dylan's overall demeanor and startling appearance – made this hard to see at the time. Not just for live Dylan "newbies" like my Finnish friends, but also for the most experienced Bob-cats such as *The Wicked Messenger*'s Ian Woodward who was particularly disappointed by Dylan's own indifference to his performance during "the glum 1987 shows".

Initially, I also preferred 1989. However, having listened to numerous shows many times since then, 1987 seems to grow better and better in retrospect. Which is not to say that the 1989 Helsinki gig I am about to focus on was a poor show, very far from it – it is just that to praise it to the rafters while pouring scorn on the previous 1987 show seems unjustified. Still, as far as 1989 is concerned, it is fair to say that Helsinki saw the first satisfactory show of what was to be a very pleasing year.

Helsinki Day May 30 1989
Jäähalli Ishallen, Helsinki, Finland

1   Subterranean Homesick Blues
2   Confidential
3   Ballad Of Hollis Brown
4   Just Like A Woman
5   Stuck Inside Of Mobile With The Memphis Blues Again
6   All Along The Watchtower
7   To Ramona (Acoustic)
8   Mr. Tambourine Man (Acoustic)
9   Eileen Aroon (Acoustic)
10   Knockin' On Heaven's Door(Acoustic/Electric)
11   Silvio
12   In The Garden
13   Like A Rolling Stone
        *
14   The Times They Are A-Changin' (Acoustic)
15   Maggie's Farm

After the standard opener, "Confidential" was a real treat. Dylan's vocals, awakened by the blistering opening song, caressed the words, extracting the most out of line endings like "*To my hee-e-e-aa-art*". He also embellished the song with a sympathetic little harp flourish.

Early "protest" classic "Ballad Of Hollis Brown" was moody and magnificent; after the words "ocean's pounding roar", there was the added effect of a thrashy electric guitar approximation of that sound. Then it was straight into a marvellous, inventive rendition of perennial classic "Just Like A Woman". And so it went on: an enthusiastic crowd served with "Stuck Inside Of Mobile With The Memphis Blues Again" and "All Along The Watchtower", the latter having a particularly atmospheric guitar opening, piercing the night air even more sharply than the harmonica that punctuated the song.

Although "To Ramona" was far from convincing, it was well received and formed part of an acoustic set that included a fine, loud "Mr Tambourine Man" and "Eileen Aroon" which was received in the silence it deserved, in contrast to the cacophony of audience chatter that had spoiled it a year before in the States. The audience's fervent applause for this classic old folk song had not subsided when Dylan and the band ripped straight into "Knockin' On Heaven's Door". This was introduced with a strange and effective start-stop-(mournful harp)-start tempo that brought the crowd's euphoria back up to the "greatest electric hits level" of the pre-acoustic slot. Dylan was experimenting with the lyrics and tempo on stage, though not for a moment leaving the audience behind.

It was a pretty special show thus far and while "Silvio" and "In The Garden" simply did not belong in this company, you could not have faulted Dylan's commitment to performing them. "In The Garden" segued into a barnstorming "Like A Rolling Stone" and when Dylan sang "kicks for you" it sounded as if he really remembered what it meant. After Helsinki – and just before Glasgow – Dylan played two nights in Dublin; still swathed in darkness and sporting the same ridiculous outfit as in Sweden. The shows were improving, though, with the first Dublin concert's splendid set-list boasting: "You're A Big Girl Now", "Every Grain Of Sand", "Gates Of Eden", "The Lonesome Death Of Hattie Carroll", "The Water Is Wide", and "Eileen Aroon", the last two traditional songs being outstanding. The electric take on "The Water is Wide" was one of the highlights of the year and would be a contender in a list of "best ever N.E.T. performances". As Dylan's vocals took off the band cut loose and proved their worth in a classic performance. The next day was a pretty good show too but had two fewer songs, a less adventurous set list and the horror of U2's Bono joining Bob on stage.

After the three already-discussed UK shows which followed Dublin, bass player Kenny Aaronson left the band to return to the States for an operation. His place was taken by Tony Garnier, who has remained in every N.E.T. line-up since. The band now consisted of G.E. Smith on lead guitar and occasional backing vocals, Christopher Parker on drums and Tony Garnier on bass.

***

After London, Dylan went a-rocking other parts of Europe, in oufits that varied from leather waistcoat to the kind of horrible jackets that he seems to specialise in. The concerts were looser than his '88 US shows, though they followed the same basic structure: a mixture of the ragged and the swagger – fun shows with some sterling rock'n'roll performances punctuated with more sensitive readings. The crowds were enthusiastic and the reviews generally good. One big difference to the US shows was Dylan's use of harmonica, though this was not always successful.

By now we were used to "odd songs" popping up in Dylan's live shows, and this leg of the tour did not disappoint in this respect. Immediately after London, the Hague got that fine traditional song "Trail of the Buffalo". There were two outings for the rarely played "Song To Woody" in July, "Tangled Up in Blue" appeared in the opening slot one night in Spain, and one of my all time favourite non-Dylan songs, Townes Van Zandt's remarkable "Pancho And Lefty", appeared on the 21st June. The 13th June concert at Frejus in France included outings for "Hey La La (My True La La)", "The Lakes Of Pontchartrain" and, most startling of all, a spellbinding rendition of Thomas Dorsey's "Peace In The Valley".[33]

Italy saw some hard-rocking shows, with enthusiastic crowds feeding back the energy. A compilation double bootleg CD, *All The Way Down To Italy*, carried the Italian electric charge around the Dylan world. Next, Dylan marked the N.E.T.'s first foray into Turkey with an extended 21-song set, including four acoustic songs in the encore.

Greece, appropriately enough, staged some classic Dylanesque drama. Patras, on 26th June, found Dylan in a foul mood; the fact that his nose sounded completely blocked didn't help. His temper completely snapped part way through "Silvio" when he stopped playing and shouted to the light engineers: "Shut that light off please!" Given the minimal lighting normal for Dylan shows in those days it meant that for the rest of the show the stage was in near complete darkness. Meanwhile the star act was more concerned with the effort of drawing breath than with projecting his voice around the darkened arena. The low point of Dylan's performing year drew predictable boos at the end.

The shouted instruction and the darkness of so many stage sets had fans worried that Dylan had a serious eye problem. A long-standing back complaint was also presumed to be playing up at the time, given his relative immobility on stage. He had also been pushing his voice to the limit with his barnstorming electric sets, so perhaps it all came to a head that night. At least the Patras audience got the first-ever live performance of "Tears of Rage" as some consolation. Technically, as neither "Quinn The Eskimo" nor "I Shall Be Released" feature on the official release of *The Basement Tapes*, this was the first performance at a Dylan show of any song from that album, 22 years after it was recorded and 14 years after it was released. ("Down In The Flood" and "Don't Ya Tell Henry" were performed when Dylan guested at a Band show in 1972).

This European jaunt came to an end at Athens on June 28th. Dylan gave an extended 19-song set and "Highway 61 Revisited" was filmed for a Greek TV special. In addition, Van Morrison joined Dylan for two of the Ulsterman's songs in the encores. These were filmed for, but not shown in, a BBC TV Arena special on Van. The programme did, however, show us the pair at large in Greece.

The Greek segment of the show opened with a shot of Dylan on the Hill of Muses. It was a great treat for fans – used to Dylan's murky appearance on a darkened stage – to see him in the brilliant sunlight so clear; though it didn't appear to be a pleasure for Dylan, who squinted uncomfortably in the glare. As the camera panned out, it revealed the marvellous classical Greek scenery in the background and Bob and Van in the foreground, performing the latter's "Crazy Love". Well, Van performed it, while Dylan hesitantly joined in – always late as he studied Van intently to glean the words as they went along.

Interestingly, during the Dylan section of this Van Morrison TV special, the camera concentrated on Bob as though he were the subject of the programme; it rarely left his face during a duet on "One Irish Rover", which once again found him trying to figure out the words as Van sang them, and then eventually giving up singing altogether. Still the film clip acts as a nice footnote to this leg of the Never Ending Tour. It provides some of the best Dylan visuals you could wish for; and, having learnt the words subsequently, Dylan would feature "One Irish Rover" some 14 times in the US legs of 1989's tour. It would also be far from the last time in the N.E.T. that Bob and Van would prove that they couldn't duet.

***

After the exertions of his European tour, you might have thought Dylan was ready for a rest. Not a bit of it. The European leg ended on June 28th, and by July 1st Dylan was on stage in Peoria, Illinois to kick off a 47-date tour – the first of two separate US legs.

Not only that, but he opened the Peoria concert with a triple surprise blast of "Pancho And Lefty", making only its second ever appearance on a Dylan set list; a debut for "One Irish Rover" and the first outing for "I Believe In You" since November 1981.

Clearly in the mood to experiment, Dylan opened the next night's show with the rarely played Glen Trout song "Everybody's Movin'" and followed it with "Absolutely Sweet Marie", "Ballad Of Hollis Brown", "Tears Of Rage", "Seeing The Real You At Last", and "Gotta Serve Somebody". One usually only expected one or two of those in a show. The next day, Gordon Lightfoot's "Early Morning Rain" (like "Pancho and Lefty", a song tailor-made for Dylan) was followed by the sole 1989 outing for both "Driftin' Too Far From Shore", and (a few songs later) "I Dreamed I Saw St. Augustine". Even more startlingly, two songs after that, Leadbelly's "In The Pines" made its first appearance since the 1960s. Things generally settled down after this, though surprises continued: from Van Morrison's "And it Stoned Me" on July 6th right through to "Rank Strangers To Me" in September. Most of the highlights – not for the first or last time on a N.E.T leg – were to be found in these covers.

Despite all this, some fans were disappointed not to have heard songs from Dylan's completed, but yet to be released, *Oh Mercy* album. It was said that Dylan was not playing this material for fear of bootleggers distributing the songs before the album appeared.

Notably for later N.E.T. developments, Steve Earle was the support act during this part of the tour and Bucky Baxter, Earle's steel guitarist sat in on some sets.

The reviews of these shows were mainly positive – though there were some familiar criticisms, especially: "It doesn 't sound like the records"; "He can't sing"; and "He doesn't speak".

A few months later Dylan gave journalist Edna Gundersen a fairly straightforward explanation as to why he doesn't talk to audiences. "It just doesn't seem relevant anymore," he told her. "It's not stand-up comedy or a stage play. Also it breaks up my concentration to have to think of things to say or to respond to the crowd. The songs themselves do the talking." Later in the N.E.T., Bob would give completely different answers to the same question.

In the meantime, *The Cleveland Plain Dealer*'s Michael Heaton was particularly enthusiastic about Bob's performance: "When Dylan's revved up as he was all night at Blossom Sunday, it's a privilege to watch him play... It was the best show of the summer so far. He's the last real deal. The genuine article. A true star." Still, like other reviewers, Mr Heaton could not help pointing out how the audience was about half the size of the previous year's 9,000.

The Boston Herald's Greg Reibman opened a rave notice with an interesting comparison that was echoed by a number of other critics. "The summer of 1989 will be remembered as a time when tours by the Who, the Rolling Stones, Ringo Starr and other veteran rockers dominated the concert stages and rock headlines," Reibman noted. "In contrast, without the now customary hype, tour sponsorships and press conferences, Bob Dylan practically snuck into Great Woods Thursday night. It turned out to be an inspired concert that his fellow '60s superstars would be hard pressed to match... The 90-minute career-spanning concert was a Bob Dylan fan's dream come true. To 15 of his best songs, he brought fresh arrangements and vitality.... The show didn't come across as a night of nostalgia nor an attempt to capitalise on past glories."

"He slammed through his 90-minute set like a small gale passing through the beach," *Newsday*'s Stephen Williams enthused of the Jones Beach show. "[Dylan's] no-nonsense posture – he'd lean forward sometimes, his guitar neck pointed at the wings like a machine gun – supplemented [his] aura of aggression." It was a posture he adopted for most of 1989.

However, not all the media coverage was positive. In the first of many N.E.T. "Bob's sold out, the Sixties are dead" stories, Dylan's decision to play at an Atlantic City casino on July 20th caused something of a press furore. This served as a stark reminder of how big an icon Dylan still was, regardless of his current record sales. The reaction of *The Montreal Gazette*'s Michael Farber was fairly typical. "The revolution is over," Farber fulminated. "We lost.... On the 20th anniversary of Woodstock the man who wrote 'money doesn't talk it swears' and meant it, sang for the first time in capitalism's playground."

Intriguingly, *The New York Daily News*'s David Hinckley saw Dylan as following in the footsteps of rock'n'roll's first icon. "It's Elvis and Dylan," he explained, "and their common ground, which begins with youths of talent, fire and charisma, when they were so good that even people who didn't understand or like them often sensed, correctly, that there was reason to be afraid of them." Dylan came out of the comparison on top as Hinckley contrasted Elvis's unchallenging casino days with Dylan "ripping into songs" at Atlantic City. The reviewer placed particular emphasis on the way Dylan used "It Ain't Me, Babe" as a personal anthem, "because it's both close to and far from the hollow 'My Way' with which Elvis tried to convince himself, and maybe the world, that he controlled his life. Dylan, more modestly and accurately, says only that he won't be what he ain't."

In the meantime, the N.E.T. resumed with one of its most exciting and rewarding legs. Much of the excitement was due to the release during that break of the *Oh Mercy* album. One of the great joys of following Dylan on tour is to observe the evolution of new Dylan originals, especially when the material is as strong as the tracks from *Oh Mercy*, though not all of them were played live in 1989.

"Everything Is Broken" was performed at all but one of the shows (26 times), which is a pity, as it is probably the weakest song from the record! However the next most played was "Most Of The Time" (23 times, at the beginning of the first encore); a majestic, searing song that grew in the playing and remains my favourite song on the LP. "What Good Am I?" featured 18 times, while "Man In The Long Black Coat" was performed on 15 occasions and "Disease Of Conceit", with Dylan on piano, 11 times. Dylan also made one under-rehearsed stab at a solo piano take of "Ring Them Bells" at the request of his manager. This left "Political World", "Where Teardrops Fall", "What Was It You Wanted" and "Shooting Star" still to be played live.

The introduction of these new songs necessitated a change in the way Dylan and the band played. The garage band sound that had the *NME* claiming earlier in the year, "This is the way the Clash should have sounded", would not do for brooding and introspective material like "What Good Am I?", "Man In A Long Black Coat" and "Most of the Time". As "What Good Am I?" was most commonly to be found as the second song, this change was noticeable almost immediately and it affected the tempo of many of the songs in the set lists. There was still room for some all-out rockers but the overall mood and pace of the shows had changed.

The first *Oh Mercy* songs were debuted in October 1989 during an enthralling residency at New York's Beacon Theatre. This was one of Dylan's most memorable series of shows. Listening to a tape of the first night, 10th October, in particular, an almost demonic rage seems to spill through the speakers.

"[On the first night, Dylan] took the stage like a wild man," audience member Peter Vincent recalls, "stalking back and forth and tearing into the first song at a furious pace. He slowed slightly for the second song, the debut of 'What Good Am I', the first *Oh Mercy* song ever to be played live, but there were no niceties like pauses for applause; one song segued into another while the musicians flogged themselves to keep up. Without good peripheral vision this would have looked like a solo electric appearance, as the band were hovering at the edge of the stage, eager to keep as far away from Dylan as the leads on their instruments would allow." No fewer than three *Oh Mercy* songs were debuted that night: "What Good Am I?"; "Everything Is Broken" and "Most Of The Time".

On tape the show sounds quite erratic in places, but when it is good it is great, and it is never less than gripping. Dylan's foul mood caused sparks to fly, not just from the rejected harmonicas he threw across the stage when he couldn't find a harp in the right key, but from his intuitive sense of theatre. This stands in complete contrast to Patras where his anger merely resulted in a sullen and lacklustre show.

Things at the Beacon calmed down on the 11th and 12th, though the first of these dates still featured a stand-out "The Lakes of Ponchartrain" – Dylan's phrasing here has to be heard to be believed – and a never bettered "It Takes A Lot To Laugh, It Takes A Train To Cry". Most especially, there was a breath-taking performance of "Queen Jane Approximately" on the 12th – the song's 9th N.E.T. outing (starting August 16th 1989). Dylan had already performed other fine renditions of the song, and would continue to do so, but it seemed to peak here. Dylan writer Robert Forryan praised it for "an opening that is all low-down, brooding guitar complemented by Dylan's slow, achingly sweet harmonica, and stately, marching drum-beat." Forryan saw the song's high point as when Bob sings "'*You want someone ... aaarrr ... you don't have to speak to*'. That '*aaarrr*' is stomach-churningly gorgeous; divinely sensual; just plain sexy!"[34]

"Everywhere they went with the music seemed totally and absolutely right," Peter Vincent recalls, "a combination of power and spontaneity the like of which I have practically never encountered. It may have been the single great-est performance by Dylan I have ever had the good fortune to attend, and no-one in the band was willing to let it go.... It seemed like they were going to keep playing 'Queen Jane' all night, endlessly finding fresh variations on the song's themes."

Bob biographer Clinton Heylin, not given to hyperbolic praise, was almost as enthusiastic, considering "Queen Jane" not just the highlight of the night, but "One of the two or three greatest performances of the Never Ending Tour". It is certainly among the contenders. The original *Highway 61 Revisited* version was stately, but in this truncated performance[35] there was a lived-in humanity mixed with a different yearning. It is this kind of performing art that makes following the N.E.T. so rewarding.

It would have been hard for Dylan to top the drama of the opening three Beacon gigs but he managed to pull out more surprises on the final night. "Precious Memories" and "Man In A Long Black Coat" were played for the first time, which may have surprised the audience, though not as much as the sight of Dylan clad in a gold lamé suit! Mr. Hinckley could have extended his "Dylan following in Elvis's footsteps" theory further had he been writing later in the year. The biggest surprise was kept until the end, though, when "Man In the Long Black Coat" led onto a hand-held-microphone version of "Leopard-Skin Pill-Box Hat". Then, during a harmonica solo, Dylan shook hands with members of the audience, leapt off the stage and walked out through a fire exit. The band was as bemused as the audience, and G.E. Smith brought the song to an end when it finally became clear that Dylan was not going to return.

Without the same dramatics, the 1989 shows that followed the Beacon fea-tured many fascinating highlights; especially, once again, in the covers (includ-ing the surprising "When First Unto This Country" and "Everybody's Movin'") as well as the *Oh Mercy* songs discussed above. In addition a number of debuts and unusual choices were unveiled, such as "Man of Peace" from *Infidels*. "Lay Lady Lay" also made its N.E.T. debut and "To Be Alone With You" made its first appearance in any Dylan live show. A number of old friends appeared in different guise: "Don't Think Twice, It's All Right" found itself, for the first time on the N.E.T., in the electric set, while "Tangled Up In Blue" popped up in an acoustic slot for the first time in five years.

In the insatiably greedy way that a fan forever demands more, my main complaint about the 1989 N.E.T. leg is that I would have liked Dylan to have spent more time at the piano. After the disappointing debut of "Ring Them Bells", Dylan used "Disease of Conceit" – when it was on the set list – as his one piano piece, other than a one-off version of "Gotta Serve Somebody". Still, as I said, I am being too greedy. Not only were the shows fine and adventurous, but they introduced a new style of N.E.T. performance and more than whetted the appetite for what was to be an extraordinary start to the new decade.

Chapter Four: 1990

Better Than Quittin' Anyway

"Don't be bewildered by the Never Ending Tour chatter. There was a Never Ending Tour but it ended... with the departure of guitarist G.E. Smith."
Bob Dylan, Liner Notes to 1993's *World Gone Wrong*

Though Glasgow 1989 was the first N.E.T show I attended, in many ways 1990 marked the true beginning of the N.E.T. for me. It was the first time I saw him in a small hall; the line-up of Bob's band began to change; and the concert locations ranged from the smallest venues to large outdoor festivals. The year also saw a huge inconsistency in the quality of Dylan's shows – from drunken rambling messes to compelling art and exhilarating entertainment. All these factors, to varying degrees, were to become integral features of the N.E.T. proper.

The year also saw a sudden key realisation dawn amongst British fans – that 1989's tour was not merely Dylan's fifth three-yearly UK visit (after '78, '81, '84, and '87) one year early; but that you could begin to count on seeing him again at a venue nearby, and soon – playing a set with a greatest hits backbone that was usually filled out with surprise live debuts of originals and delicious covers.

Before the first real 1990 leg of the N.E.T., Dylan pulled a major surprise by booking into Toad's Place, a 700-capacity US venue, and playing four sets, across five hours, from 9pm onwards, in a single night. Once word started to travel about the content of those sets ("Key To The Highway" – *are you sure*? "Tight Connection To My Heart"? – *you are kidding!* Bruce Springsteen's "Dancing In The Dark"? – *are you mad?*) the eagerness to get one's hands on the tapes was incredible. The hype just grew and grew as those lucky enough to have been there talked about Dylan chatting at length between songs and the special feeling there was between performer and audience.

All this raised fans' already heightened anticipation of the forthcoming Paris and London shows – due after Dylan spent a brief sojourn in South America for massive, six-figure festival audiences. When the Toad's tapes finally arrived, it soon became apparent that, extraordinary event though it was, that marathon night had been merely a public rehearsal. Nothing wrong with that – I wish he would do it every year – but it is just ironic that this most sought-after of tapes was soon blown away by recordings of proper gigs.

Two warm-up shows in the States acted as a kind of half-way house between the rehearsals and the real concerts. The first of them was, like Toad's, all-electric and found Dylan still working on "Tight Connection To My Heart", as well as making a stab at "You Angel You". Both of these held significance for the shows to come, though Dylan's recollection of the latter's lyrics at this point stretched to the title only.

The UK dates were scheduled for the Hammersmith Odeon in West London. By one of those weird coincidences I had recently moved house to the Hammersmith area – which left me a mere 15-minute walk away from both venue and box office. I was all set to rush there the minute Lambchop contacted me from the head of the queue.

Naturally, life did not go so smoothly.

***

Once again you find me taking a course in Eastbourne, while my pager is going wild with so-called urgent messages. The only really urgent one was from Lambchop, telling me that those in the know were queuing all night for Dylan tickets just up the road from my flat. Stunned ain't the word. Anyway, the excitement of the approaching concerts sends my training course on an eccentric path and all is halted while I dash off a letter to the Hammersmith Odeon, carefully following Lambchop's detailed instructions.

Days pass slowly.

Cousin Andy then phones to say he has six tickets for various parts of the venue. Lambchop phones to say he has his tickets and is heavily into swapping them around to get the best possible seats for every night.

But I have no tickets.

Fear sets in; I should have heard something by now; by this time everyone else has tickets. So I trot off to the Odeon. There are short tempers and confusion a-plenty at the ticket desk, with Dylan fans much in evidence.

Finally the Odeon staff locate my letter. They've not sent out any tickets! Because I appear to have asked for seven in my first paragraph, one over the limit per application, they have ignored the rest of my letter.

Just as I break into a state which only the similarly obsessed can possibly imagine, along comes yet another agitated Dylan fan in the identical predicament. The staff are getting a bit fed up with this, while the rest of the queue look on in bewilderment.

Eventually pity wells in the breast of one member of staff and I get my seven tickets. They're for all over the place, so after many phone calls, and much frenetic swapping and buying, I'm calm(ish); two very good seats, two in the balcony and two in the middle and various others for those I am taking along.

As the opening London show approached, mouth-watering reports filtered back from France, culminating in a call from Lambchop in a state of ecstasy at the latest Paris date. I assumed he was exaggerating in understandable post-concert excitement, but was impressed that he was so blown away by the show. The subsequent arrival of a tape proved that he was telling it just the way it happened.

Eventually the great day of the first concert dawned. My wife Pia and cousin Andy were going with me. Andy was down for the week with his usual goodies. An inspired electric "Pretty Peggy-O" on video was the last song he played for me before leaving the flat. It was the best version I'd ever heard – an opinion I would shortly have to revise.

On the way to the show, we stopped at the Novotel, which was full of people I would get to know over the next year or so, involved in a massive ticket swapping session. All of this activity had the added benefit of filling the time before Dylan came on stage.

Hammersmith, 3rd February 1990
Hammersmith Odeon, West London

1	Stuck Inside Of Mobile With The Memphis Blues Again
2	Pretty Peggy-O
3	Tight Connection To My Heart (Has Anybody Seen My Love)
4	Political World
5	You're A Big Girl Now
6	What Was It You Wanted
7	Leopard-Skin Pill-Box Hat
8	All Along The Watchtower
9	Love Minus Zero/No Limit (Acoustic)
10	It Ain't Me, Babe (Acoustic)
11	The Lonesome Death Of Hattie Carroll (Acoustic)
12	Gates Of Eden (Acoustic)
13	Everything Is Broken
14	Queen Jane Approximately
15	It Takes A Lot To Laugh, It Takes A Train To Cry
16	Man In The Long Black Coat
17	In The Garden
18	Like A Rolling Stone
	*
19	Mr. Tambourine Man (Acoustic)
20	Highway 61 Revisited

As show-time approached, the whole front area could hear Lambchop shouting at the top of his voice, *"Bobby Bobby Bobby ... Stand-up"*. Then Dylan took to the stage and the opening guitar lines signalled the arrival of "Stuck Inside of Mobile With The Memphis Blues Again". The screams of joy were pure teeny-bopper stuff, as was my stunned wonder that He was so close. The music pounded in my eardrums and when Bob started singing, the hall erupted all over again.

It was to be too much for some; near the beginning of the show two people actually ran onto the stage. Bob looked momentarily alarmed but then just stepped out of the way and kept playing his guitar.

The energy poured from the stage as Dylan and the band tore into the song like your favourite garage band. By the end of the first verse I could have died and gone to heaven. As the song continued, I revelled in Dylan's every word; his every facial expression; his every movement. My senses were in overdrive. I tried to tell myself that there were six whole nights of this to come, to pace myself. But such reserve was inconceivable. Then the guitar break brought another outbreak of fan hysteria.

"*Stand-up for Bobby.... show some respect*", shouted Lambchop as the song ended to tumultuous applause. "*Show some respect! Bobby's standing for you, you stand for him...*"

The clapping died down as the opening chords of "Pretty Peggy-O" emerged. Back at the flat, Andy and I had joked about how wonderful it would be if Dylan played this, and how wonderful it was indeed! This was the most heavenly part of heaven itself. My reverie afterwards was broken by Lambchop's dulcet tones:

"*Fuck 'em all Bobby, fuck 'em all, they don't fucking deserve it. Show them who is boss*".

"Tight Connection To My Heart" followed. Dylan slowed down enough to give a pointed delivery, making the audience actually think about what he was saying – even as they continued to act like love-crazed teeny-boppers. In the 1,200-plus shows of the N.E.T., the coming together of these two elements is what Dylan appreciation is all about. Bob repeated the "Tight Connections" line "*Has anybody seen my love*" so many times that it became the *de facto* title of the song in this guise – a format far removed from the *Empire Burlesque* prototype. As it drew to a close, Larry Lambchop was off again.

"*Bobby, Bobby, Bobby...*" he started to scream. At which point, Lambchop's voice suddenly packed in (it was amazing it had lasted so long). Then, after a pause during which it sounded like it had cracked for the very last time, he was back at full throttle:

"*Too good, too fucking good for them... Bobby you are the best*".

Dylan then swung into a breathless run-through of "Political World" – his performance so unlike the depressing, staged video that had been used to "promote" the song. In contrast to the album version's biblical mood, this sounded contemporary.

As the tightly-rocking band finally ground to a halt, above all the male roars and female screams, there was Lambchop:

"*Fuck 'em Bob fuck 'em!*"

An utterly classy "You're A Big Girl Now" ensued, with the phrase "*singing just for you*" bringing cheers from the crowd. "What Was It You Wanted?" started suddenly, before the applause for the previous song had tailed off, while the insistent beat made the questions seem menacing rather than contemplative.

"*ThankyouBobbyThankyouBobbythankyouthankyouthankyou*", Lambchop yelled without pause for breath.

The driving intensity of "Leopard-Skin Pill-Box Hat" was beyond belief. If the 1989 version had been fine, this was pure ecstasy. The band were playing fabulously and everyone in the hall was having a ball.

By the time the band abruptly slammed into "All Along The Watchtower" Larry's throat was getting pretty hoarse, but he hung in there:

"Thanks for coming! Anything you want Bobby, anything you like."

A woman cried *"We love you"* as the band launched into a beautiful perform-ance of "Love Minus Zero/No Limit".

Much as singing along at concerts is anathema to me, I found it hard to decry the spontaneous crowd accompaniment to the first chorus of "It Ain't Me, Babe" – for all I know, I was joining in.

"We're going change the title now to 'Ain't it me babe'?" Dylan quipped at the song's conclusion.

"Thank you Bob thank you Bob", replied our feather-in-the-hat-friend.

"The Lonesome Death of Hattie Carroll" was almost perfect. Although Dylan forgot some words, he was firmly in control and his illuminating harmonica break preceded a great, guitar-driven end to the song.

"Gates Of Eden" was attacked at a break-neck pace and then the whole crowd was clapping along to "Everything Is Broken" – all *Oh Mercy* songs were cheered back then!

"God bless you Bobby God bless you", cried Lambchop.

Bless Bob indeed, for going into the transcendent "Queen Jane Approxi-mately". His voice hit a high note on the crest of a wave in the song's open-ing, and then there was the totally wonderful Dylanesque-to-the-nth-degree vocalisation of the stretched-out line endings.

At its end we were breathless, but Bob was not: with hardly a pause he was into "It Takes A Lot To Laugh, It Takes A Train To Cry". As he ended the lines *"And if I don't make it/ You know my baby will"* by stretching the last word to *"willlllllllllllll"*, a classic was reinvented in front of our eyes.

Could life get any better? Throw in a "Man In the Long Black Coat" and, yes, it could. After which, a showstopping "In The Garden" had everyone par-tying.

As for "Like A Rolling Stone" – well, it had to be experienced rather than heard. We could tangibly feel we were at an *Event*, a pinnacle even in Dylan's peak-strewn career. "Like A Rolling Stone" had to be the closer, and we all went crazy.

"Thank you everybody"

"Bobby Bobby Bobby" – it was no longer just Lambchop who was shouting thus.

The encores opened with some lovely guitar picking to introduce "Mr. Tam-bourine Man". Bob was back in vocal control with an ambitious staccato deliv-ery changing the pace of the song completely. It finished with a splendid Dylan harmonica break.

Finally, a storming finale of "Highway 61 Revisited" brought this perfect evening to a close.

***

So many things shone out on the opening night: Dylan's mobility (in such contrast to 1989); his happiness; the great reception given to *Oh Mercy* songs; the brilliant "Tight Connection". "It Takes A Lot To Laugh" alone would have been more than enough to satisfy me for the entire week. Instead, the residency was to supply jewel upon jewel, night after night.

There were many highlights for me. On February 5th, I got lost on my way out of the venue, finally alighting by a side door that led straight to the waiting tour bus. I got on it and chatted to Chris Parker, the drummer. On the 6th we got one of the week's highlights: "Dark As A Dungeon", performed in a dark, deep voice that croaked and crackled with emotion and emphasis.

The February 7th show featured a rapturously received "Forever Young" that brought memories of 1978 and would have made a fitting finale. Dylan began it as a benediction to the audience, but it grew into a defiant declaration of intent. That same night, there was also an oddly arranged "Tonight I'll Be Staying Here With You" (making its first appearance since 1976) – the almost shouted lyrics, intimating that the narrator was moving on rather than staying. Still, most people's favourite on the 7th was probably "Most Of The Time". "*I can survive, I can endure*", Bob was singing, but his voice made clear that it was at a terrible cost.

As for my favourites that night, well "Dark As A Dungeon" from the acoustic set and, from the electric set, the quintessential city blues, "It Takes A Lot To Laugh" – with additional guitar embellishment, it was even better than on the opening night. The walls of the Hammersmith Odeon seemed to vibrate as bass lines snaked and drums relentlessly pounded; above it all soared Dylan's vocals in tandem with the lead guitar. Exhilarating, exhausting, magic.

It was a worry that the last show would have to be an anti-climax. It seemed impossible that Dylan could top the previous performances; but that is exactly what he did. As in Paris, good hands were played during each show, but all the aces were saved for the final night.

Hammersmith, 8th February 1990
Hammersmith Odeon, West London
1	Absolutely Sweet Marie
2	Man In The Long Black Coat
3	Positively 4th Street
4	Ballad Of A Thin Man
5	Pledging My Time
6	I Want You
7	Political World
8	You Angel You
9	All Along The Watchtower
10	Boots Of Spanish Leather (Acoustic)
11	To Ramona (Acoustic)
12	She Belongs To Me (Acoustic)
13	Mr. Tambourine Man (Acoustic)
14	Disease Of Conceit (Piano)
15	I'll Remember You
16	Where Teardrops Fall

As the band stormed through the opening "Absolutely Sweet Marie", Dylan steered the song through the electric maelstrom. "Man In A Long Black Coat" was next, understandably similar to the opening night.

A complete mood change was wrought with a driving "Positively 4th Street". As the aisles swayed in hymnal response to this most cruel of put-downs, Dylan sounded more resigned than overtly scornful: the cawing sneer of the young man was replaced by a more mature voice – so used to being let down that he accepts it as part of life.

"*Kyou*", Bob told the enthusiastic audience and launched straight into a monumental "Ballad Of A Thin Man". Menacing, dark and wonderful, the questions pierced the thick air like stabs of lightning. A harmonica break slowed things down before Dylan had us all just staring (or dancing) in awe as he exploded through the final verses.

"*Kyou*".

"Pledging My Time" made a rare and welcome appearance, as somehow Dylan conjured up a sense of intimacy in the crowded, stuffy auditorium. At the gorgeous harp break the crowd went nuts all over again.

Next was the third *Blonde On Blonde* song of the night, "I Want You", taken far too fast, but the sound of celebration in Dylan's voice made it clear he was having a ball and wanted us to have one with him.

"Political World" provided us with a needed break from the intensity, before "You Angel You", so surprisingly played in response to a request at the warm-up show on January 14th, reappeared to a roar of shocked delight. Dylan had clearly been re-learning the lyrics and gave an exuberant performance, following it with a menacing version of "All Along The Watchtower".

"*Play anything you like, Bob*", Lambchop wisely suggested over the ensuing hubbub of requests. What we got was a sharply focused "Boots Of Spanish Leather" that quietened everything down again.

Dylan's punchy delivery sounded simultaneously ravaged and sensuous on the following "To Ramona", and "She Belongs To Me" continued our acoustic feast.

"*ANKYOU*," expounded Bob at length.

Some hesitant guitar playing strengthened into the unmistakable sound of "Mr. Tambourine Man" – a fine clear version with a lovely brief harp break early on.

"*Thank You*", said our man, becoming positively verbose, before walking over to the piano that had remained untouched throughout the residency. A huge roar went up. All week long Dylan had been teasing us by circling the piano without ever touching its keys. As Dylan now approached the piano once again, the crowd's anticipation was tinged with apprehension that this was another put on. The cheer re-doubled when we realised that this time it was for real. Dylan briefly returned to the front of the stage to revel in the applause before returning to the piano, for an inspired rendition of "Disease Of Conceit".

"I'll Remember You" was followed by "Where Teardrops Fall" – the next glorious surprise of this week of never ending treats. I was brought back to earth with "Seeing The Real You At Last". Even Bob in this resplendent form couldn't redeem this bombast, occasional good lines notwithstanding.

"Every Grain Of Sand" is one of those songs that should never be played live because the studio versions are so perfect. At the end of this week, however, it seemed he could do anything, and he pulled it off with gusto.

A change of mood followed with "Rainy Day Women" – from metaphysical insight into all-out rave-up in one easy movement. The song sounded fresher in those earlier N.E.T. years and this was great fun. Dylan's voice almost gave out at one moment but he just came back with a big, bear roar of a *yeah-eah!* and ended the song, before instantly ripping into "Like A Rolling Stone". It was a tangible a-rocking climax to an entire week of euphoria. Never have such scathing lyrics sounded so celebratory. It felt as if the energy both on and off the stage could fuel a starship to the farthest reaches of the galaxy. As G.E. Smith went through his showcase solo I would never have imagined that this would be the last time I'd see him on stage with Dylan. The band seemed so happy and so together.

Suddenly, unbelievably, the residency was approaching its end. We had reached the encores of the last show. Each passing moment was becoming ever more precious.

"It Ain't Me, Babe" found Dylan's vocals restored for a strong version of the acoustic classic that has grown into one of his most bonding live songs: both singer and audience aware of the irony of greeting its lyrics of denial with such a rapturous reception.

The traditional "Hang Me, Oh Hang Me"[36] found his voice a throaty, but deeply satisfying, growl. Deep bass lines and simple guitar strokes lent gravity. For a man who had been criss-crossing continents for the past five years, the sentiments of "*Lord, Lord, I've been all around this world*" seemed fitting. A hush came over the hall. It was one of the most perfect moments of my life.

Then a blistering, rip-the-paint-off-the-walls "Highway 61 Revisited" brought the whole thing to a rousing, exhausting finish. It was a long time before many of us left the hall, so reluctant were we to leave the scene of our extraordinary experience.

There was a huge over-reaction from fans in the following weeks. "The best since '75", said many; "since '66", said others. I joined in this daft game, to a slightly lesser extent, by affirming it "the best I'd seen him since 1978". Though easily dismissed by later perspectives, these heady claims certainly felt right at the time. The high standard of performance and the intimacy of the venue provoked an immediate need to elevate Hammersmith 1990 over past triumphs such as the 1979 and 1980 tours.

In any case, the experience was far from over. Hammersmith 1990 may have ended on stage but the tapes were already out and the videos, vinyl and CDs would follow. To this day, I find it hard to accept that these were just "six more shows in the N.E.T". For me they were the turning point, and the beginning of a time when I could regularly see Dylan in concert at close range; when all sorts of weird and wonderful things would happen to the set lists; when I would start to know more and more of the audience who, like me, were going to a number of shows and listening to them all. My own N.E.T. had started with a vengeance.

I had discovered the door to a magical kingdom and felt like Charles Ryder in *Brideshead Revisited* when he first encountered the world of Sebastian Flyte.

"I went there uncertainly. But I was in search of love in those days, and I went full of curiosity and the faint, unrecognized apprehension that here, at last, I should find that low door in the wall, which others, I knew had found before me, which opened on an enclosed and enchanted garden, which was somewhere, not overlooked by any window, in the heart of that grey city."[37] This "enchanted garden" of endless touring and Bob watching was open to anyone who wanted to step into the enclosure.

From now on I'd be collecting as many shows as I could on tape, and subscribe to all those Dylan magazines I'd heard so much about, Hell, I'd even start one myself. So I did, and the first issue of that magazine, *Homer, the slut,* came out later in 1990. Producing and distributing it would take up most of my free time over the next four years.

***

While we were still enthusing wildly over the Paris and London shows, Dylan popped up as a guest at some US shows, recorded a new, killer, version of "Most Of The Time" and laid down tracks for a new album of his own, as well as working with the other members on the second Traveling Wilburys record.

Then, on May 29th he picked up the N.E.T. again, starting a North American tour in Montreal. Changes had been made; most significantly the band now remained on stage during the acoustic set, providing Dylan with a sympathetic backing that allowed him to concentrate on his vocal delivery. Almost as surprising was his use of the harmonica, which resumed its status as an important element in his performances. The opening show also featured the first "Desolation Row" of the N.E.T., a development dramatic enough to make me redouble my search for every tape. As it happens, it was a couple of months before I heard the opening night, but meanwhile I kept getting tapes from other dates. The second show, on 30th May, was one of the first and one of those I played most.

N.E.T. NORTH AMERICAN TOUR: 30th May 1990:
Kingston Community Memorial Hall, Kingston, Ontario, Canada

1   Most Likely You Go Your Way (And I'll Go Mine)
2   Ballad Of A Thin Man

3	Stuck Inside Of Mobile With The Memphis Blues Again
4	Just Like A Woman
5	Masters Of War
6	Gotta Serve Somebody
7	Love Minus Zero/No Limit (Acoustic)
8	It's Alright, Ma (I'm Only Bleeding) (Acoustic)
9	She Belongs To Me (Acoustic)
10	Ballad Of Hollis Brown (Acoustic)
11	One Too Many Mornings (Acoustic)
12	Mr. Tambourine Man (Acoustic)
13	Where Teardrops Fall (Piano)
14	Everything Is Broken
15	I Shall Be Released
16	All Along The Watchtower
17	What Good Am I ?
18	Like A Rolling Stone
	*
19	Blowin' In The Wind (Acoustic /Electric)
20	Highway 61 Revisited

This is the setlist, but that isn't really how I recall it...

My own memories of that show only run from the middle of the acoustic set to the end of the show (not including the encores), because the second side of my tape, which became a particular Walkman favourite, began in the acoustic set with "She Belongs To Me" and ran until just before the encores.

At that time my journey to work was approximately one hour; 45 minutes of which I'd be sitting down listening to a tape. I'd run my latest tape in one direction, and my most recent favourite in the other (I was usually reliving the excitement of the Hammersmith shows).

"She Belongs To Me" was lovely, in spite of the crowd's determined efforts to clap along. " Ballad Of Hollis Brown", like "Gates Of Eden" in 1988, seemed to benefit from a brief foray into the electric set before returning to the acoustic. "One Too Many Mornings" was truly compassionate and the wild enthusiasm that greeted "Mr Tambourine Man" was fully merited by its performance. The latter segued into "Everything Is Broken". (By this point there was only "Shooting Star" from *Oh Mercy* still to be aired on the N.E.T.. It duly appeared at Alpine Valley in a great version where, instead of finishing at the end of the song, Dylan returned to the last verse and repeated it after an instrumental break, building to a magnificent conclusion. Since the last verse is one of my favourite verses on the whole of *Oh Mercy* I was obviously delighted that this version worked so well. Alpine Valley was another tape I played again and again.[38])

As for the other shows, the tapes from three nights in Toronto were also much sought after, not just for the gorgeous "Early Morning Rain" tribute to Toronto native Gordon Lightfoot, but for yet another live debut, "One More Night", more than 20 years after he had written it. This featured a guest appearance by local rock 'n'roll warrior, Ronnie Hawkins. By now Dylan had taken to chatting to the audience from the stage, and he introduced The Hawk at some length:

"Yeah we got a friend here who's actually a hero of mine. One of my all time heroes now, Ronnie Hawkins. He's coming to the centre of the stage and sing a song called 'One More Night'. It would be awful nice if we can clap him on. If we do perhaps he'll play two. Cause otherwise it's gonna be up to me to sing it. All right. We did it. Here he is, oh here he comes."

That was not the only example of Dylan's new-found verbosity. Earlier in the show, he'd introduced "Boots Of Spanish Leather" somewhat patronisingly: "There's more and more young ladies coming to my show so we're starting to do a lot of love ballads now."

Somewhat more revealingly, between "It's Alright, Ma" and "Hang Me, Oh Hang Me" he interjected: "Yeah! 'Put my head in a guillotine'. Actually guillotine wouldn't be a bad way to go. Considering some of the kind of ways they got these days. Better than quittin' anyway."

At first, I couldn't understand why Dylan had suddenly started this between-song patter but the change could be traced to the 2nd June show in Ottawa where he addressed two matters which had clearly upset him. First came an appeal for the return of a stolen guitar:

"Somebody worked his way in here and stole a guitar last night.... Anyway if any of you know who did it just let somebody know. Nothing's gonna happen to the thief.... We'd just like the guitar back. It was inside on the job. That's what this next song's about, something like an inside job."[39]

Ottawa also found Dylan mulling over a hatchet review of the previous night's show. The critic's incredibly inapt demand that Dylan stop playing harmonica and bring back the pre-N.E.T. backing singers provoked Dylan to another extended intro:

"Well here's another song that has a lot of harmonica playing on this. There used to be a bunch of girls used to play on this instead of harmonica. But they decided they'd let me play harmonica for a while whilst they stay home. Anyway hmm. Seemed like there was an article written in the paper about me saying that the girls should come back, and the harmonica should go. Nobody showed me the article but they told me about it though. Anyway so, the girls might be back next time. But it's OK to play harmonica in this one, right?"

Unsurprisingly, there was a thunderous affirmative.

As this leg of the tour approached its climax, the shows lost a little of their sparkle. Voice and energy levels often suffer at the end of a long touring schedule and this had been a very busy year already. Nonetheless, I think this fails to explain why this period is often overlooked by so many fans. Perhaps, they were still entranced by the heights that Paris and London reached.

The first half of the opening year of the decade had gone marvellously well. In the N.E.T., though, you never know what is just around the corner.

It is hard to credit that a year that had gone so well was about to hit problem after problem. It is even harder to believe that the summer 1990 edition of *The Telegraph* opened with an "Address from the Secretary", written by the late John Bauldie, that asked "Isn't Bob's recently acquired 'need to play' getting a tad tedious, even for some of the keenest of Bobcats?" Bauldie was particularly scathing of the European leg of the tour that climaxed with two 60,000-capacity festivals in Belgium, and dubbed it "The Horrible Tour".

This much maligned leg had begun on June 27th in Reykjavik, Iceland. The rest of the short summer jaunt consisted of festivals. Lucrative, no doubt, but far removed from the engaged performances at real Dylan shows.

"'Everything Is Broken' and 'Silvio' were delivered as meaningless babble," Bauldie complained of one Belgian festival date. "And many of the other tunes were tossed off with not a hint or a hope of subtlety or communication. G.E.Smith has turned into a heavy-handed parody of himself – all guitar-thrash and noise and none of the sympathetic interaction that made him so wonderful a sparring partner at past shows, Parker is drumming through the motions in the manner of a bored session player and Tony Garnier was always as interesting as a wet fish. Are this band played out? I mean, don't you just find yourself wanting a 'Like A Rolling Stone' without the mechanical Smith lead lines or an acoustic song without the extra guitar bashing Bob's into oblivion?"

That these comments seemed at least partly true at the time demonstrates how quickly the N.E.T. can change, from intimate hall and focused Dylan to a disinterested parody in a large, muddy wasteland.

Not that these shows were completely without merit. One of the best of these dire summer outings was at the beautiful Stadtpark in Hamburg, and included a cover of "No More One More Time" and a curious one-off item called "Old Rock And Roller". This latter was introduced by Dylan as a song about, "What happens to people like me."

As a tale about a star from the past, largely forgotten by the world he relentlessly tours, it was stunningly apt for this particular leg. Although Hamburg was one of the better shows, Dylan looked extremely the worse-for-wear as the show opened. If his body began to sober up, you had to wonder about his mind – and doubt the wisdom of his new penchant for chatter – when you heard him say:

"I'd like to say a lot of people in America, they're concerned about Germany reuniting. But when you think about it, why should they ever have been disunited, really? Lot of people, they don't know that Hitler wasn't a German anyway."

Mr. Bauldie's criticism[40] no doubt stemmed partially from the fact that these summer money-earners were not a regular feature back then, that Dylan had been playing so well and that we were used to tours with different bands, not repeated visits from the same line-up.

Admittedly the Belgian shows were a prologue for the shambolic Dylan of 1991 and other depressing festival performances throughout the N.E.T. Also, tramping through endless muddy Belgian fields, tired and hungry, and being jostled by thousands of frankly odd fans[41] of headline band The Cure, is hardly a scenario for "enjoying yourself".

Festivals aside, Dylan's deterioration since February was so marked that it appeared essential he take a break. What Dylan didn't need was to keep touring, and drinking; and for G.E. Smith to leave, with prospective replacement guitarists being auditioned in front of paying audiences.

So guess what happened?

***

Dylan followed his short summer tour of Europe with a double blast in North America. Firstly, there was a month of dates beginning on August 12th in Edmonton, Canada. Fans were shocked to learn that G.E. Smith was soon to quit. Two years and some 200 concerts is a pretty fair stint by any normal reckoning but looking back it seems way too short. Dylan believes that the "Never Ending Tour" ended with G.E.'s departure, but for convenience's sake fans have retained the label to refer to everything since 1988. Either way, many feared that the tour itself would not survive the loss of the guitarist. And things certainly did not progress smoothly. During the next month a number of new guitarists were auditioned – live on stage! John Staeheley (August 12-18), Steve Bruton (August 19-29), Miles Joseph (August 31-September 3), Steve Ripley (September 4-9), and guitar technician Cesar Diaz (September 11-12) were all given this trial.

Some of these men also took part in pre-tour rehearsals in late July and early August. The songs they covered were many and varied, giving an insight into the range of material that Dylan was considering for his set lists, despite the unreadiness of a lead guitarist.

Despite all this chaos, late 1990 was not at all bad. If not as consistently impressive as the first half of the year, it certainly shook off the "Horrible Tour" tag. Much like the previous year, the last leg of 1990's touring was, if looser, full of surprises and successes.

After the departure of G.E. Smith, shows that were great from the first to the last song – with no filler, no mumbled lyrics, no coasting along for a few numbers – could no longer be expected. Being searingly, life-changingly, on the ball for every moment of a complete performance no longer seemed within Dylan's grasp – certainly not on a regular basis.

The closing leg of 1990 produced mighty swings between the shambolic and the transcendent – sometimes from one song to the next. Notable moments in mid-August to mid-September included some astonishing covers. The first show featured the Beatles' "Nowhere Man", a song that seemed to have been composed under Dylan's influence. It's nice to know that Dylan covered it, but not so nice to actually hear it. It is hard to know what prompted these one-off covers, but the Beatles had been on Dylan's mind at the Hamburg show in Germany. Besides rabbiting on about Hitler, Dylan introduced his final song that day like this:

"Thank you. It's always a pleasure to play here in this city here. Hamburg, where the Beatles started. Anybody remember the Beatles? Shout 'Yeah', if you remember the Beatles...[Nobody did]... Nobody knows the Beatles?...They started right here. This is one of their songs, which they inspired way back when."

The song he actually then played was his own, "Highway 61 Revisited". Perhaps even more surprising was his performance of Otis Redding's "Sitting

On The Dock Of The Bay" on August 18th. It was another eccentric effort, with Dylan sounding somewhat drunk. Which stands in contrast to another cover that hardly anyone else seems to like but I love unreservedly. That being a moving tribute to Stevie Ray Vaughan who had died the night before[42], Dylan introduced the song to the audience, saying:

"OK I guess everybody here knows about Stevie, so. This is for Stevie. Wherever you are."

And then played a poignant version of the Mercer/Mancini classic, Moon River. Given the song's history and its reference to Huckleberry Finn[43] it seems a fitting one for Dylan to cover and provided a most moving and memorable tribute.

Other covers included a one-off "Stand By Me" and a swaggering version of the Grateful Dead's "Friend Of The Devil". Another cover that sounded like a song ready made for Dylan was Little Feat's "Willing" which reappeared later and improved with successive outings.

The shows were uneven, perhaps not surprisingly given the guitarist situation, and even a song like "Lakes Of Pontchartrain" could turn out (relatively) poorly. At Portland, Oregon on August 21st, for example, it was painful to hear Dylan just tiptoe through the song. All the energy and glory of 1988 had dissipated in the wind.

***

In the month's break between tour legs, *under the red sky* was released to unfairly scathing reviews and disastrous sales. During October rehearsals, the band attempted several of its songs: "Wiggle Wiggle", "10,000 Men", "Under The Red Sky", "2 x 2", and "Unbelievable" (the single from the album). But only the title track, "T.V. Talkin' Song" and "Wiggle Wiggle" would be played before the year's end.

If Dylan's 1989 casino show provoked a newspaper debate, Dylan's decision to play the military academy at West Point, New York, on October 13th 1990 led to an avalanche of press. Although the set-list included "Masters Of War" and "Blowin' In The Wind", Dylan laid no special emphasis on them or on the venue – the standout track, in fact, was "Trail Of The Buffalo". For Dylan, it was just another show.

As is often the case, while Dylan drew no significance from his actions, others were more than willing to do so. *The New York Times* could not overlook the irony of the man "who galvanised the 1960's anti-war movement" performing "Blowin' In The Wind" for an audience of future army commanders.

"Many hard core Dylan fans shook their heads in disbelief as they entered the auditorium," the paper's critic continued, "walking under banners for the Screaming Eagles (101st Airborne Division) and Hell on Wheels (Second Armored Division). They said the concert, in a setting they variously described as 'weird', 'bizarre' and 'the belly of a beast', had a special intensity."

Well it may have for them, but there is no indication that for Dylan it was any more than another show on the N.E.T..

After the West Point gig, Dylan stayed in New York for another Beacon Theatre residency, starting on October 15th. This was G.E. Smith's last stand, with John Staeheley and Cesar Diaz being tried out onstage too.

For the five-night series of shows Dylan veered from the sublime to the ridiculous via the successful and the awful.

"He shuffled his song-deck with dizzying inconsistency," David Fricke wrote of the opening night in *Melody Maker*, "alternatively flashing aces and jokers like a schizo cardsharp – all too willing, it seemed, to play a losing hand just to upend our expectations. The Protest Prince, The Voice Of A Generation, The Folk-Rock Avenger – none of those Dylans showed up tonight. What we got was the Imp Perverse."

There were various highlights throughout the residency, as there were throughout the remainder of the year. I was collecting all the shows by now and listening to them avidly, but as the N.E.T. progressed and more and more shows clamoured for attention, I returned to compilation bootleg CDs when I wanted to hear late 1990.

With an average of some 100 shows a year, it was almost impossible to keep listening to all the shows (as well as all the other material), so compilation CDs became very popular. The summer and fall US tours spawned a double-CD selecting the best or most unusual performances, while the Beacon shows were represented by discs presenting a full show plus the highlights of each night.

N.E.T. – Last night of the 1990 Beacon Theatre Residency
19th October 1990, Beacon Theatre, New York, New York, USA
1   Dixie (Daniel/ Decatur/ Emmett Instrumental)
2   To Be Alone With You
3   Joey (Dylan/ Levy)
4   Silvio (Dylan/ Hunter)
5   Masters Of War
6   Under The Red Sky
7   Wiggle Wiggle
8   Dark As A Dungeon (Merle Travis) (Acoustic)
9   She Belongs To Me (Acoustic)
10   It's Alright, Ma (I'm Only Bleeding) (Acoustic)
11   Love Minus Zero/No Limit (Acoustic)
12   TV Talking Song
13   Shooting Star
14   Tight Connection To My Heart (Has Anybody Seen My Love)
15   Gotta Serve Somebody
16   All Along The Watchtower
17   Like A Rolling Stone
        *
18   It Ain't Me, Babe (Acoustic)
19   Highway 61 Revisited
20   Maggie's Farm

All the Beacon shows started with a short instrumental, usually "Dixie", though even "Old MacDonald Had A Farm" and "The Battle Hymn of The

Republic" were tried. The 19th October show had a subdued start with "To Be Alone With You", which was strangely at odds with the "Dixie" opening. It was a lovely choice as first song, though, and we had become accustomed by now to Dylan taking time to warm up. Warm applause greeted the song's close and also the opening of the next song – the great, and unfairly maligned, "Joey". The fire of Hammersmith and Paris way back in February was now replaced by a more sombre shading.

An instantly forgettable "Silvio" at least got Dylan and the band going before "Masters Of War" launched the show properly; there was a good range to Dylan's vocals, from punchy to cantillating. This set him up for a powerful, deep-voiced rendition of "Under The Red Sky". Sticking with the new album, he then gave us an enjoyable, up-tempo "Wiggle Wiggle".

The acoustic set opened with the impressive "Dark As A Dungeon" sung with great feeling. "She Belongs To Me" was followed by a rapturously received "It's Alright Ma (I'm Only Bleeding)". This sumptuous acoustic set ended with "Love Minus Zero/No Limit", with an experimentally exaggerated melody.

"TV Talking Song" sounded more like the menacing outtakes that dwarf the released version, without being as powerful. However, Dylan was a bit unfair to *under the red sky* when he followed one of its lesser songs with one of *Oh Mercy*'s heavyweights, "Shooting Star". Then it was another outing for the re-christened wonder from the start of the year: "Has Anybody Seen My Love". It was very welcome here although Dylan could not match February's control.

Things loosened up with "Gotta Serve Somebody", which saw saxophonist Karl Denham, from support act Lenny Kravitz's band, come onstage. He remained for "All Along The Watchtower" and made a positive contribution to a chaotic, urgent version.

"Like A Rolling Stone" closed the set, but for a song that has changed minds if not worlds, this fell into the category of live grunge. Similarly, the encores lived up to their normal standard – great when you're there, but less impressive on tape. On "It Ain't Me, Babe", to his great credit, Dylan made a determined effort to raise the song above a mere singalong, but no-one told the crowd!.

There was a slam bam thank you ma'am "Highway 61 Revisited" and then the evening came to a close with an even more raucous "Maggie's Farm", with Kravitz and his band onstage for a full-blast rock-out.

***

The last leg of an incredibly packed year saw Dylan and the band pull out many fine performances. The October 25th show in Oxford, Mississippi opened with a great rendition of ZZ Top's then current single, "My Head's In Missis-sippi", and he also performed, for the only time, his 1962 cry against injustice, "Oxford Town". Other treats included a moving "One Too Many Mornings", an understated "Visions Of Johanna", an interesting new take on "Every Grain Of Sand", and a surprising cover of Hank Williams's "Hey, Good Lookin'".

The year's touring ended on November 18th at The Fox Theater in Detroit. This show opened with yet another surprising live debut, "Buckets Of Rain", of all things. This gem from *Blood On The Tracks* was a most welcome fare-well present to mark the end of 1990.

Chapter Five: 1991

You've Got To Give It Your All

"You hear sometimes about the glamour of the road, but you get over that real fast. There are a lot of times that it's no different from going to work in the morning. Still, you're either a player or you're not a player."
Bob Dylan talking to Robert Hilburn, November 1991[44]

Despite a hectic 1990, Dylan was back on the road again by late January 1991. With another Hammersmith residency beginning on February 8th, we had the dubious pleasure of queuing up all night for tickets in freezing weather. After 1990's problems I was determined not to miss out but I could have done without having to queue overnight three times. This was necessitated by the way the tickets went on sale – first for five nights, then later two more shows were added and then, after that, another one. I say "necessitated", but this was only the case if you were so obsessed that you needed to be those few extra rows closer to the front.

At least the queuing gave you plenty of time to meet other Dylan fans, renew old acquaintances and make new ones. The morning after the first batch of tickets went on sale, I noticed someone joining the queue between 5 and 6 am. Within minutes he was moaning about the cold. Since I had been there for over six hours already, and in much colder weather, I kindly suggested that he should be grateful to be only three places behind me. This was my first meeting with a certain Joe McShane, whose acquaintance I suffer to this very day. I think I have been to more Dylan shows with Joe than with anyone else.

As the new year dawned it brought news of band personnel changes. Tony Garnier was still playing bass, and Cesar Diaz was still around, but the main guitar duties now fell to new recruit John Jackson. Meanwhile, Chris Parker had been replaced by Ian Wallace on drums, who had an approach that was so consistent it seemed like he played the same on every song, every show, every time.

Still, there were encouraging noises emanating from the first leg of the year's touring. The opening show in Zurich on January 28th gave a debut to "God

Knows" from *under the red sky* and more surprisingly also featured "Bob Dylan's Dream" from his *Freewheelin'* days, which had not been performed for nearly 30 years – talk about whetting your appetite!

After all the queuing, the ticket swapping, the late requests, and organising seats for family and friends, the shows drew nearer, slowly (very) but surely.

Before the Hammersmith residency Dylan played two shows in Glasgow and one each on Dublin and Belfast. They did not augur well, as the band appeared under-rehearsed, or to be more precise, completely unrehearsed.

"Bob Dylan shuffled onstage wearing a tartan jacket and looking like he's had a drink," Michael Gray observed in his review of the first Glasgow date. Dylan certainly seemed to be the worse for alcohol at the second Glasgow show, dropping his guitar a couple of times and wandering off stage during "Positively 4th Street", leaving his astonished band to continue without him.

"Muttering into a microphone," Gray continued, "hiding in the oblivion of the guitars and under lights so low it was hard to see him even from the front, Dylan was obviously suffering. 'God knows it's a struggle' was his most heart-felt line last night. It surely doesn't have to be this way."[45]

Alas that's the way it was for much of this early bout of 1991 touring though. Many people laud the second Glasgow show, which benefited from the most varied and interesting set list of February. What people seemed to like most was the experience of watching a man teetering on the brink. There's an end-less fascination in seeing whether he can keep going, and on the second night in Glasgow it wasn't so much teetering on the brink as falling over the edge.

As for Hammersmith, it was more of the first night Glasgow, though there were a few positives. One was that Dylan had come at all, as the Gulf War had seen a sharp decrease in any "names" travelling from the States to Europe. Another was that Dylan wasn't sullen – all the time. For much of the time he was having fun, clowning about on stage. He seemed to veer from being very drunk to – well, sober might be overdoing it, but certainly well in control. The band though were terrible. John Jackson did nothing but grin maniacally at the audience while playing the same thing on every song. I'm not at all sure what the other guitarists were doing, and the drums sounded like a drum machine with a replay button that had got stuck. Hunched up in the darkness over his microphone, Dylan offered no help, muttering and mumbling his way through the electric sets.

The acoustic sets, as usual, were better, and we got to hear "Bob Dylan's Dream". It was also exhilarating to see Dylan so close up again, with the mannerisms and the facial grimaces that are so much part of his act. Overall though, it was mainly bad memories of bad shows, and I don't mean "bad" just by Bob's standards. These were bad performances by any measure.

Not that you'd have known I thought so from the reviews I wrote at the time. Buoyed up by having just seen Dylan and in the full flush of running my own Bob fanzine, I wildly accentuated the positive. In addition, I chose for two of my three reviews the Saturday shows which were the best of [what I now acknowledge as] a sorry bunch.

However, in spite of my immediate euphoria, my wildly enthusiastic show diary did contain one major initial reservation. After "The Man In Me" on Friday 8th, I noted amidst my joy that "It was about then that I realised how pedestrian the band are and how it was restricting Dylan. He seems about to step up a gear and really fly, but is brought back to earth each time."

I didn't have any tapes to listen to until later the next week so I was still caught up in the "live" experience, and the Saturday show was much better than the opening night, which I probably didn't yet rate as low as it deserved, so you can imagine that I was still very up for things on the first Sunday of the residence. Yet my notes from the time also betray a touch more realism creeping in.

"'Lay Lady Lay' doesn't take off," my tour diary states in black and white. "After a promising opening, the temperature is lowered and it just sounds as though she's not gonna stay and that knowing this, he just goes through the motions.

"A grunge-rock version of 'All Along The Watchtower' gets its first London airing. Half the audience and band thought it was 'Masters Of War' at the beginning. Well, the same tune is being used for a lot of the songs this week, or so it seems. Maybe they don't know any others?"

My notes betrayed other words of caution. After revelling in the "goose-pimple" delights of "Bob Dylan's Dream" I admonished our hero to "just forget bands like these and do an acoustic tour next time, Bobby". Other highlights were "Man In A Long Black Coat" and "Shooting Star". I was pleased Bob seemed to be enjoying himself, but even back then I couldn't "help noticing that some of the gestures and mannerisms that look so spontaneous are being repeated in an obviously predetermined manner".

***

These initial doubts were compounded as the gigs passed. On the Tuesday night I was centre front row and was startled and delighted when Dylan stormed to the microphone, sans guitar, for a hand-held harmonica and vocal "Tangled Up In Blue". Except this was not a statement of artistry à la 1975 or years later in 1995, just a hopeless mess. I'm still not sure if Dylan had deliberately set aside his guitar, or simply didn't realise he had left it behind.

At the time I was most excited by the Saturday show on the 16th – which probably was the best of the Hammersmith run – despite the depressing rumours amongst fans that suggested Dylan had been seen that very afternoon being walked around the Odeon car park to sober him up. Anyway, the comparatively above-par Saturday raised my hopes for a good ending on the second Sunday. Joe remarked shortly before the concert that this was "Dylan's last chance to pull the series of shows out of the fire", but Dylan either did not realise this or did not care. A humdrum performance of yet another standard set-list sent the fans home disappointed and disgruntled. I kind of cheated in my magazine, anyway, because I had already read how others had reviewed the other nights so felt it incumbent upon me to lighten the blow of some of their comments. Comments such as: "Desecrate ... negative ... lack of imagination ... shambles ... crushing disappointment"; complaints about Dylan being drunk and uninterested; and unanimous agreement that the band either couldn't play at all, had never rehearsed properly, or both. It was all very dispiriting.

Another major complaint was the lack of variety in the set lists. Clearly if the band were so unfamiliar with these "standard" set lists, changing them would be (even further) beyond them. I was still clinging to the belief that there were some positive performances, but reality dawned with the tapes, when the inevitable comparison with the previous year was highlighted in all its damning clarity.

My co-reviewers had been more truthful and direct. This was at a time when I said – with no hint of a lie – that I'd be happy to see Dylan walk on stage and read from the telephone directory. As time went on and the fanzine became more established, I, in turn, felt confident enough to be more pointed in my comments and, in fact, my information line (up and running by now) was, in later years, to lean completely the other way.[46]

There were defenders of the shows, as there always are of anything Dylan does, and a lively debate ran on for the next few issues. Most tellingly for me was that I stopped playing any tapes from this period soon afterwards and have never enjoyed returning to them. Allan Jones in *Melody Maker*, however, managed to find much to praise in the first Glasgow show in a review that offered more insight and creativity than Dylan managed most nights on stage:

"...The group had apparently not distinguished themselves in either Switzerland or Belgium. They had obviously prepared only a limited repertoire, and for the first time in years Dylan had been forced to play identical sets at successive concerts. Furthermore, there are sinister rumblings about Dylan's drinking. In Belgium he was allegedly pissed virtually senseless, singing off-mike throughout most of the show. When you could hear him, his singing was apparently slurred, more incoherent than ever. Those lyrics he could remember were delivered with an off-handedness that bordered on bored indifference."

Mr Jones found himself, at the Glasgow show, unable to tell what song was being performed (it was "Stuck Inside Of Mobile, With The Memphis Blues Again"). He compared the "vandalisation" of the song to that witnessed during the 1987 UK tour, and continued:

"Dylan looks as much a mess now as he did then. The ragged comanchero look has been abandoned, however. Dylan now resembles nothing so much as an alcoholic lumberjack on a Saturday night out in some Saskatchewan backwater, staggering around the stage here in a huge plaid jacket and odd little hat. The band, meanwhile, have all the charisma of a death squad in some banana republic... these people aren't so much under-rehearsed as almost complete strangers to each other and Dylan's music specifically. Dylan, hilariously, doesn't seem to give a f***."

Well, maybe it was hilarious that first time but, it became less so with each repeat viewing as the tour stumbled on.

To see and hear how the band looked and sounded in February 1991, you just need to view television footage of the Grammy awards ceremony from New York on the 20th, when Dylan was given a Grammy Lifetime Achievement Award. Dylan's appearance caused a media stir par excellence on two counts. Talking point one was his performance; number two was his acceptance speech.

Dylan performed his damning anti-war indictment, "Masters Of War" – a brave choice given that the Gulf War was still going on and Hawkish jingoism was rife. However, since he chose to sing it without a pause for breath, and backed by this hapless band, no-one who did not already know the song would have got the message. In fact, many who did know the song didn't even recognise it here. Not only did Dylan's nasal passages sound blocked (he later revealed he'd had a cold) but it seemed he had swallowed a burst of helium before starting to sing. Many observers thought he was singing in Hebrew. The tuxedoed crowd looked on in utter bewilderment. The next day's papers marvelled how only Dylan had performed a song with any meaning and purpose, but then, being Dylan, he had made it completely incomprehensible.

So far this was all quite funny, but pure comic genius was still to come in the form of his acceptance speech.

After taking his trophy from a deliriously happy Jack Nicholson, Dylan peered out at the lights and cameras, and hesitantly, began to speak:.

"Thank you ... well ... alright ... yeah, well, my daddy he didn't leave me too much ... you know he was a very simple man and he didn't leave me a lot but what he told me was this ... what he did say was ... son ... he said uh ...."

Then Dylan paused, and the pause seemed to go on forever. Time hung still; it appeared as though Dylan had lost it completely. The crowd began to stir, a few titters were heard, then full nervous laughter. The audience seemed embarrassed for Bob, for themselves, and for the Grammies that were supposed to go so smoothly to a pre-determined schedule of mutual back-slapping. But Dylan hadn't lost it: his timing was perfect as he extended the pause to a tension-filled breaking point and then concluded:

"He said, you know it's possible to become so defiled in this world that your own father and mother will abandon you and if that happens, God will always believe in your ability to mend your ways. Thank you."

With that Dylan walked off, leaving many a dropped jaw in the bewildered audience, who gave him a standing ovation – probably because they were relieved to see the back of him.

For me, watching this in the UK, it was a great, great moment. Somehow Dylan had performed live on TV down to the level of his recent Hammersmith shows but, just by his choice of song, had made that noteworthy. This person who had seemed so out of it, so not in control, had then pulled off a marvellous little Dylanesque wind-up. I was basking in the glow when my phone rang. It was someone asking me what the hell Bob had thought he was doing, why did he "sing" like that and what the hell was his speech all about? Oddly enough, I knew then, for sure, that it had been a success and that Dylan had stirred things up again. Once people found out what song he'd been singing, "Masters Of War" was much discussed.

It worked a treat: newspaper after newspaper carried the story along the lines of, "Want to know what Bob Dylan was singing last night, it was.....", then acres of print about Dylan, about the war, about the Grammies. Most comment was pretty favourable too, praising Dylan for being an individual, for resisting the cloying show business approach and for still, all these years later, being a rock'n'roller who made you think. The only downside to all this was that I knew that "Masters Of War" had not been made incomprehensible just for this one-off appearance; it was just one of many incomprehensible renditions we'd already heard this year. But the choice of song was perfect and the timing in his speech was superb. At this point I, and nearly everyone watching, thought it was an off the cuff speech, another glimpse into the totally unique way he looks at life. Someone on the internet,[47] though, recognised the text as "almost a verbatim account of the commentary of Rabbi Shimshon Rafael Hirsch [the spiritual leader of traditional Jewry in Germany in the mid-19th century] on [Psalms 27:10]":

"Even if I were so depraved that my own mother and father would abandon me to my own devices, God would still gather me up and believe in my ability to mend my ways."

Now, we have no way of knowing if Abraham Zimmerman really taught this to his son or if Bob simply picked it up from a commentary on the Jewish prayer book (Psalm 27 is recited at the morning and evening prayer services during the month before the Jewish New Year), but in any case, the wording is too similar to Hirsch's to ignore.[48]

***

The release of *The Bootleg Series*, in the last week of March, was a major illustration of what I talked about in my introduction to the N.E.T. – the way Dylan always lives with his past. Not that as an artist he can afford to dwell on things like this – indeed the great Dylan "achievements" of this year, this compilation and the "Series of Dreams" video occurred without his input – but, whether he likes it or not, he cannot escape them. The poverty of his current touring was shown up not just by the memories and tapes of the '88-'90 shows and his impressive back catalogue, but by the release of this three-CD career retrospective, consisting of out-takes, oddities and live tracks – a feast of "bootleg" material including some never heard on the hundreds of Dylan bootlegs released to date. The compilation was a treat not only for fans but for anyone interested in popular music, especially given Dylan's rather strange principles that had allowed, for example, one of his finest ever songs, "Blind Willie McTell", to remain the preserve of bootleggers until this official unveiling. What for anyone else would have been a collection of cast-offs was instead a release of serious artistic worth. *Record Collector* considered it "The most important archive release we have ever reviewed. Album of the year? It seems certain. Any takers for best compilation of all time?"[49]

It would be no exaggeration to say that the performances on this compilation alone show Dylan to be the best lyricist and greatest interpretative singer in the whole of recorded popular music. At the same time it seemed an acknowledgement of the wisdom of those die-hard fans who had collected bootleg after bootleg, tape after tape; the fans who also knew that, magnificent though this collection was, it was just the tip of a staggering iceberg.

Unfortunately, though, these same fans had to endure the nadir of the N.E.T., indeed Dylan's whole career, at the same time as the *Bootleg Series'* vindicating appearance. The contrast between the past and the present was never crueller.

Undeterred by, and seemingly unconnected to, the release of these back pages, Dylan continued the dismal start to 1991's touring with a ramshackle 15-date jaunt in America, starting on April 19th. Cesar Diaz, the roadie-turned-guitarist, had left the stage by now, not before time. However, it might have been an idea if someone else had replaced him. This most forgettable period of the N.E.T. – or forgettable if your therapy works – thankfully drew to a close on May 12th.

That date was less than two weeks before Dylan turned 50 (on May 24th). The welter of publicity for *The Bootleg Series* was nothing compared to the tidal wave of books, magazine articles, newspaper features and editorials, TV programmes and news clips that greeted this landmark. The coverage was exceptional, and exceptionally varied, from the trite to the ultra-serious and every shade between. If Dylan had begun to seem marginalised in the '80s, the N.E.T., the box set and his 50th birthday were pushing him back into the limelight he seemed to both detest and court.

Anyway, back to the shows, and you may think that we Europe-based Bob fans had cooled in our frantic need to see the Great Man, after bemoaning the February shows and each of the succeeding leg's tapes as they arrived. Not a bit of it: the mere mention of more dates in Europe in early summer had us scurrying about to secure tickets and arrange travel. It takes a lot to really dampen a Dylan fan's expectations, and nothing at all can dilute the hope that he can turn it around again at any given time. He had done it so often in the past and would again in the future. And, although it may sound odd now, we never knew when his last visit to Europe might be. That long gap between 1966 and 1978 was hard to forget, even all those years later. After all, this was the third consecutive summer: we hardly thought that it would continue that way.

June 6th found Dylan in Rome, kicking off a three-and-a-half month stint that would take him from Europe to the USA and then on to South America. In the eternal city he opened with an N.E.T. debut of "When I Paint My Masterpiece" (appropriately enough, as that song also begins in Rome). We also got rather lovely acoustic renditions of Paul Simon's "Homeward Bound" and John Prine's "People Puttin' People Down". It seemed that Dylan and the band had been working to extend their repertoire and were more focused than on those dismal February nights. It would be going too far to say that this hope was repaid but there were some stronger shows than earlier in the year and some genuine highlights. Dylan always seems to be raucously received in Italy and has a good time there. Van Morrison was around for a few of the Italian dates; the twosome even playing a couple of "double headers", but the only duets were in Milan, where Dylan added harmonica to two songs during Van's opening set.

A standout for me from this tour was "When First Unto The Country" in Budapest. Dylan was still, unfortunately, swallowing some of his words; nonetheless, his performance was so good that for years I thought it came from 1992.

Although these shows displayed a degree of improvement, disaster never seemed far away and as the European jaunt progressed, it struck on various occasions, including a dire show at Denmark's Mitdfyn Rock Festival on June 29th.

The Stuttgart show was remarkable for a number of reasons. It was the first time in about 300 shows that the set list did not feature "Like A Rolling Stone". The old war-horse was replaced in the last pre-encore slot (both tonight and for the immediate future) by that, er, other old war-horse from the same album, "Ballad Of A Thin Man". The set structure changed too – instead of six electric songs followed by the acoustic set and six more electric, it was now eight in the first electric set and four in the latter. After a catastrophic attempt at playing the piano on the first song, Dylan abandoned it.

Another exceptional thing about this show was Dylan's silly between-song patter. Dylan introduced "Leopard-Skin Pill-Box Hat" as "my fashion song". "Anybody here into fashion?" he asked us. "Like, you know, clothes." Prior to "Knockin' On Heaven's Door" the questions got even easier: "Anybody here hear of Heaven? Well here's a song about Heaven. Heaven's in the title." [50]

Stuttgart also produced one of my favourite N.E.T. fan stories. David Bristow's experience there sums up the worst of the N.E.T., 1991 style. "The show did not go well," Bristow wrote to me.

"The good citizens of Stuttgart were leaving by the third song. I went to a bar after the show, where many of those brave folk who had survived to the end had gathered. Next to me was a serious looking German guy writing down the track list, although one or two songs had eluded him. This was a solemn exercise being conducted by someone who took life, and such lists, very seriously. He asked me to help him fill in the blanks and seemed quite pleased that I recalled a couple of numbers that he had missed. The problem came with the first song of the night, which I informed him was 'New Morning', as indeed it was and was, no doubt, identified as such on the cue sheet given to the band. At least, three members of the band played 'New Morning', but the one at the front had some difficulty with it. As I recall, Bob tried to play the piano/organ and having failed, he decided to sing into the mic on the piano to discover that, very like this version of this song, it wasn't working. He then made his way, perhaps a little unsteadily, over to his guitar before finally arriving at the main mic to deliver a vocal performance that made any live version of 'You Angel You' sound, by comparison, word-perfect.

"Hence my German friend's difficulty in identifying the opener that night. However, when I had to insist that the song was indeed 'New Morning', or at least that is what would appear in the set list once published, things turned a little ugly. 'But I am knowing the song 'New Morning', he tried to explain in his broken English, 'and that is not it'. When I had to confirm it was, he became insistent that he was compiling an authoritative document and that it was essential only accurate information be included. He had the album *New Morning*, he knew the song and whatever else that was tonight, it was not

'New Morning'. He knew I was a fan and must therefore have thought that I was withholding this important information, the correct name of the song, as an act of spite... Hence I had to leave a Stuttgart bar rather quickly as otherwise I may have suffered the kind of assault that Bob had launched on the song in question. There were no survivors of that assault and I feared a repeat."

After inflicting two more festival sets on Scandinavia at the end of June, Dylan was back touring in the US, beginning on Independence Day and ending on the 27th. Following a shockingly lengthy break of almost two weeks Dylan then found himself playing nine shows in South America, performing mainly greatest hits to crowds that varied from under 2,000 to over 20,000. Dylan sent a "wish you were here" calling card to his regular touring fans by including "Ring Them Bells" for the first time since its botched debut in October 1989.

By the end of the summer, even Dylan was tiring and, after ending the South American jaunt on 21st August he did not resume the N.E.T. until October 24th in Corpus Christi, Texas. Exactly a week prior to that, however, he made a high-profile, filmed stage appearance at the '60s night of the Guitar Greats Festival in Seville, Spain, though without his regular N.E.T. band.

The Jack Bruce Band backed Dylan on his opening song before Bob switched to acoustic mode for the next three songs. (Richard Thompson was on stage for these but seemed unsure of what Dylan was up to.) Finally Dylan introduced his former Live Aid partner in crime Keith Richards for a criminal deconstruction of "Shake Rattle & Roll".

Given his poor performances in the year so far, trepidation levels – both amongst audience members and TV viewers like myself – were sky-high as Dylan took the stage. In the opening song, "All Along The Watchtower", he was clearly struggling – not particularly badly by 1991 standards, but struggling nonetheless. For a Guitars Legend event the guitar playing sounded, to put it mildly, inappropriate. No one seemed to know what they were supposed to be doing, and Dylan was having too much trouble of his own to give any directions. "Boots Of Spanish Leather" (a predictable choice!) started very shakily too, and it looked for all the world as if tomorrow would once again be spent excusing Dylan's TV appearance.

Then, out of nowhere, something magical happened. Dylan began to find his voice and his control. The improvement continued apace with a decent stab at "Across The Borderline" and a magnificent reading of Mutterlein, Winkler, Rausch and Sigman's "Answer Me, My Love". He had suddenly rediscovered the power of enunciation and seemed engaged in his performance in a way that had been lacking previously. It was not enough to get him good reviews – and to be fair, of the four songs we'd had two poorly performed, one quite decent and one good, so that's hardly surprising – but it gave people like myself hope that the year was not going to be a complete wash out.

After the closing chaotic Keith Richards "duet", I spun the video back and watched "Answer Me" again, and again, and again. It was a charming harbinger of better nights to come in 1991.

Seville proved a crucial turning point. Dylan steadily improved in the last week of October before unleashing his new found enthusiasm. I am not saying it was all plain sailing but if we look at the show from Tulsa, we can see the contrast to earlier in the year, and the way he turned the November shows into triumphs.

It should also be noted that the band had transformed themselves into a much better unit. According to Olöf Björner they had taken to calling themselves "the undesirables" in response to all the criticism they had received. Perhaps it was this "us v them" spirit of unity that inspired them to greater heights.

Tulsa, 30th October 1991
Brady Theatre, Tulsa, Oklahoma

1	New Morning
2	Lay Lady Lay
3	All Along The Watchtower
4	Early Morning Rain (G Lightfoot)
5	I'll Remember You
6	Gotta Serve Somebody
7	Simple Twist Of Fate
8	I'll Be Your Baby Tonight
9	Trail Of The Buffalo (Trad)(Acoustic)
10	Mr. Tambourine Man(Acoustic)
11	Answer Me, My Love (Mutterlein/Winkler/Rausch/Sigman) (Acoustic)
12	It Ain't Me, Babe (Acoustic)
13	Every Grain Of Sand
14	Everything Is Broken
15	Man In The Long Black Coat
16	Maggie's Farm
	*
17	What Good Am I ?
18	Ballad Of A Thin Man

"New Morning" was still the opener and, even though Dylan now seemed to know more of the words than he did in the summer, it was still dreadful; even his "thanks" at the end sounded weary.

On a messy "Lay Lady Lay", Dylan's self-parodic whining was punctuated by ham-fisted instrumentals. Dylan seemed oblivious that things sounded as bad as earlier in the year."

An impossible-to-identify intro led into a passable "All Along The Watchtower", before a throaty but stoic take on Gordon Lightfoot's "Early Morning Rain" raised the show to a new level. "That's one of my real old songs," Bob told the audience. "So old it wasn't even written by me."

"I'll Remember You" was OK, while "Gotta Serve Somebody" saw Dylan having his usual fun with this song. "That's my response to, er, Arlo Guthrie's song called "Alice's Restaurant", Dylan quipped afterwards. The audience were then treated to a wonderfully understated "Simple Twist Of Fate", enlivened by daring experiments with the line endings. The opening few bars of this magical song, even before Dylan started singing, were worth the whole show thus far. Even the ending harmonica solo and band playing in this seem to have a point rather than the mindless doodling evident earlier. It disinte-

79

grated at the end, alas, as a coughing Dylan excused what he called "a trick ending".

"I'll Be Your Baby Tonight" was a lazy-good-time-Bob. Dylan then found an assured voice for "Trail Of The Buffalo" – "my animal preservation song". He always performs this well, but, even so, the contrast between his vocals here and on the preceding song was extraordinary.

"Mr. Tambourine Man" started somewhat hurriedly, then there was a nice little conspiratorial whisper on the second line ending word of "you". Dylan seemed to play the song around it, eternally circling the song for further new meanings and intonations.

Still in whimsical mood, Dylan introduced "Answer Me My Love", the song that had so impressed me at Seville, as "My new song, we've got a single coming out". Despite still being bedevilled by an intrusive throatiness he was in full expressive mode, ably abetted by some nifty guitar work. It was a good example of what going to shows on the Never Ending Tour is so often about: a working musician going out night after night and attempting to convey to the audience the very core of what a particular song means to him at that particular moment.

As though it had inspired him as well as us, Dylan got thoroughly into the succeeding – and lyrically contrasting – "It Ain't Me, Babe". He was now singing in an impassioned, deeper, voice. The (successful) attempt at fully communicating "Answer Me" had freed him from the tinny wheeze that had plagued the earlier material. "It Ain't Me, Babe", along with "Simple Twist of Fate", "Answer Me" and "Trail Of The Buffalo" was light years ahead of the rest of the show, and they all hinted at Dylan's newly re-discovered commitment to his performing art.

This tape kicked off a period of shows which I have played and enjoyed ever since. To this day when I hear the names Ames, Wichita, South Bend, Evanston, Dayton, Wilkes-Barre or Madison, it is Dylan's great November 1991 shows I think of. At Madison, Dylan gave a revealing interview about the N.E.T. to Robert Hilburn of *The L.A. Times.*

"Dylan paces impatiently backstage at the Dane County Memorial Coliseum in Madison" Hillburn began. "A snowstorm had snarled traffic, and it has taken Dylan's bus four hours instead of two to get here from Chicago. He seems anxious to get the whole evening over with. Finally, he goes back to the bus to wait out the opening act." After the show, Dylan tells Hillburn flatly, "That was a useless gig." When someone mentioned that the audience seemed to enjoy it, Dylan dismissed them with a wave of his hand. "Naw, it just wasn't there. Nothin' wrong with the audience. Sometimes the energy level just doesn't happen the way it should. We didn't invite this weather to follow us around." Dylan then lapsed into silence.

This is fascinating as, far from being "useless", the gig was quite excellent. And, as for "it just wasn't there", Dylan could hardly have been more unfair on himself. Still, it was refreshing to hear him demanding more and more of himself. What a contrast to the shambling, disinterested figure that had visited the UK back in February.

"The night before, after the Northwestern show, he had been more talkative, and more philosophical about the ups and downs of touring," Hillburn was relieved to report. "'You hear sometimes about the glamour of the road,' he said then, 'but you get over that real fast. There are a lot of times that it's no different from going to work in the morning. Still, you're either a player or you're not a player. It didn't really occur to me until we did those shows with the Grateful Dead (in 1987). If you just go out every three years or so, like I was doing for a while, that's when you lose touch. If you are going to be a performer, you've got to give it your all'."

1992 beckoned, and Dylan continued to give it his all.

Chapter Six: 1992

It's Hard To Shut It Off

"There comes a point for everything, playing music is a full-time job you know. It's hard to shut if off and turn it off and on again like a faucet".
Bob Dylan talking to Stuart Coupe, 1992

The end of 1991 and the opening of 1992 were dominated for Dylan fans by rumours that the tour was going to end altogether, or that there would be a long gap before he resumed touring or, more encouragingly, that Dylan was going to get together with the surviving members of The Band for a tour of Japan. None of these rumours came true in 1992; nor have they since, despite re-appearing with regularity over the ensuing years.

1992's Never Ending Tour legs kicked off with some 20-odd dates in Australia and New Zealand before Dylan returned to the States to play his first shows in Hawaii since 1966. Bucky Baxter, from the Steve Earle band that had supported Dylan back in 1989, had joined the band providing steel guitar and mandolin to flesh out the sound.

The opening show, in Perth, Western Australia, featured Jimi Hendrix's "Dolly Dagger"[51] and the traditional "Little Maggie", neither of which has been played live since. Another "first" was the Grateful Dead's "West L.A. Fadeaway", which was rehearsed in February 1989 and appeared twice more in 1992 before re-surfacing in 1995.

After the first show, the format for the standard 18 song set list changed from 8 electric songs followed by 4 acoustic, 4 electric and then two electric encores to a main set consisting of 7 electric songs, followed by 4 acoustic, 2 electric, 1 acoustic, 1 electric. The encores became 2 electric, 1 acoustic solo.

The really big news, though, came soon after, with the story that "Idiot Wind" had been played on 2nd April. It is hard now to accurately describe the excitement that boomeranged around the Dylan world at this news.

The song is a central masterpiece in what most fans consider Dylan's greatest album, *Blood On The Tracks*. It was central, also, to the *Hard Rain* album and film and it seemed almost inconceivably great tidings that Dylan had decided to play it again after so many years. It is a song of such transcendent brilliance and weighty impact that it was bound to be the engine room of the new shows, the song which all others in the set-list would play off.

Dylan fans were also much engaged by the news that our man had apparently "broken down with emotion" as he sang the lines "he was famous long ago" in "Desolation Row". Dylan had to stop singing and retreat from the microphone to compose himself before finishing the song. Like worried nannies, fans speculated that Dylan was overcome by the fact that he was not as famous as he used to be. Their concern mounted when he next attempted the song (14th April) and again his voice broke at the same line. Whatever the reason[52], Dylan sang the song on May 4th in the United States without any problems, as he has done many times since.

As for myself at this time, I was mainly still listening to the tapes from late 1991. In 1992 I was not in a position to acquire tapes very rapidly from Australian shows. Technological and contact changes since then mean it would make no discernible difference today whether the shows were in Manchester, Milwaukee or Melbourne. However, back then I had to wait a bit longer. I was, though, working reasonably close to the Australian Embassy in London (UK), and used to go there a few times a week to follow the decidedly mixed Australian press coverage of the tour.

Around the same time, journalist Stuart Coupe asked Dylan why he still spent so much of his time touring. "There comes a point for everything, playing music is a full-time job you know", Dylan muttered. "It's hard to shut if off and turn it off and on again like a faucet". Mr. Coupe observed:

"Possibly that's the (unlikely) key to it all – that it remains in his blood and he feels he has no choice but to continue. That doesn't however explain Dylan's extended period away from touring, some breaks punctuated by occasional performances, lasting as long as 7 years. In his biography of Dylan, *Behind The Shades*, Clinton Heylin suggests that this is only one of 3 periods in his career when Dylan has combined frequent studio activity with prodigious bouts of touring. All have coincided with periods of turmoil in Dylan's personal life, almost as if the road becomes an easy escape from the issues he must face head on in life away from the road. If that is the case with the Never Ending Tour, Dylan certainly isn't saying anything."

The Australasian leg saw the usual number of one-off's and special performances. Tasmania witnessed a one-off "I Want You", and perhaps not so luckily, an electric "John Brown". Sydney's shows were blessed with "When I Paint My Masterpiece", "Union Sundown", "Sally Sue Brown" and perhaps most surprisingly of all, another beautiful traditional song, "The Lady of Carlisle". Bob had last sung it in 1961 and it is so perfect a song for him that even some of the phraseology seems Dylanesque. We also got "Delia" (last sung in 1960, but to be released a year or so later on Dylan's *World Gone Wrong* album in a different version).

"Delia" is perfect for the register left in Dylan's vocals – something he clearly relished. So much so that he maintained the same vocal register for one of his own songs, like "If Not For You" at the Sydney shows too.

Another Sydney 1992 treat was Dylan in top form on "It's All Over Now, Baby Blue". As for "Idiot Wind", certain lines in it were so heart-brokenly and tenderly sung, the regret expressed could have filled the entire universe. Nonetheless his voice was also strong when reassurance was needed or when steelier emotions were demanded. The band was completely on top of this song and it quite gloriously echoed past victories in Dylan's delivery.

When emphasis was expected at the end of a line Dylan sometimes, in fact quite often, hit the middle of the line with the same emphasis instead. Somehow, he made this work. Somehow, he kept the same overall meaning of the original song, but built up new tensions and new resonances.

The line *"Blood on your saddle"*, was a long drawn out moan that took up the same musical space as *"Visions of your chestnut mare shoot through my head and are making me see stars"*. No mean feat for someone in their 50s. An additional highlight was "Cat's In The Well" played as a low-down dirty, full-out rocking blues.

However, I am running ahead of myself. By the time I did eventually get to hear these shows from Australia Dylan was already in the States and reports and tapes from those shores were flooding in. Charlie Quintana[53] was now on drums, making the band a quintet and thereby allowing a wider range and a more dynamic sound. The contrast with the same period a year before was enormous. Here was a band who could kick ass, then revert to a subtler, country sound and then rave things back up again when necessary. Dylan himself was singing and playing guitar with much more purpose. Some of these shows were excellent and "Idiot Wind" was growing in stature with each outing.

The early weeks of May found Dylan in resplendent form – some of the best shows of the Never Ending Tour are claimed to have come from these particular dates. Most people's favourites probably include the show on the 9th at San Jose, where Dylan gave a magnificent version of "Most Of The Time" and what many feel was the best "Idiot Wind" of the year, (though arguably an even better version of the latter had been performed just before at San Francisco's Fox Warfield Theatre). The Fox Warfield show was also notable for an advance in technology. This was the first audience video I received that had been recorded on a digital camera, allowing its operator to focus in on Dylan even if standing quite far back from the stage. Despite still having many of the inherent drawbacks of the video medium – and the added drawbacks inevitable with unofficial audience tapes – it is quite watchable.

***

San Francisco 5th May 1992
Fox Warfield Theatre, San Francisco, California

1	Rainy Day Women # 12 & 35
2	Lenny Bruce
3	Union Sundown
4	Just Like A Woman
5	Stuck Inside Of Mobile With The Memphis Blues Again
6	I Don't Believe You (She Acts Like We Never Have Met)
7	Shelter From The Storm

8	Love Minus Zero/No Limit (Acoustic)
9	Little Moses (Bert A Williams/Earle C Jones) Acoustic
10	Gates Of Eden (Acoustic)
11	Mr. Tambourine Man (Acoustic)
12	Cat's In The Well
13	Idiot Wind
14	The Times They Are A-Changin' (Acoustic)
15	Maggie's Farm
	*
16	Absolutely Sweet Marie
17	All Along The Watchtower
18	Blowin' In The Wind (Acoustic)

The video opens with a garishly bestriped Dylan singing "Lenny Bruce". He appears to be just going through the motions (which is unusual, as he often pulls out a good performance of this). The following "Union Sundown" is just dreadful. But things soon start to get better.

"I Don't Believe You" shows the first signs that it could be a good night. Dylan then tackles a fast-paced, instrumentally driven "Shelter From The Storm" with gusto. His vocals are far stronger, richer and more expansive than in the opening songs. A carefully played harmonica leads a band running like a freight train into the song's close.

"Gates Of Eden" changes the emphasis and pace. Dylan is now the solitary figure picked out by a single spotlight in the centre of the darkened stage – strumming his guitar, hunched over the microphone, barely moving. An enduring image.

During the following song, "Cat's In The Well", Dylan gives a lovely, knowing smile when he glances back to see Jerry Garcia on stage strapping on a guitar. Garcia was certainly one of the few who could walk onto Dylan's stage and instantly be in tune to what was going on. Not just a pal, Garcia was able to add something musically to the overall sound. The Grateful Dead man may have joined "Cat's In The Well" for a standard blues-type jam, but it gave him time to settle in before the evening's – if not the entire leg's – tour de force.

As if by an act of God, the video's picture becomes clear just before "Idiot Wind" begins. The performance is so good that it overcomes even the painful sound quality of the audio track. In fact, this performance stands up well even when compared with the *Hard Rain* version. This song, clearly so important to Dylan himself, is performed with such energy and passion that it is like witnessing a wild stallion ride and wondering who is trying to buck who – the rider or the horse. Garcia on guitar embellishes the song perfectly as Dylan is driven to ride that demon horse harder and harder.

"Idiot Wind" is clearly presented as a centre-piece. "You're on the bottom" was sung with a lived-in knowledge unequalled even by the wry couplet from "Love Minus Zero/No Limit"; "There's no success like failure, and failure's no success at all".

Dylan then seizes the harmonica almost desperately: music just erupts through it. It is a marked contrast to those occasions in 1991 when he played the harmonica simply for the sake of it.

The American leg finished on the 23rd in Las Vegas where Dylan, appropriately enough, played his gangster song, "Joey". This meant that Dylan was in Las Vegas for his birthday; something that was much commented on at the time.

For most of June, Dylan was off the road, not that he spent the entire month resting. Instead, he found time to record some intriguing sessions with Dave Bromberg, covering a number of old standards some of which have since appeared on the N.E.T., and one of which at least, "The Lady Of Carlisle", he had already played in 1992.

Then it was back to Europe, but not to the UK. The closest he came to Britain was three dates in France on June 30th, July 1st and July 2nd – all of which I duly attended. The last of these dates was not a full show, but at a festival at Belfort. Both Dylan and the band sounded played out. The fire was gone from a lot of the performances, particularly the electric sets. However there were a number of high points, including "Girl On The Green Briar Shore" from the opening show on June 30th. Yet another traditional, acoustic, classic, wrought with Dylan's incomparable interpretative powers. The acoustic sets were better all the way through. Dunkirk also boasted a lovely "Love Minus Zero/No Limit" and the next day at Rheims instead of "Girl On The Green Briar Shore" we got the even better, "Newry Town" (aka "The Roving Blade").

Dunkirk marked the last time "Idiot Wind" appeared as a regular feature of the set. However, lovely though it was for me to finally witness this great song live, there's no denying that this was a poor rendition. It was no surprise that Dylan would henceforth only play it occasionally, before dropping it altogether.

At the last show in Belfort Dylan was due to headline but he swapped places with Bryan Adams at the last minute. Apparently this was so that after he played, Dylan could still get to his favourite restaurant before it closed.

Dylan's Belfort set was consequently brief, but it did include a marvellous rendition of "Little Moses" in the acoustic set – Dylan referred to this as "the spiritual part of the show" and it was certainly one of the year's great treats. In fact, of the three shows I saw in France, the three best songs by a mile were "Girl on the Green Briar Shore", "Newry Town" and "Little Moses". On the way back to the bus I ranted that Dylan should restrict his sets to acoustic performances of pre-19th century traditional folk songs!

Certainly at Belfort, the spiritual heights of the three traditional gems were not reached elsewhere. Though I remember being profoundly moved during the closing "Blowin' In The Wind": standing on a French hill, Joe McShane beside me, both dragging in every iota the man on stage was giving out; both wistfully wondering when (or if) we'd see him again. Even after all these years, we lived in fear of the N.E.T. actually ending.

The 5th of July in Italy saw the first live version ever of the song "2 x 2". It clearly needed more work, but by now Dylan was running out of steam. This European leg ended on July 12th in Antibes, France at the Juan-les-Pins festival. Dylan opened the show with Jimi Hendrix's "Hey Joe", sending our thoughts back to Australia and "Dolly Dagger". In this case Dylan was prompted by the previous band ending their set with the song. It was a neat idea but Dylan did not seem to remember the song too well. This was the first disappointment of many in a very depressing show. Dylan's voice was shot and the band seemed clearly spent.

It was a sad end to this leg, but Dylan seemed undaunted. After a mere month's break, August 17th found him beginning another North American jaunt at Toronto's Massey Hall.

Dylan was back in top form with a very adventurous list on the opening show, including "Wiggle Wiggle". He also surprised the audience with "Heart Of Mine" and provided another stunning acoustic treat, the traditional "Female Rambling Sailor", which had also been performed earlier in the year. This was another in a long line of maritime songs where Dylan had his audience seeing, smelling and tasting the sea air.[54]

"Like A Rolling Stone" surprisingly re-appeared after a long lay-off, before vanishing again, while one of the other highlights was an electric "I Dreamed I Saw St. Augustine". As was to become a fairly usual custom during legs of the N.E.T., Dylan's audacious opening sets were not repeated afterwards – though some surprises continued to pop up here and there.

If the set lists were not particularly adventurous, the performances were. Refreshed from their post-Europe break, Dylan and the band had returned to the road in fine fettle; the highlight being a marvellous five-night Minneapolis residence at the "Historic Orpheum Theater" which Dylan had once co-owned with his brother, David. Dylan pulled out all the stops, watched on the final night by both his brother and mother. There were sad farewells too – "Idiot Wind" was played for the last time to date during these shows, and Charlie Quintana left the band to be replaced by Winston Watson. However, this resi- dence still stands as one of the highpoints of the N.E.T.; every night seemed special in its own right but the greatest pleasure is to listen (and re-listen) to all five shows in sequence.

Twenty shows later Dylan took a four-week break before rounding off the year with another 20 shows in America, and a short performance at an extraor- dinary event in his honour on October 16th: "Columbia Records Celebrates The Music Of Bob Dylan". Extraordinary because it seemed such an un-Dylan- like affair. An air of self-congratulatory phoniness hung over the proceedings, and it was dispelled only by a furore surrounding Sinead O'Connor and the party atmosphere engendered by Neil Young.

This tribute show was broadcast on pay-per-view TV in the US and clocked in at approximately three and a half hours. During the concert, more than two dozen musicians, backed by Booker T and the MGs with G.E. Smith on extra guitar as "musical director", sang about 30 Dylan songs (and two non-Dylan songs).

Most of the guests were predictable: Lou Reed, Johnny Cash, Eric Clapton, George Harrison, Tom Petty & the Heartbreakers, Roger McGuinn and Neil Young were all present and correct. However some acts, such as O'Connor, were considerably more removed from the Dylan story, while the likes of Joan Baez, Bruce Springsteen and Van Morrison were notable by their absence.

Performances were generally worthy at best, though Neil Young lit up the event with an incendiary "All Along The Watchtower" and an impressive "Just Like Tom Thumb's Blues". Lou Reed deserves praise for his brave attempt at the difficult "Foot of Pride" though it may have helped if he had not had to strain to read every line on his autocue. At least this was one of the few songs not from the 60s canon. Another was to have been Sinead O'Connor singing "I Believe In You", Dylan's song of how his faith in Jesus had brought scorn from former "friends". It would have been apt, as scorn had been heaped on Sinead after she recently ripped up a picture of the Pope on *Saturday Night Live*, in protest at the Catholic Church's stance on sex and abortion.

Introduced by Kris Kristofferson as someone whose name has become "synonymous with courage and integrity," O'Connor was greeted with scattered cheers but mostly boos. As the booing continued, the 25-year old singer stood motionless on stage until Kristofferson tried to offer encouragement. "Don't let the bastards get you down," he said, his words picked up by the microphone. "I'm not down," she answered in a steady voice. But the hostility took its toll. Apparently too shaken to attempt the Dylan song, O'Connor launched into a defiant, a cappella version of the song she had performed on *Saturday Night Live*: Bob Marley's "War," a battle cry for equality taken from a speech by Haile Selassie, the late Ethiopian emperor. Afterwards, Kristofferson again tried to comfort her as she left the stage in tears to the sound of more mixed boos and cheers.

It was a galvanizing segment in an otherwise mostly predictable event. A number of journalists later pointed out the irony of a young singer-songwriter facing a hostile crowd at, of all events, a tribute to Dylan. Sinead herself bitterly complained that Dylan had not come out and defended her. This controversy and recrimination fortuitously distracted the media from Dylan's own performance.

Dylan took the stage dressed smartly but as nervous and uncomfortable as you would expect him to be on such an occasion and in front of the cameras. His choice of songs was fine, if totally rooted in his pre-electric days, but his performance of them was abysmal.

Dylan's voice takes some time to warm up.[55] It is usually only after a lung bursting rendition of the regular third song "All Along The Watchtower" that he can shake off a rusty croakiness. One can only surmise that he had not warmed up here, as that croak was all too evident. He opened with "Song for Woody", a doubly apt choice, being his own tribute to an artist who influenced him and because it was from his 1962 debut album. Unfortunately it was his worst ever performance of the song, his voice sounding shot to pieces.[56]

Dylan's vocals were no better on the plodding "It's Alright Ma" that followed. His verse of "My Back Pages" – various guests sang a verse each –

was so poor he had to re-record the lines after the event before the "video single" could be released. After the grand finale Dylan returned to the stage and performed a creditable "Girl From The North Country". It sounded utterly transcendent in the light of what had gone before, and at least hinted at what the whole night had been in tribute to.

Dylan's performance aside, the question that lingered was why on earth had he gone along with this whole deal? For a man famed for not looking back this was surely anathema? He was certainly well rewarded for his efforts; to the astonishment of many this was not a charity event. Tickets ranged from $50 to $150. Pay-per-view was just under $20 and the inevitable double CD and double video soon followed. The event generated a huge profit and the main beneficiary was Bob Dylan. Not that I begrudge him the money – all the better if it allowed him to keep touring small halls on the N.E.T. – but he could have raised similar sums from a more challenging event – perhaps more Dylan, perhaps Dylan interacting with his guests more. A roster list could have been organised that properly reflected Dylan's influence over the three decades.

Obviously it would have helped too if Dylan had looked and sounded in better health. The tabloid press ventured that the event had been quickly put together before Dylan left us altogether; his press office even had to issue a denial. "It's just the way he looks after 30 years in the rock business," Bob's spokesperson told the press. "OK, he looked a bit confused, like he'd been let out of the cage for a while, but that's him."

That's him at events like this maybe, but Dylan's life for years had consisted of touring, rather than being in a cage, almost unable to perform. Without pause, he was back on the N.E.T. in proper concert settings, and back on form. For example, nine nights later in Providence a much more Dylan-like night opened with Muddy Waters "I Can't Be Satisfied" and included a live debut of "Dear Landlord" from the flawless *John Wesley Harding*. For most of the rest of the show Dylan's vocals remained excellent – "Mama, You've Been On My Mind" being particularly affecting.

"The Providence tape is an absolute delight," fan Guy Borg enthused in a letter to my fanzine. "He seems to be trying to do something special with every phrase – and pulling it off!... The solo acoustic slot simply knocked me out – it could've been 1962, but it was better!"

It was hard to believe that this was the same man who had croaked his way through his part at Madison Square Gardens. How like Dylan to perform so poorly at a celebration of his career and yet so well either side of it. How like Dylan too to answer that bloated celebration of his incomparable writing talents by releasing an album of covers, *Good As I Been To You*, on 30th October. The track listing was:

Side One: Frankie & Albert; Jim Jones; Black Jack Davey; Canadee-i-o; Sittin' On Top Of The World; Little Maggie; Hard Times.

Side Two: Step it Up And Go; Tomorrow Night; Arthur McBride; You're Gonna Quit Me; Diamond Joe; Froggie Went A Courtin'.

Many Dylan fans were disappointed that the album contained no Dylan originals. However, my first reaction was to be thrilled that he had done a whole LP of N.E.T.-type acoustic songs; and that they were all new. (One performance of "Little Maggie" in Australia, earlier in the year, excepted).

However, this first reaction wasn't the full story. The L.P. did not follow the blueprint of Dylan's live interpretations of "Eileen Aroon", "Little Moses", "Female Rambling Sailor" etc... Instead these album tracks saw Dylan mimicking – his inimitable tones aside – other performers of these, mostly traditional, songs. Fans swapping tapes of possible source songs (the track list was known prior to the album's release) uncovered many treasures, but there were no doubts which versions were Dylan's sources. Rather than giving us interpretations, he gave us copies – of Nic Jones doing "Canadee-i-o", of Paul Brady doing "Arthur McBride", of De Dannan doing "Hard Times", and so forth.

I have a CD of each of these "source songs", followed by Dylan singing his take. It's uncanny and certainly not what one would have thought from the N.E.T.'s transforming performances of songs drawn from the same well springs of inspiration. Presumably Dylan did this in tribute to the originals. If so, though, it seemed strange that there were no credits on the sleeve notes and that the songs were copyrighted – rather laughably – as Dylan originals. This was a source of some disquiet.

This is not to say that the LP doesn't work. Admittedly Dylan's voice is a bit strained, and pitched at times a little too high, but there's not really a "bad" track on it, which differentiates it from Dylan's mid-80s albums containing covers, the lamentable *Knocked Out Loaded* ("Brownsville Girl" aside) and the slight *Down In the Groove*.

This was not surprising, however. After all the songs themselves are great, and mostly within Dylan's 1990's vocal range. A more unpredictable highlight was Dylan's excellent musicianship; it seemed a long time since he had played guitar this brilliantly. The same man that had merely strummed his way through countless acoustic sets was now suddenly dexterously picking the guitar strings, providing effective, understated embellishments. How I wished he'd played guitar like this every time I'd heard "Boots Of Spanish Leather", "It Ain't Me, Babe" etc. In fact, there was a noticeable improvement in this regard in the live shows that followed *Good As I Been To You*. The harmonica playing on the L.P. was pretty sharp too, though it was not as prominent a feature as I'd presumed it would be on seeing the track listing.

Tribute shows and albums come and go, but the N.E.T. rolls on unhindered and the year's touring continued on to a formidable climax at West Palm Beach on November 15th. The previously discussed Providence show was only one of a series of top notch performances. It was as though getting through the "Tribute" night, Dylan could once again dedicate himself to giving the N.E.T. his all. Wilkes-Barre from November 1st 1992 remains a personal favourite, while Clearwater on the 11th found Dylan in fine form with a splendidly inventive set-list.

The night after Wilkes-Barre saw Dylan perform, "Farewell to the Gold". A mournful testament to the lot of the miner, Dylan sang it with conviction. (One presumes it had once been destined for *Good As I Been To You* as it featured on Nic Jones's *Penguin Eggs* album that had clearly affected Dylan around this time.

Other highlights included two powerful readings of "Disease of Conceit" two outings also for the ever-welcome, "I Dreamed I Saw St Augustine" and a one-off return for George Lowell's "Willin'".

By the time he had stormed through Florida, Dylan's voice was so ravaged at the final show, (West Palm Beach on November 15th), that he had to omit the electric encores. Notwithstanding this, he was in spell-binding form, compensating for vocal shortcomings with a tour-de-force of harmonica playing as though determined that 1992's almost ton up of shows would come to a glorious conclusion.

Chapter Seven: 1993

Before

"The songs I recorded in my past, they're almost like demos. I'm still trying to figure out what some of them are about. The more I play them, the better idea I have of how to play them."

Bob Dylan, 1993

1993 began with a live prelude to the N.E.T.'s resumption on January 17th, when Dylan appeared at the Bill Clinton Inauguration Concert at Lincoln Memorial in Washington, D.C. There was something moving about seeing Dylan in such a setting; so many echoes and memories resonated that one hardly had time to reflect on Dylan playing for a President younger than himself. The times sure had a-changed since Dylan had sung "Only A Pawn In Their Game" at the same venue during the Washington Rights March some thirty years ago.

The performance, of "Chimes Of Freedom" was splendid enough in a completely Dylanesque way; that is, it did not kow-tow to the setting nor the unfamiliar audience. The President seemed pleased that Dylan was there, Hilary seemed to think the whole thing was a joke (a view shared by many, I'd venture) and Chelsea looked as though Bob had descended from another planet (potentially another popular view).

With Dylan's inaugural duties completed, it was time to pick up the threads of the N.E.T.. By now Ian Wallace had quit and for the entire year the band comprised of John Jackson, Bucky Baxter, Tony Garnier and Winston Watson.

The year's touring began in Ireland before returning once again to the Hammersmith Odeon – now renamed the Apollo. Again there was a great build up, and again a few dozen queued for front row seats. Expectation was high, especially with this series of shows coming so soon after last September's acclaimed Minneapolis residency. As far as Hammersmith memories went, the glamour of 1990 offset the disappointing 1991 memories. It was an exciting time at our flat too, as family and friends plus old and new Dylan acquaintances again came to stay.

After all the build up, at last it was time for the first show. Perhaps the opening minutes should have warned us that this was not going to be an easy ride. Dylan took to the stage, glowered at the microphone for being at the wrong height, adjusted it, stood back, prepared to start the opening song and stepped forward to the microphone again which promptly fell to its lowest setting with a loud clunk. A brave roadie scrambled on to try to rectify the problem as Dylan retreated to the back of the stage.

As it turned out, this was one of the highlights of a night that – "I & I" aside – was as dull as ditchwater. Oh, the acoustic stuff was OK but the rest was a real disappointment. Winston Watson looked and sounded great on drums; unfortunately he drummed the same way to every track. There was no variation between songs, or portions of songs, and no acknowledgement paid to melodies.

Now, this is not all Winston's fault; either Dylan purposely hired a drummer with no flexibility or he hired a quite capable drummer and instructed him to play this way. It would appear the latter was closer to the truth. Watson was not necessarily a hapless drummer but a drummer haplessly following orders.

Such a waste, especially as there can rarely have been a band member more obviously in love with Dylan's songs and singing. In the times when he wasn't required in the acoustic set, night after night Winston stood at the stage side and listened intently and with pleasure to Dylan's performance. He claims he never missed a single song, and I believe him. It is a great pity he wasn't allowed to express his love of Dylan's music by playing with, rather than against, the spirit of the songs.

Ironically, the band had been crying out for a new drummer before Winston joined in late '92. It seemed then that he would be the answer; but as those shows progressed the worrying tendency to have him overplaying – or playing at the wrong time – began to surface. Soon songs were being stretched out not just by unnecessary drum breaks but by all the instruments on stage: inane doodling and ill-timed thumping forever threatened to draw a song to a painful close, only for the musicians to go back and repeat themselves in ever-expanding loops of mediocrity. By Hammersmith 1993 the only thing more stretched out than the songs was my patience!

These long "endings" were bad enough; even worse were the obtrusive "instrumental passages" during the songs. These deadening interludes sapped any pleasure that could have been gleaned from a week of rigid set lists. Sure, theoretically Dylan's creative experimentation with song structure could be applauded as much as his experiments with set lists. However, in practice, it didn't work. There's a difference between musically inventive instrumental passages transforming songs into something new and vibrant (or giving songs space to breathe in new ways) and the meaningless doodling and uninspired scratching of these 1993 dates.

Taking 8th February as an example, Dylan and the band gave us a near 12-minute "Tangled Up In Blue", a "Pretty Peggy-O" at 7 minutes 33 seconds, an "I&I" and a "Highway 61 Revisited" both at over 9 minutes. Plus, "Simple Twist Of Fate" and "Mr. Tambourine Man" were both over 8 minutes and, for

God's sake, "It Ain't Me, Babe" was almost so. Duration isn't everything, of course; a 16-minute "Simple Twist Of Fate" would do nicely, thanks, if the minutes were spent constructing a performance that moved the listener, rather than just extending it for no apparent reason.

"Pretty Peggy-O" started well enough; it is a great song and Dylan sang it – as he nearly always does – with tremendous empathy. The first two minutes were really moving and I was well into it. Then the band played "doodle doodle" for a minute; which was just about acceptable, it gave Bob time enough to rest his voice before coming back with the concluding two verses. Then, at about 3 minutes 45 seconds, the song was over. Except it wasn't; it was back to "doodle doodle doodle" for nearly another minute before the first verse was repeated. A further bout of "doodle doodle doodle drum drum doodle doodle" brought the song past the 6-minute mark with all impetus lost along the way. Even then we weren't finished, though by now no-one seemed to know what to do next. More arbitrary doodling took the song staggering to an end at 7 minutes 12 seconds. Each musician stopped playing at a different moment, so there was a little guitar flourish of some other melody and a cymbal arbitrarily hit to bring it to a ragged close.

From the same night, we can hear how Bob and his gang vandalised quite possibly the best song he has ever written, "Tangled Up In Blue". It started, and started, and started... whipping the crowd into an excited state of expectation. Then, still it started and started, to no effect, the build up was over-extended and the anticipation gradually waned. There was some nice harp after a while and it sounded like Dylan was finally going to start singing... but he didn't. The intro began all over again. Finally, just before 3 minutes had elapsed, Dylan croaked the first line.

This is a Dylan crowd favourite and Dylan sang – albeit hoarsely – with some intensity. The crowd's excitement seemed to culminate at about the 5:40 mark, when there was an instrumental break. That wasn't the problem, there was every reason for it to be there. The problem was that rather than end where it should, it just went on and on, sounding like the interminable opening all over again. By the time Dylan eventually returned to the microphone for that great last verse, he sung it without an iota of feeling. The song's real end came after just under 12 minutes – but it sure felt a lot longer than that.

These arrangements, and particularly the long song endings, contributed to make this the dullest residency I have attended or probably even listened too. Not the worst, this was far better than Hammersmith 1991, but the most uninteresting. Even the actively bad has at least some kind of life force behind it. Sure there were intermittent silver linings in '93 – an electric "Under The Red Sky" and the aforementioned "I&I" – but overall this was a boring week of shows; and "boring" is simply not a word I ever thought I'd have to use to sum up a set of Dylan performances.

So we were bored[57] – but was it our fault for going every night? Maybe, I would not have minded the instrumental fooling-around as a one-night experiment. Another thing that irked us greedy fans was a lack of originality in the set lists. To counter that though, as ever with Dylan, there were many more changes over the nights than you would expect from anyone else. They lacked, however, the truly surprising; a new song, one not played for years, a cover you never expected to hear.

After Hammersmith I followed the tour on to Utrecht in Holland where, thanks due to Wilhelm Meuleman's hospitality, I saw two more shows and was rewarded with slightly better performances and the surprise choice of Hank Snow's "I'm Moving On" as the set opener.

Dylan continued through Europe, ending in Belfast on the 25th February. The shows were improving, though not radically so. Even better than anything on stage, though, was Dylan's arrival in Belfast the day before his show – or at least the few minutes of video footage that circulates amongst Dylan fans and collectors. In a scene that Beckett or Pinter would have given their right arm for, Bob in full "dressed-as-a-bum" mode ambles around near a bus stop. A woman waiting on the bus looks decidedly – and understandably – worried by his appearance and demeanour. Dylan seems very confused. For one glorious moment I thought the woman was going to hand him a coin!

Not one to rest for long, Dylan resumed touring in the States in mid-April for a short run of shows leading up to an appearance on Willie Nelson's TV broadcast 60th birthday bash. Dylan, unusually for a TV programme, was in magnificent form, contributing wonderful vocals on the sublime "Pancho and Lefty" and performing a sterling version of the heartbreaking "Hard Times" with his touring band.

Six weeks later Dylan was back in the UK, kicking off another summer European jaunt with an appearance at the Fleadh festival in London's Finsbury Park. Now, a day spent waiting on Dylan at a festival is not usually to my liking, but this one was enlivened when I bumped into John Jackson and Winston Watson outside one of the beer tents. They were very friendly and we chatted about the year's shows so far and passed some pleasant time in the sunshine. By the time Dylan hit the stage the weather, predictably, had changed to a downpour.

Dylan played a truncated but fairly standard set. Non-Dylan fans left in fairly large numbers. Not Paul Stevenson though – if you remember back to the Glasgow show in 1989, Paul stood in for me at work so I could attend the show. He and his girlfriend thought Dylan was pretty good, though he did also tell me that the other couple he was with thought Dylan's singing was a joke and fell about laughing. It would be reasonable to say that Dylan's unique enunciation was not at its clearest and that the rain and the lack of any particular brilliance on stage had people running for transport home.

Years later I had another boss at work who had been at the show and she remembered Dylan's performance as being "rank rotten", so bad that she left after a few songs. I tried to explain that with Dylan, often the audience has to put in a bit of work to contribute to the occasion. She replied, not unfairly, that it was more than she was prepared to do.

This is part of the problem with these festival shows. It is one thing for Dylan to expect his experienced fans to be players in the N.E.T.'s never ending drama; but for the curious, the one album-owning, and the Greatest Hits crowd, it is asking too much. Paradoxically, Dylan has throughout the N.E.T. built his set around a spine of classic '60s hits as though he wants to attract these people. He then turns up each summer and performs his hits in a way that drives them away.

There was one saving grace at this performance, though, and it came in the last song. Just as the only good thing of Dylan's at 1992's Madison Square Garden tribute had been his closing, solo "Girl From The North Country"; so at the Fleadh 1993, he opened his true voice only on the last song, a magnificent "It Ain't Me, Babe". Full of yearning, knowledge and courage, it somehow paid tribute to the need for interdependence while simultaneously declaiming the sovereignty of the individual. Very moving, but by now the only witnesses in the pouring rain and sodden, muddy field were those who always knew he could perform this well anyway.

The press, no doubt alienated by both the weather and Bob's performance, were merciless in their criticism. Meanwhile, as his fans reacted to the adverse reviews by proclaiming the gig to be far better than it was, Dylan was trekking around Europe again, via a few dates in Israel. In Lyons, a back problem that had been plaguing him for years caused that great rarity, a cancelled show. Dylan has often performed shows even when quite ill and has been known to stick to the phrase "the show must go on" even with a raging temperature. Understandably then, the Dylan fan world was worried this was something serious. Fortunately Dylan was back on stage the next night and the N.E.T. continued. This leg came to an end at the Gurten Festival in Berne, Switzerland on July 17th.

Dylan, however, did not fly straight back to the States. He was not finished with Europe yet and had saved one final "performance" for Camden Town[58] in London where he appeared, unheralded, on July 21st to film a promotional video. It turned out to be my favourite Dylan "show" ever.

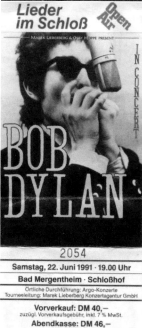

Lieder im Schloß Open Air

MAREK LIEBERBERG & OSSY HOPPE PRESENT

IN CONCERT

BOB DYLAN

2054

Samstag, 22. Juni 1991 · 19.00 Uhr

Bad Mergentheim · Schloßhof

Örtliche Durchführung: Argo-Konzerte
Tourneeleitung: Marek Lieberberg Konzertagentur GmbH

Vorverkauf: DM 40,–
zuzügl. Vorverkaufsgebühr, inkl. 7 % MwSt.
Abendkasse: DM 46,–
inkl. 7 % MwSt.
KEIN SITZPLATZANSPRUCH!

Wichtiger Hinweis siehe Rückseite!

Above: Paris Grand Rex Theatre 30-1-90.
Photo: © Duncan Hume

Left: Ticket to Open Air 1991.

Below: Paris Grand Rex Theatre 29-1-90.
Photo: © Duncan Hume

Above: Juan-Les-Pins, Antibes France 12-7-92.
Photo: © Duncan Hume

Above: Lyon, France. 5-7-94. *Photo: © Duncan Hume*

Opposite top: Paris Grand Rex Theatre. 29-1-90. *Photo: © Duncan Hume*

Opposite bottom: Juan-Les-Pins, Antibes France. 12-7-92. *Photo: © Duncan Hume*

Below: Guitar Legends, Seville, Spain. 17-10-91. *Photo: © Duncan Hume*

Above: Juan-Les-Pins, Antibes France 12-7-92.
Photo: © Duncan Hume

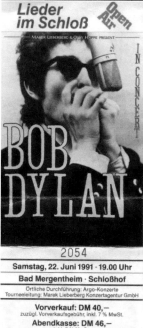

Above: Paris Grand Rex Theatre 30-1-90.
Photo: © Duncan Hume

Left: Ticket to Open Air 1991.

Below: Paris Grand Rex Theatre 29-1-90.
Photo: © Duncan Hume

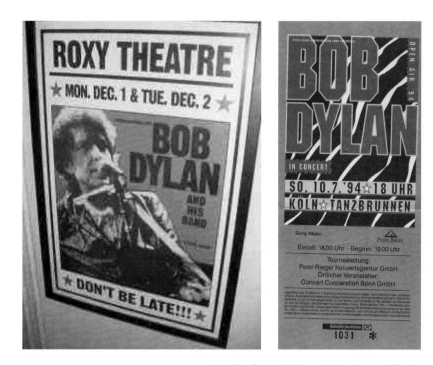

Above: Roxy Theatre, Atlanta Advert. 1/12/97.
Photo: © Duncan Hume

Right: Tickets for Koln, 94 and Liverpool, 96.

Below: Wembley Arena October 1987.
Photo: © Duncan Hume

THE LIVERPOOL EMPIRE

LIME STREET, LIVERPOOL, L1 1JE

STALLS

Barry Dickins &
Rod Macsween Present
BOB DYLAN

AA8

WED 26 JUN 96

CSTR 20.00
B.FEE 0.00

TICKETS BOOKED BY:
FAN CLUB

8:00 PM

Above: Lyon France 5-7-94. *Photo: © Duncan Hume*

Below: Posters for Vienne, France. 28-7-95 . *Photo: © Duncan Hume*

Above: Juan-Les-Pins Stage by the sea. *Photo: © Duncan Hume*

Below: Tickets for two of Dylan's Prague gigs in the 90s.

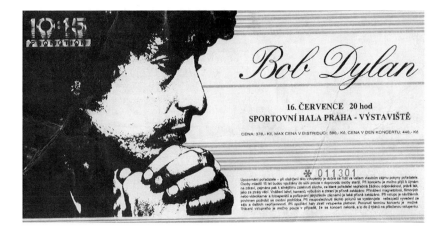

Above: Prague Sportshalle Czech Republic. 16-7-94. *Photo: © Duncan Hume*
Below: Tickets and press cuttings. *Photo: © Duncan Hume*

Chapter Eight: 21st July 1993

Hey, that's great...

I am due to return to an important meeting after a short lunch break. I get a message that Alex, my brother-in-law, wants me to call him immediately. I gather it is something very urgent indeed. I have to go into the meeting as I'm already late. I reckon that it can only be one of two things: an illness in the family or something Dylan-related. If the former he surely would have said so. I have to assume it is the latter and sit in a ferment of worry and nerves (I presume that Dylan is on telly or that some big news has broken) for the eternity of the 100 minutes that follow.

The minute the meeting ends, I rush out to phone Alex. I'm more than stunned to hear that Dylan has been in Camden and that Alex has stood next to him. Although he had had no opportunity to speak to Dylan, he was at least rewarded by seeing Dylan walk backwards into a cafe as part of the video shoot. One of Alex's colleagues even spoke to Bob and obtained an autograph with a lovely little personal message for Alex. Overwhelmed, pleased, a bit jealous – all those feelings at once with the nagging question: could he still be there?

Alex is still talking: of a song possibly called "Blood In My Eyes"; of Dylan singing with a busker; of the autograph he has. This is all too much. He goes. I call Larry. General disbelief and astonishment later, Larry says he cannot possibly get there but will phone Mike Sutton[59] in Camden to see if anything is still happening. He tells me to call back in 20 minutes. Five minutes later I call him back. He hasn't got through to Mike. I ask him – very precisely – to tell me that there is no possibility that Dylan is still there and that I've to be sensible and go home. He follows my instructions to the letter; I hang up, step into the street and hail the first taxi I see.

Within three minutes we hit a traffic jam. I gnaw at my fingernails, knuckles, wrists and arms, still the taxi crawls along. I have the bright idea of calling Compendium Bookshop[60] who sell my fanzine, *Homer, the slut*. I tell the driver that I'll be back but must run & make a 'phone call; I have no worries that I'll catch him up. I think that I'd better appear cool and collected – after all Dylan probably left ages ago.

After a few rings, I'm greeted by the familiar voice of Compendium's buyer, Mike. I interrupt him hurriedly:

"Hello, I supply you with *Homer, the slut*, a Dylan magazine, do you need any more copies?"

"Funny you should ring just now, he's sitting straight across the road at the window of a restaurant....." click, *BRRRR*!

Within seconds I am back in the cab, impressing upon the driver that, traffic jam notwithstanding, I have to be in Camden High Street *NOW*. I expect he couldn't make out any of my words, but he got the idea. Sooner than I'd thought possible, we were in Camden High Street.

I get the taxi to stop straight across from Compendium Bookshop. Sure enough there is a restaurant there, called Flukes Cradle.[61] I walk in. For Mike to have seen him from the bookstore, Dylan would have had to have been in the room where I now stand.

The room was empty of Dylan, bereft of Bob.

I trudge across to Compendium to ask when he left, what they saw etc. They kindly grab me at the door and say:

"He's still there, he's in the back now, having a meal."

"Can I have a *Homer, the slut*?"

"Yes, but don't take the top one, it's dog-eared. Take two and bring one back signed."

"On your bike!"

I take two and go back across to Flukes Cradle. My plan is simple – I'll go into the restaurant and sit as close to Dylan as possible, and ask for his autograph if there is a convenient opportunity as he leaves. I pass through the bar, thinking that above all I must be inconspicuous. I go into the restaurant and... *Oh my God He's really there!* OK, I went in knowing he would be there but seeing him really there, like really him, really sitting there... too much! (I've read that in moments of shock the body is supposed to have a kind of automatic defence system; I've obviously been programmed wrongly as when I went into shock my body went on the attack. Knees buckling, head spinning and heart attempting to smash through the ribs!)

He's wearing a top hat, sitting in profile, that nose, those curls; visions of Blackbushe and all that '78 meant to me seeing him live for the first time, visions of so many years before and after that. I stand stock-still. I somehow remember that I am supposed to be inconspicuous.

Dylan's table was down a few stairs to the left. I go to sit at the nearest table to him on my level of the restaurant (a whole other level) and try to be cool. I pick up a menu, though I know I'll never swallow anything I order. The menu slips through my sweaty paws. I decide I'm too conspicuous so I move to the next nearest table which just happens to have a better view of our man. I realize I am, in fact, totally conspicuous as Dylan and his entourage are the only people in the restaurant apart from me. Maybe I'm not supposed to be there? I think, and this thought prompts others that remind me I'd always said I'd never disturb him in this way and that I was acting very stupidly. I leave the dining area and go back to the front bar.

I'm still feeling pretty happy though, seeing Him so close is a big thrill.

I order a drink. I sit down. I stand up. I sit down again. I move table. I decide on an alternate strategy. I could go downstairs again and ask someone if they could get Dylan to sign a *Homer*. This I do, whispering my request and stressing that I only want it if it will not unduly trouble Dylan.

"Go and ask him yourself."

I glance up at Dylan, a mere four seats away:

"No, I don't want to disturb him and anyway it isn't physically possible."

"OK, maybe."

"I'll be sitting in the bar if you manage to get it signed. Thanks a lot."

I sneak back out and wait. A few minutes – or eternity – pass. My *Homer* is returned, this person doesn't feel it is right for him to present it to Dylan. "Fair enough," I think. I'm happy enough and have remembered all the stories about him being pestered by fans. I'll just sit and watch him leave.

A few more minutes pass and someone comes over to me and says:

"Go now! Now's a good time."

I stand up, hesitate, look doubtful.

"You'll never have a better chance in your life, go now."

I go. Back in the restaurant only Dylan's table is now occupied. The furthest away table; Dylan, naturally, the most difficult person to get near to. To get to him I'll I have to push past someone I don't recognise and then Dave Stewart.

If I'd thought that my heart was pounding before – and, hey, it had been – it was doing something else altogether this time. There were four young looking people at the table; three on the far side, one nearest me, then next to him Dave Stewart and next to him, Himself. Looking absolutely gorgeous. You know what they say about "an aura around him"? Well, I'd always thought that was nonsense – or, rather, a projection of our feelings. I was wrong. The aura is almost tangible. My legs are threatening to give way before my rib cage. I try to detach my tongue from the roof of my mouth and my jaw from the floor.

At this moment there is a babble of conversation in the room. Dave Stewart is facing Dylan – who is staring straight ahead in profile (and what a profile) – asking a series of questions quite vehemently. I cannot make the questions out due to the conversation amongst the others. Dylan is not responding at all. I push past the first person between me and Bob.

A silence falls around the table with the exception of Dave Stewart's drumming questions. I cannot make out the words because my heart is beating so hard that my ears are drumming louder. I try my pen for the last time – but I'd tried it once too many times and it ran out – luckily I'd brought eight with me, so I fished out my seventh last. I'm now standing right beside Dave Stewart's chair. Dylan is within arm's reach.

The movement in getting *Homer* and the working pen out alerts Dave Stewart to the fact that there is someone behind him and that everything has gone quiet. He stops talking and looks around and up at me. His look is marvellous: it says "Oh no, not another one of these Dylan nutters". (In a kindly way however, and later I admire his ready acceptance of himself as a mere pop star beside someone who is a real Star.) He moves his chair slightly, I help him move it a little more. I am now standing right beside Bob Dylan.

There is total silence.

Dylan just keeps staring ahead, not reacting to the sudden silence or anything. This lasts for 7 zillion aeons, or about two seconds in real time.

Well this is it, after 18 years of interest – some have called it obsessive – in the Man, I'm at the point many of us have dreamed of over and over. What am I going to say? I have no idea. Staying alive is only barely within my grasp at this moment. Thinking stopped some time ago. I tear my tongue from the roof of my mouth.

"Excuse me, Mr. Dylan," I squeak.

HE MOVES – and *how* – the head swivels round in an instant. Dylan is staring me in the face (or, at least, the rivers of sweat where my face should be) and says – "says" is the wrong word but, since the real description does not exist, it will have to do – pointedly and interrogatively:

"Yeeaah?"

I am dead. It is not a pleasant feeling. I want my mummy and daddy. I want the ground to swallow me up and never let me out again.

Suddenly I am reborn and mysteriously function.

I hold out a copy of *Homer* issue 9. I force the Sahara Desert above my chin to respond; the sand becomes a torrent of burbling water. Something along the following lines pours out:

"Could you please sign this? Of course, it doesn't matter if you don't and I'm very sorry for disturbing you, I realize it is a stupid thing to do, and it has been great being this close to you and I'll leave now."

I don't know how much of this Dylan made out; maybe "please" and "sign" or possibly he just guessed what the pen and magazine were for!

"Yeah, sure..."

He took the magazine in his left hand and the pen in his right I was pleased to see. However, the pen was upside-down! A tale flashed through my mind of someone asking for his autograph who didn't have a pen and his devastating response... maybe if he tries to sign it now he'll get annoyed. Oh No...

Fate, however, intervened. Or perhaps it was the whole point of the suggestion that I "go in now" (if so I owe that gentleman so much I could never, ever repay him). Dylan laid the magazine down and jabbed a beautiful finger at the embroidery on the jacket sleeve pictured on the front cover:

"That's it, that's the jacket I'm talking about."

They'd been discussing that very jacket???! Someone says from the far side of the table:

"Well, that's it then, it's Hammersmith."

I answered, in a very small voice, without taking my eyes off Dylan's right hand which was signing the front cover of Homer at that very moment: "Actually it is Belfast. But, hey, if you guys want it to be Hammersmith, then Hammersmith it is."

I take the signed copy from Himself and slither backwards out of the room. I am aware of acute physical pain. But the thought resounds that IT HAS HAP-PENED.

I sit in the bar again. Stunned. Staring at *Homer*. More stunningly stunned. Slowly the brain tries to re-establish a modicum of control. "Sit where he'll have to pass you on the way out" it urges. I do. I get crafty, I get a table where they'll have to pass in single file as they approach the door. I take away the second seat and wedge myself into a perfect viewing position as they leave the restaurant. I place the signed *Homer* by my right hand and lay the other one on the table in such a manner that anyone looking as they passed would have to see it.

Another few zillion years (2 minutes) later they start to leave. Stewart and some of the others (three, I think) are talking quite animatedly and, gesticulating over to me, one says something along the lines of: "Oh yes they still do, look at that lad over there."

They all laugh, in a friendly fashion, I keep my eyes glued straight ahead waiting for You Know Who. However, attracted by the laughter, the next person out – a young American – stops at my table (thereby blocking the passageway, so I have another hero) and, pointing to the unsigned *Homer*, asks:

"Do you subscribe to all of these?"

"Yes, and, actually, I run this one."

"Really, how?"

"Well I type it up on computer and I've a photocopier at home..."

As those last three words came out, every sensory input in my being went into overdrive again. Dylan had majestically walked up the stairs and was now heading straight for my table. Do not believe he is 5' 7", this man is at least 95 feet not including the top hat.

He rests one hand on the table and lifts *Homer* from the young man's hands. The youngster backs off a little, Dylan moves in. I self-liquidise.

Dylan starts reading the inside cover page. He says something about the information line number and laughs and then flicks a few pages, sometimes pausing to read. There's a smile, a grunt, an "uh-huh". Some of my senses are still working, I realise that behind me everyone has left except Dylan and the youngster who first stopped at my table. He is shifting his feet as though to leave, Dylan is still reading but I feel he is about to go.

"Please take it Bob.[62] And thanks for a great year..."

"Yeah". ("Heard it a million times before" voice.)

He is still standing reading.

"Did you write this?"

I have no idea what page he is on. Remember I am sitting down, wedged in, he is right ahead and above me. I can see the front and back page and *him*. Having written virtually none of Issue Nine, I answer anyway:

"No, I edit it...it's not a very good issue anyway Bob..."[63]

He raises an eyebrow and flicks a few more pages, keeps on reading. Suddenly he realises it is time to go, very regretfully he says:

"This is eh, uh, really interesting but you know I just don't have time..."

"Please take it, Bob, take it with you..."

He leans towards me with a look that says: "There's a puddle on this chair and it is trying to speak to me, but I don't know what it is burbling". Thankfully the young man translates:

"He's trying to tell you it is yours to take, Bob."

(How can he say that so easily, I wonder)

Bob, still pretty close, in a very surprised and grateful voice:

"Really? I can take this one?"

Utter panic, his face is now too close for its own safety. I gasp/scream/whisper whatever:

"Nothing would give me greater pleasure in life...."

He – Bob FUCKING Dylan – puts the hand with *Homer* (his left) toward my right shoulder and his right hand squeezes my left shoulder as he leans forward and says gratefully:

"Hey, that's great...."

I am now beyond death, beyond rebirth, beyond Nirvana. I am also almost completely incapable of movement. However, Dylan is still nearby so I manage to get up and follow him to the car waiting outside.

I notice Dylan is still being generous with his time, a denim-clad man is shaking his hand and they are exchanging greetings. I notice too that Dave Stewart is in the back of the car video-ing everything. But mostly I notice Dylan and how friendly he's being and how people are drawn to him and, finally, something which even he may never understand, how even the ordinary things he does do not lessen the aura, the mystique. He is doing normal things, but he is set apart. I never believed such a thing possible; but he just doesn't walk and talk like anybody else. He is Bob Dylan.

He walks around the back of the car and goes in the far-side back seat. (They let him walk near the cars? – dear Christ, I wouldn't.) He is waving to people on the street, unfortunately this brings too many of them across the road, and they press against the car, staring in at him. He opens the *Homer* and buries his face in it as the car speeds away.

I have a feeling that I will never be able to describe the way the fear, pain, hesitation, wonderment changes to an unbelievable rush of adrenalin.

I want to tell everybody in the world what happened. I realised that I could start at Compendium and Alex's office and thank them at the same time. I ran across the road to Compendium. In my delirium I had forgotten such things as traffic. It was coming straight for me. Screeching brakes, burning rubber. Chaotic hubbub. My hero from the entourage shouting:

"*Hey watch the cars!!!*"

I spin round in the middle of the road and yell back:

"What the hell does it matter now?!"

***

This meeting, as you have probably gathered, had a profound effect on me. There wasn't much time to stop and analyse its impact then though, as I seemed to have been transported into a Bob-filled universe. Suddenly the TV news programmes, newspapers and magazines were full of his attempts to buy a house in London's unfashionable Crouch End. We found out where his favour-ite Indian restaurant there was, and his favourite choice from their menu. Fans camped out in his prospective purchase's lawn. Needless to say all the atten-tion meant the deal never came to fruition.

I was still wandering about in a happy daze at having met the Man when he hit the road again on 20th August, for a near two month stint in the States.

Chapter Nine: 1993

After

By mid-1993, Dylan's constant touring was having an obvious effect on his ability to sell tickets, so the trick this late Summer/Fall was to have a joint tour with Santana. This had a number of effects; there was heightened media attention and tons of newsprint were spent on comparing the current times to the sixties. Dylan's songs seemed tighter as he had less time to play and, when performing next to Santana no-one is going to sound like they are the ones serving up the meaningless instrumental doodling. Dylan was actually roped in to do some interviews to help promote this tour.

"My whole thing has been about disallowing demagoguery," Dylan told *The Chicago Tribune*'s Greg Kot. "The songs I recorded in my past, they're almost like demos. I'm still trying to figure out what some of them are about. The more I play them, the better idea I have of how to play them."

N.E.T. followers may feel, as Kot himself pointed out, "This may explain why Dylan seems perpetually inclined to tamper with his classics, messing with chords and altering his phrasing as he turns 'Like a Rolling Stone' into a shuffle or 'All Along the Watchtower' into a dissonant rocker. "

In response to Kot's musings, Dylan responded rather tellingly:

"My audience has changed over a couple of times now, Dylan says. A lot of 'em don't even know 'Like a Rolling Stone'. They're not enchanted by the past, and I don't allow the past to encroach on the present."

Meanwhile, Gene Stout of *The Harmony Detroit Free Press*'s attempt to find out why Dylan was touring with Santana provoked a straightforwardly honest, and therefore comically revealing answer:

"Somebody just asked me about it one day, and I said I'd do it," Dylan told Stout, trailing off.

The obvious explanation was that it was being done to try and shift tickets. In this it was only partially successful. Some venues were half – or less – full; Sacramento's Cal Expo Amphitheatre apparently had 6,000 in a 14,000 capacity. According to the reviewer half the audience left during Dylan's set and he ended up playing to 3,000. It barely needs pointing out that those 3,000 would have preferred a two hour Dylan-only set in a smaller auditorium, and that this would have been better for Dylan too.

It seemed more of a touring event than a touring experience and is not one of my favourite periods performance-wise. Dylan's constricted set time also meant there was less manoeuvrability in song choice. "It'll be difficult cutting it down to an hour," Dylan told the press.

Yet Dylan did still pull out a few surprises, such as ending a show with "One More Cup Of Coffee", or introducing "Black Jack Davey" (to very good effect at that) from *Good As I Been To You*. Most astonishing was "Series Of Dreams" on 8th September at The Wolf Trap, in Vienna, Virginia.

"Series of Dreams" is an out-take from 1989's *Oh Mercy* album, and how it was left out, Bob alone knows. It appeared as the closer to *The Bootleg Series* and a magnificent video was created to promote it. Dylan himself, alas, was not involved in these activities – other than appearing in a nice little cameo for the video. However, he had clearly been thinking about the song creatively before Vienna, for the version he played that night was a radical re-arrangement. It was far from an unqualified success but showed immense promise. Unfortunately Dylan did not try it out again until 1994. The Wolf Trap show also gave us another of those "on-stage foul-ups" that fans so love to recall. In this case it was when Dylan started playing "Boots Of Spanish Leather" as the thirteenth song; unremarkable, except that Dylan had already played the song as the ninth one that night. Rather shamefacedly, and amidst general mirth, Dylan acknowledged his error, stopped and played "It Ain't Me, Babe". Never mind, Bob, a lot of your old acoustic songs had begun to sound so alike it was an easy mistake to make.

Which is not to say they were all played by rote, the peerless "The Lonesome Death Of Hattie Carroll" brought some transcendent moments to a few of these shows; and again to the Wolftrap. Also on that stand-out Wolftrap set were notable versions of "God Knows" and "Born In Time".

Dylan's vocals on the former were fabulous, from fragile to menacing within a few lines. It was a marvellous and varied delivery; in places its demon edge called to mind that great *under the red sky* out-take version of "TV Talking Song". Meanwhile, the band was producing some real visceral, teeth-on-edge interplay. John Jackson was never finer. This is the kind of thing defenders of Hammersmith 1993 talked about as being the point of the arrangements there. It never worked back then, but here I see what they mean: I hear it, I feel it – this instrumental jam adds truckfuls to the song; this is superb hard driving rock.

This was the best performance of "God Knows" I'd heard and, earlier in the set, there was certainly the best live performance of "Born In Time" (though the rejected *Oh Mercy* sessions version is unlikely to ever be bettered). By the time Dylan got around to releasing "Born In Time" on *under the red sky*, he seemed to have lost the feel for it – certainly the released track is a disappointment.

Dylan's delivery at the Wolftrap reclaimed the song in masterly fashion from the self-consciously "poetic" LP version, transforming it into something natural and affecting. It is a gorgeous performance and overall Vienna, 8th September 1993 was a night to treasure. In the main though, this leg of the tour was short on shows that really sparkled.

There had been some great song performances and some solid, if not spectacular, sets; but by September 1993, nothing in the year to date could stand alongside, say, the Greek Theatre '88, Beacon '89, Hammersmith '90, Fall '91, Spring '92, or Minneapolis '92. In fact, the best live shows of 1993 were yet to come. Before that though, Dylan was again in the news. After he finished touring with Santana, there was the release of a new album, *World Gone Wrong*.

This was Dylan's second consecutive album of traditional covers, but it felt much more like a Dylan album than its predecessor. It was more cohesive. While it was often faithful to the originals, it was not all pure mimicry, unlike *Good As I Been To You*.

Dylan returned to performing on November 16th and 17th for two nights of free concerts (two sets each night, each set approximately one hour long) at New York's Supper Club. These were shows intended to be filmed and every song was played acoustically, so it seemed for all the world that this was to be Bob Dylan's version of MTV's Unplugged series of acoustic shows. The idea of an Unplugged-type show by the most famous unplugged artist in popular music (who became even more famous by plugging in) was irresistible. So were Dylan's spellbinding performances.

A mixture of old classics, songs he hadn't played for a while and tracks from World Gone Wrong were all treated to the true, authentic voice of Bob Dylan. Not only that but each show seemed better than the previous one and some songs, such as, "Queen Jane" and "Ring Them Bells", were performed nearly as well as they have ever been, either before or since. Unsurprisingly fans couldn't wait to see the film and hear the released record. Unfortunately, Dylan refused to sanction the release of the film, apparently unhappy with the results. One can only speculate there must be something particular in the film that he really hates, because this wonderful testament to his abiding talents as a performer would have done a great deal more to boost his reputation and credibility than the actual MTV Unplugged that he eventually released.

As a coda to these fabulous, yet sadly unreleased, performances, Dylan did appear on the Letterman show the day after the last Supper Club show to perform a very fine "Forever Young". It was another unusually assured TV performance – as long as you could drag your attention away from his ridiculous hat – and a spectacular end to what was by Dylan's high standards, an indifferent year of touring. As 1993 drew to an end, all Dylan fans were looking forward to the sixth year of the N.E.T. and the eighth of non-stop touring. Or should I say "nearly all", as one of them was still looking back to a certain day in July.

Chapter Ten: 1994:

You Do Wonder If You Are Coming Across

Edna Gundersen (USA Today)*: "Was playing at Woodstock a special moment?"*

Dylan: "Nah, it was just another show, really. We just blew in and blew out of there. You do wonder if you're coming across, because you feel so small on a stage like that."

Nineteen ninety-four began with an announcement that disappointed many long term Dylan fans and caused a surprising amount of press coverage. It was another of those "Dylan sells out", "final death knell of the Sixties" stories; this time prompted by Bob's decision to allow international accountancy giant Coopers & Lybrand to use Richie Havens' recording of "The Times They Are A-Changin'" for a TV commercial.

Given all that had happened since the song's release over 30 years previously, I imagined that to most people this seemed a bit of an over-reaction. On the other hand, in all these years Dylan had never allowed such a thing before. Now, Dylan stated he had no problem with doing this, nor did he see anything to regret afterwards.

Stories like this made my Dylan information line busier and busier. I had to change the answering machine to a digitized one as the endless clicking on and off of the tape through the night was starting to keep me awake. I used to lie there and guess that one sudden rush of calls was people in the UK returning from the pub, later it would be opening time in offices on the US East Coast, then move Westward and so forth: the endless need to know, and to know as soon as possible. The service relied on someone getting the information to me and there were a few regulars who did the majority of this work. Disturbingly for me, none of them was going to be able to call me from Japan, which was where 1994's opening leg of the N.E.T. was going to begin.

Fortunately, fan Jon Casper stepped into the breach, and thanks to him, I'm proud to say, the set-lists were updated on my information line as they happened. Or, as someone pointed out, due to the weird effects of the time differences, I had one set-list on "before" the concert had started!

Fans soon forgot all about the Coopers and Lybrand controversy in a united, delighted reaction to the opening two songs of the year. Dylan had begun his first set with "Jokerman", from 1983's *Infidels* album, one of his major songs of the past decade, but not played in almost as long. (Ironically, later I can clearly recall groups of us fickle fans being desperate for him to open with anything other than "Jokerman").[64]

"Jokerman" is one of the most important Dylan songs of the last quarter century. It was the single from *Infidels*, had a fine video and also featured on Dylan's TV appearance on the Letterman Show on March 22nd 1984; an appearance most Dylan fans rate as one of his best.

It suffers, as do many of Dylan's later career "major songs" from one flaw – that of being self consciously a "statement" carrying deep import. It is a difference in his writing that Dylan astutely noticed and described back in 1978[65] as:

"Now, in the old days, they [the songs] *used to do it automatically, but it's like I had amnesia, all of a sudden in 1966. I couldn't remember how to do it. I tried to force re-learn it, and I couldn't learn what I had been able to do naturally, like* Highway 61 Revisited, *I mean you can't sit down and write that consciously.*

"To do it consciously is a trick, you know, and I did it on Blood On The Tracks *for the first time....I knew how to do it because it was a technique I learned, I actually had a teacher for it.* Blood On The Tracks *did consciously what I used to do unconsciously."*

Ironically, in *Blood On The Tracks* this appeared far from a problem; in fact the very opposite seemed to be the case. This testament from the author's own lips seemed the only explanation for how that album had superceded even his classic albums of the 1960s. However, that album turned out to be the exception to a rule that has bedevilled him often since. As he moved away from the teacher and the lessons that had so successfully resurrected his writing skills so the "trick" of the "technique" would become more visible. The "unconscious" touch was often replaced by carefully constructed songs that betrayed or even drew attention to the craft necessary to write them.

This is not to say there was no craftsmanship before – far from it – but that the intuitive touch which led to a naturally formed, cohesive web of imagery and symbolism that had lit those songs from within their crafted stanzas was missing. This has afflicted a great many of Dylan's best later songs. Some still stand above and beyond this reproach, if reproach it be, – "Blind Willie McTell" and "Every Grain Of Sand", for example. Others though, including some of his finest songs, such as "Jokerman" are affected by it. It is a great rock song but it also is too obviously a carefully thought out explication of theological intent, drawing self-conscious attention to its meditations on the nature of humanity, belief and theology.

In concert "Jokerman" did not need to concern itself with such considerations; instead it was a perfect, full-on introduction to a regalvanised Dylan. It yelled that Bob was back on stage and meant business.

Perhaps even more surprising and exhilarating was the second song on the opening three nights: "If You See Her, Say Hello", nearly sixteen years after it had last been played. In 1994, it quietened things down after the explosive opener.

The live history of this breathtaking song from *Blood On The Tracks*, although brief, had been one of the most dramatic in Dylan's canon. In 1976 Dylan unveiled a remarkably vicious live re-write. No-one who knew anything of Dylan's life in the mid '70s could listen to this version without thinking it had been affected – or directly inspired – by the state of his relationship with Sara. The pivotal verse on the album version reads as follows:

"If you get close to her kiss her once for me
I always have respected her for doing what she did and getting free
Oh whatever makes her happy I won't stand in the way
Though the bitter taste still lingers on from the night I tried to make her stay."

The live '76 outing was changed to:

"If you're makin' love to her, watch it from the rear
You never know when I'll be back, Or liable to appear
Oh it's as natural to dream of peace, as it is for rules to break
But right now I got not much to lose, so you better stay awake."

The song was rewritten again for the 1978 tour, though rarely performed, and quickly dropped altogether. By this point, the lyrics had returned to the same emotional area as the album version, though the crucial pivotal verse was missing.

So, what a pleasant surprise it was when Dylan re-introduced "If You See Her, Say Hello", in Japan (where it was performed in 1978 too). The "difficult" pivotal verse was still absent and he had returned to the *Blood On The Tracks* version in the main, with occasional couplets from the 1978 version.

The greatest surprise of the Japanese '94 dates was saved for February 16th, when a reworked acoustic "Master of War" was performed in Hiroshima. This was the first acoustic performance of the song since April 12th 1963 in New York City. An apt, if harrowing, choice, it received a breathtaking performance. Dylan once again sounded like an angry young man: the folk singer rebelling with cause after cause. Here he was in Hiroshima, an American in the first Japanese city obliterated when the U.S. dropped The Bomb, singing out against the terrible sufferings of the innocent in war. I have rarely been as moved. How strange that such a blunt, unforgiving, adolescent piece should achieve that effect. Or rather how strange it would have been in almost any other location.

"Since Hiroshima, of course, 'Masters Of War' has become a regular choice in Dylan's acoustic sets... but at the time this acoustic performance was a revelation," Dylan writer Robert Forryan enthused, "A gentle, haunting, melodic instrumentation; not at all angry, this time, and a voice from which the years have dropped away. This is the voice of a young man. It sounds as if for one night, and for one song, Dylan has done a deal with the Devil. 'Let me have my youth back for this song in this place – let me be inspired.' A pact with the Devil – or maybe a prayer to the Lord."

Things were moving so fast that soon local stores carrying dodgy merchandise had racks of double CD Dylan bootlegs from show after show. It was round about now that I – and a number of others – stopped collecting *every* show on CD or vinyl. There were just too many. Don't get me wrong though, we had them all on DAT or analogue tape, anyway – how else could we have come to such a cavalier conclusion!

In all seriousness, the N.E.T. was becoming difficult to keep up with. 1994 was another very busy year and I find it hard to remember exactly how I felt when the tapes came in from the opening shows of that year now.

So, I have now picked a tape at random from them (it is the 12th February; Castle Hall, Osaka) and placed it on the tape deck, to tell you how it feels listening to it now, six years further down the N.E.T. tracks.

***

The show starts with "Jokerman" and it is a great opener. Dylan is singing it with a sly intonation – by turns humorously and with a more meaningful edge. His voice rides over a driving beat. This gets everyone up and going. The second song by now is not, "If You See Her, Say Hello" but "If Not For You" and a very good performance it is too. Dylan is on top of the song, allowing the new melodic structure to portray a different side to the song.

"All Along The Watchtower" opens to great cheers – there is a fabulous delivery of the opening lines which is much better than I had remembered from any of these shows.[66] It does suffer a bit from the 1993 type of over-elongation musically, but it can work on this song as arranged, here, with the heavily acknowledged ghost of Jimi Hendrix behind it.

Dylan's vocals continue to impress on "Ring Them Bells". It is a bit overly clamorous but Dylan is in command and this declamatory shouting is part of a new, more defiant version that does not, however, completely overturn the original song's feeling.

Again we are given an extended version but at least (like "All Along The Watchtower") this is done at the end only. In any case, if Dylan is going to sing with this power throughout the show, his voice will need to take the occasional breather. February 1994 sounds so much sharper all round than February, 1993.

I picked this tape up by chance and it is throwing a curve ball at me, this is more exciting than I had remembered these shows. Years of listening to hundreds of shows from the N.E.T., must have dulled my memory of this period. I include this confession as it is in itself, part of the N.E.T. experience. The very non-stop nature of it means that all the dedicated fan can do is absorb as much as possible before the next wave hits. One is always most eager for the new shows, the new covers, the latest developments.

Next up there's a tumbling, rushed "Tangled Up In Blue". It is done as a crowd-pleaser and although this still retains some of the freshness that has so often been battered out of it in the years since, it is still hurried and shrill. It is also the 5th song in a row with a long jam at the end.

"Under The Red Sky" gets us back on track, with Dylan allowing the luscious melody the room to breathe that it demands. The opening chords of "Tomorrow Night" get a very good reception, The band play it well, though it is nothing dramatic. "Mr. Tambourine Man" is the next song; it is almost impossible for me to be fair to this. I now cannot but help compare it to the 1995 versions of the song. There's nothing *wrong* with this performance as such, though there is a touch of insincere sounding "sobs" in the vocals at times.

During "Don't Think Twice, It's All Right" the audience tries to clap along, mingling these attempts with applause. It seems such a huge favourite with the crowd that Dylan has to show real persistence to keep the song on course.

"Series Of Dreams" is played with a very weird syncopation. Dylan is putting a great deal into the vocals (as he had at the Wolftrap, Vienna, in 1993) changing the whole nature of the song as he veers from some kind of tonal experimentation to a shrill cry via an exercise in cantilation. All the while the disquieting percussion plays behind him. Brave, if flawed. It's a very unsettling version (which is no bad thing) and if I don't really think it worked, I certainly applaud the spirit in which it was undertaken.

In "I & I" the drums are still driving the song as they were in 1993; but Dylan's focus is not always as melodramatic as it was that year. He sounds as though he has doubts about what he is saying, and the arrangement features a discordant ending in the same experimental mood as the backing to "Series Of Dreams". "Maggie's Farm" is a cacophonous thrash, you would have to have been there to have enjoyed it. I hope the audience got up and boogied in their seats and in the aisles. It certainly sounded from earlier audience noise as though that's exactly what they were looking forward to doing. One hopes too that they kept on their feet for "Ballad Of A Thin Man" before being sent out into the night with the ironically placed, touching closer, "It Ain't Me, Babe".

***

All in all an impressive tape, I think now that I probably did not pick the 12th of February by chance. A deep Dylanial memory of my tapes probably guided my hand to this particular show. I played a few others immediately afterward and, although they all had good moments, I would have to say that none impressed me as much as the 12th. It was beneficial to return to them all, I had not done so in too long. One of the effects of the never ending part of the N.E.T. is that there is a concomitant lack of time to spend on each leg, on each show – because there's always another leg, *just around the corner*....

After Japan, Dylan ended this Asian leg by making his first ever performing visits to Malaysia, Singapore, and Hong Kong.

Back in the U.S, as Dylan prepared for another American trek, he gave a journalist a glimpse into his motivations for keeping the N.E.T. going.[67]

"It seems as if you're always doing new things and reinventing yourself. What keeps you moving and motivated?" the reporter asked Bob.

"Just life itself," Dylan replied. "There's a certain non-transparency to life that keeps me motivated. I try not to work in a linear way. That's incumbent on what's given to you at any given moment. There might be inconsistencies to that, nevertheless, it does give you a degree of independence you might not get any other way."

This resistance to working – or, indeed, perceiving existence – "in a linear way" is something Dylan has returned to again and again.

On April 5th, Dylan began a US tour in Springfield, Illinois. The shows drew widespread praise from the media. Long-term fans however were bemoaning unchanging set lists. Tim Hardin's "Lady Came From Baltimore", at Davenport, Iowa, on April 6th, was the only song debuted live in the whole year. At least it was a good one!

Dylan began another US leg with song numbers 1, 3 and 5 still firmly fixed. Even the "new" opener was soon caught up in the misery of repetition. As the US tour progressed "Senor" unexpectedly appeared as the second song and remained there throughout. This initially caused a bit of a stir, but ultimately gave us four out of five unchanging opening songs.

Once you added the standard inclusions of "It Ain't Me, Babe" and "Maggie's Farm", my information line started to sound the same day after day. My punters were getting restless. I could feel the discontent breathing out of the answering machine. The same thing recurred in the fall leg. Whether this is a problem for Dylan, or just for overly obsessive fans who attend too many shows, is a question that rears its head throughout the N.E.T. The argument that any criticism was just the inevitable result of jaded, hyper-critical fans who have seen too many shows was dealt a blow by Dylan himself, however, soon after this leg ended.

The catalyst was Dylan's appearance at The Great Music Experience in Nara, Japan. This was a three-day, UNESCO Cultural Development Project, where local artists were joined by representatives from the West, including Joni Mitchell, INXS, Ry Cooder, Jon Bon Jovi – and Bob Dylan.

The entire show was the same each day, Dylan's contribution being "A Hard Rain's A-Gonna Fall", "Ring Them Bells" and "I Shall Be Released". (The latter was reprised as the all-star finale every night.)

For the first time ever, Dylan was backed by a full orchestra, the New Tokyo Philharmonic Orchestra. The final day was widely televised around the globe and Dylan was in magnificent form. I remember being near tears as The Voice – which had seemed lost forever – returned in all its full, expressive, raging glory. I watched the footage again and again, transfixed at what seemed the best ever rendition of "A Hard Rain's A-Gonna Fall" and a magical and magisterial "Ring Them Bells", with Dylan filmed beneath a huge image of Buddha.

Somehow, the discipline of playing the same songs each day and marrying his vision to the backing of these accomplished musicians – who would not alter their playing just because he glared at them – had brought out the best in Dylan. For the first time in years he was being stretched. It made an amazing difference.

The Nara shows exceeded anything from the '93 and '94 legs of the N.E.T.[68] Because he was either unwilling or unable to pay for top-rate musicians, Dylan had become used to having a band at his beck and call. At best they could sound like a fired-up garage band, at worst like a motley crew from your local pub. Either way, they were at the mercy of the whims of their idiosyncratic and demanding lead singer. These bands have grown in time to produce some sparkling shows, but they have never been allowed to stretch Dylan, to push him into higher performance levels, to challenge him to come out and sing it.

How ironic that we fans ache for novelty, changing set lists and debut songs, when playing the same set nightly in Nara brought the best out of Dylan. It's a reminder that Dylan's greatest years of performance – let's take 1966, 1975 and 1979 as irrefutable examples – were built on unchanging set lists (largely in the case of 1975, almost entirely for the two other years). The shows from these periods were so dramatic and intense and consummately performed that there was no need for novelty in song selection. This is not to decry the N.E.T.; those earlier tours were driven expressions of a clear artistic goal. They were presented by a white-hot Dylan on top of his game, ably backed and extended by top-notch musicians. The N.E.T. is not like that. You might get a night of searing drama, or you might be confronted with a series of standard run-throughs by a limited, cowed band and a singer who will swallow his words, sing off mike, mumble along – do anything *but* articulate. It's all part of the ongoing N.E.T., and the reason one needs to sample a number of shows to puzzle out what is going on.

***

July brought Dylan back to Europe for his now customary summer appearance. Exceptional shows included Prague on July 16th, where the Czech President Vaclav Havel (longtime admirer of Dylan, Lou Reed and The Rolling Stones among others) joined a large and hugely enthusiastic crowd. Dylan is held in great esteem in some Eastern bloc countries where his words and music fuelled hope in days of oppression. His reception here may have inspired him to start 1995's shows in the same city.

Good though Prague '94 was, the outstanding show of the summer was the second date, on July 4th, at Besançon, France, which featured an especially moving rendition of "Tears Of Rage" for Independence Day. This stand-out show featured a fine vocal performance and a set list that included "Under The Red Sky", "Lady Came From Baltimore", "Mama, You Been On My Mind", "She Belongs To Me" and "What Good Am I?"

Sadly, I only caught two shows that summer, both in Germany, at Balingen and Cologne. They were not memorable: Balingen was, as festivals nearly always are, more of an endurance test than an enjoyable experience.

Meanwhile, with or without me, the Never-Ending Tour continued to wind its way through July. After a short break, it was back to the States in August, for a brief set of dates that encompassed Woodstock II and Dylan's controversial decision to play there. Having taken the moral high ground and avoided the first Woodstock – which was held there in honour of his residence nearby – Dylan saw no contradiction in lending his name to this corporate and phoney re-run of an event he'd decried in the first place. Needless to say he was enormously rewarded in financial terms. The event took place on August 14th, and besides engendering a media blitz, was broadcast around the world.

Woodstock 2 Festival, 14 August 1994
North Stage, Saugerties, New York

1	Jokerman
2	Just Like A Woman
3	All Along The Watchtower
4	It Takes A Lot To Laugh, It Takes A Train To Cry
5	Don't Think Twice, It 's All Right (Acoustic)
6	Masters Of War (Acoustic)
7	It's All Over Now, Baby Blue (Acoustic)
8	God Knows
9	I Shall Be Released
10	Highway 61 Revisited
	*
11	Rainy Day Women Nos. 12 & 35
12	It Ain't Me, Babe (Acoustic)

Finnish television, in a move that was enough to make me want to move back there, showed Dylan's Woodstock set a few days after the event. No other performers were shown, there was no commentary, no presenters. There was just Bob. The programme started with Dylan's opening words to his first song "Jokerman".

It was brave of Dylan to retain his standard set opener rather than switch to something the crowd would recognise, and he looked great. His trademark hair was still not falling out or greying, somewhat miraculously at his age. It was good to see him in a clear light, not wearing any shades. There he was, on a massive stage before a crowd numbering in the hundreds of thousands, consisting mainly of youngsters. Bob must have been nervous, but he and his band looked as though they knew exactly why they were there. Bob made his trademark moves and lovely little sideways glances as the crowd went mad beneath him.

Next was "Just Like A Woman". The audience responded so enthusiastically, Dylan gave an almost shy smile and bent his legs in a classic guitar pose before attacking the vocal with even greater power. "It Takes A Lot To Laugh, It Takes A Train To Cry" – saw the witty blues-drenched lyrics welded with snaking blues guitar lines. This was electric city blues steeped in wise old magic. Dylan added some good guitar work and looked great too, with his little guitar step dances and an occasional menacing move towards the microphone. He did the whole knee-bending, guitar-hero bit, playing the crowd successfully as he turned them to an all-out cheering mass as he thundered out a blues riff, then reeled them back in with a quiet harp. This was then in turn built into a more aptly sinuous blues phrase, while the drums turned up the heat and Dylan and John Jackson traded guitar solos before the song came to a close. You could see the crowd's excitement and expectancy.

"Don't Think Twice, It's All Right" got a cheer, but even for Dylan this was a big, big place to quell acoustically. He retreated into the song and, looking out above the massed heads, projected it as best he could. During "Masters Of War" the crowd's enthusiasm could be heard throughout the song: individual lines were clapped; approval was hollered. Dylan was deep within himself, singing the song with true conviction, as if this new generation needed to be as compelled by his rhetoric as those who went before.

Dylan followed it with a startling, mesmeric, version of "It's All Over Now, Baby Blue". The exact thing he'd been aiming for and missed in a "warm-up show" the week before was hit bull's-eye here, as a thousand flash bulbs popped in his face. Harmonica brought a song that was damn close to a benediction to its conclusion.

"God Knows" ushered in an electric guitar maelstrom and heralded full scale moshing around the front of the stage in the dimming lights. Then the lights came up for "I Shall Be Released" and the spectacle of hundreds of flags being unfurled and tens of thousands of peace signs being flashed. As Dylan threw his guitar hero shapes, the band played tight and loud. A rapturously received "Highway 61 Revisited" brought the main part of the set to an end. There followed a pause filled by an American TV female presenter, gushing enthusiastically, if somewhat patronisingly:

"750,000 watts of Dylan, this must be heaven. We were all kinda holding our collective breath to see how he'd be received tonight, but it was great. I feel very, very proud of Generation X tonight: showing the whole world they are full of patience, wisdom and tenderness, they are INTO Dylan big time tonight at Woodstock '94. And it looks like Bob Dylan will be returning to the microphone."

The mosh pit during "Rainy Day Women", or "Everybody Must Get Stoned" as Americans under a certain age refer to it, has probably rarely been more apt nor less needed as an exhortation. Then, to close, Dylan performed a gentle acoustic "It Ain't Me, Babe", turning the vast bowl into an intimate stage, while he gazed at the lights high above the stage, lost, it seemed, in a private reverie. When he glanced back down he was confronted by a sea of young faces, all obviously loving his performance. It was a sight that must have buoyed him, even after all the adulation he had received in his life.

Dylan was later to dismiss this as just another show,[69] and though the audience was 100 times the size of the N.E.T. 's usual nightly capacity, this widely broadcast show is fairly representative of the Never-Ending Tour, though with a curtailed set. Somewhat typically, in the history of disappointing live Dylan releases, the official recorded release from Woodstock II featured only one Dylan track, and that was "Highway 61 Revisited".

Meanwhile, Dylan continued to tour the U.S., passing the 600 mark for N.E.T. shows soon after Woodstock. He took a break after finishing the late summer leg, but was back on the road by October. My information line now informed listeners that my wife Pia and I were off to see the shows at the Rose-land Ballroom in New York; but not to fear because I had a very special guest to take over the telephone news while I was away.

Lambchop had agreed to deputise, and proved a great success, as I knew he would. I joined about half the people I met in New York in phoning my own line just to check his latest rants on the brilliance of Dylan and his dia-metrically opposite views of the Grateful Dead and their fans.

The Dead were appearing around the same time in New York, at Madison Square Gardens. In fact, on the day prior to his opening concert at The Rose-land Ballroom. Dylan appeared on stage with the Grateful Dead in the Garden and proceeded to join them in sleepwalking through a turgid "Rainy Day Women #12 and 35".

New York, 18th October, 1994
The Roseland Ballroom, New York, New York

1	Jokerman
2	Senor
3	All Along The Watchtower
4	Shelter From The Storm
5	Tangled Up In Blue
6	Man In The Long Black Coat
7	Mr. Tambourine Man (Acoustic)
8	Masters of War (Acoustic)
9	To Ramona (Acoustic)
10	Highway 61 Revisited
11	Joey
12	Maggie's Farm
13	Ballad of a Thin Man
14	The Times They Are A-Changin' (Acoustic)

I thought Dylan was in excellent form from "Masters Of War" on the first night onwards. I felt the first electric set was not very good – but Pia hadn't seen him since the last Hammersmith show in 1993 and was more impressed with this segment than she'd expected to be.[70]

Nonetheless, I'd not swap any part of that first concert for any of the next two, even though the shows probably got progressively better. I find it hard to be definitive: "Masters Of War", "Knockin' On Heaven's Door", "Tears Of Rage" and "My Back Pages" thrilled me on the 18th but the 19th was much more consistent. From the little I could hear in peace it sounded like it could've been one of my favourite shows. The show on the 20th had some peaks but I would hazard a guess that it wasn't overall as impressive as the 19th. I don't really know, however.

The main reason I "don't really know" and that the first show is my best memory is that the venue and crowd conspired to make the other shows more an endurance test than an enjoyable, far less a meaningful, experience. For the second show, I was standing with Dylan biographer Clinton Heylin and N.E.T.

chronicler Glen Dundas, fairly close to the stage but way out to the side. My position had worsened considerably in the last few minutes but I could still just about see the centre mike on the stage. Someone behind me is telling his friends what he thought of yesterday's show: "He only played for one hour 40 and his voice packed in after the first half-hour." Odd, I thought he only picked up after the first half-hour... but this train of thought came to an abrupt end as there was a sudden rush of people pushing in as Dylan's arrival became imminent.

Glen and Clinton had warned me that the crowd might make our position untenable but I wasn't prepared for this. I was trying to hold my ground when a booming voice declared "COMING THROUGH" and I felt the people behind falling back and tried to hold my place. (Not easy since any of this guy's four chins probably weighed the same as me.) The only thing helping to keep him back was his sheer bulk: he couldn't get through on my left side as Clinton refused to budge. Alas, he boomed "COMING THROUGH" again and barged by my right hand-side by bowling over whoever had been standing there. He had a couple of friends in tow. I could now only see a patch around Dylan's mike.

Dylan hit the stage and was right into "Jokerman'. More people pushed forward, and it transpired that the recent interloper had a few more friends situated right behind us. They tried to push in, we refused to let them. Much pushing and shoving later they decided they were not going to get through so stayed where they were. This wasn't the end of our problems, though. They proceeded to continually shout across us to their friends, whooping and talking at an incredible volume, straining to keep their inane conversations going over the noise of the unhelpfully intrusive band.

We were about three quarters of the way through "Jokerman", I vaguely sensed that Bob was in excellent voice when I suddenly found myself being thumped on the shoulder. While no direct violence was intended, one of this obnoxious set was pointing out that he had set my T-shirt alight trying to pass a joint forward to his friends. Helpfully he put the flames out, and nearly did the same for my collarbone.

Attempts to pass the joint around were repeated interminably through the next two songs, often my first glimpse of Dylan in ages was suddenly blocked by a spliff-holding arm. Those in front of us spent as much time facing us and their friends standing behind us as they did the stage. They shouted and pushed and shoved through what sounded a potentially great "If You See Her, Say Hello". Glen had already given up and moved elsewhere, I told Clinton I'd go to the back sometime near the end of "All Along The Watchtower". This I did.

The back of the theatre was amazing, the noise level absolutely extraordinary. People stood in little groups, not facing the stage, bellowing to each other primarily about their sex lives and endless family problems. Others were trying the most pathetic chat-up lines; you'd have thought Dylan fans would have a better store of them.

The hall itself was also a major part of the problem, clearly it was not designed for live music. A little slope and some thought to the acoustics might have helped. I had by now walked all around the hall and found nowhere that I wanted to see the show from. I met other Dylan fans that I knew who were struggling to see and hear; all frustrated by the antics of Deadheads who presumably couldn't get into Madison Square Gardens.

The electric set passed, Clinton appeared having given up his spot near-ish the stage – things had just got worse – and reported that he too had been unable to find a bearable spot to watch from. We resigned ourselves to observing the crowd's increasingly bizarre behaviour and catching whatever glimpses we could of Dylan.

I had brought binoculars with me but every time I used them at the back of the hall someone came and either bumped into me or stood right in front of the binoculars – this in an area with plenty of space. I'm glad to say that it wasn't just me. The minute Clinton tried to use them someone came up and head-butted the binoculars.

During the acoustic set's opener, "One Too Many Mornings", Dylan sounded in good voice. But there was so much chattering going on around us that it was difficult to tell how good. "It's All Over Now, Baby Blue" sounded Wood-stock-ish but by now the six people directly in front of me had formed a horse-shoe facing away from the stage, their conversation having reached a critical point. So it goes. The night dragged on and on. By the time Dylan had got to "It Ain't Me, Babe", I had returned to the back of the hall, binoculars trained on Bob, when a Deadhead grabbed me and shouted in my ear "Do you think Jerry will come on?" I suspected he was at the Dead show but just replied, "I hope not."

The Deadhead thought I was joking, his mouth was now right to my ear as though he was really worried that I might hear a bit of the show I had travelled 3,000 miles for. "Maybe Jerry and Bob will do 'All Along The Watchtower'?!" He was getting excited. I didn't point out that the song had been played already and that I knew Dylan was about to end his show for the night. I didn't say anything. Dylan was approaching the final words of the night. Fittingly, I didn't get to hear them. The unwanted voice bellowed "Wouldn't it be a gas if they played 'All Along The Watchtower' at two in the morning, wouldn't that be a blast, eh?" masking the last words from the stage.

End of show, goodnight.

***

I was luckier with the third night, (the 20th). Bits of the evening were almost tolerable. The majority of the crowd were there in the hope of seeing Jerry Garcia though, and I wish to God they'd stayed away, or that the Dead had played one more night at Madison Square Gardens to spare us this onslaught. The one thing they did do was make tickets for the night very valuable. Which was a pity for me, I'd had 5 spares for the first two nights and could hardly give them away. Tonight was a scalper's feast.

I enjoyed the show as much as I could with the constant chattering and ceaseless moving around of a crowd who rarely seemed to care about what was happening on stage and the Never-Ending questions of "Can you see Jerry yet?". "Jerry who?" became my standard reply. The Roseland shows closed with extended encores as both Neil Young and Bruce Springsteen joined Dylan and the band on stage. Musically forgettable it may have been but the sight of the three together was one not to be missed.

Still the opening night had been great, because I was right in front of Bob, with Pia by my side, at my first ever New York show. Around us were people who were there for Dylan; there to enjoy the show. We got there only thanks to the generosity of friends Andy and Michelle, who not only persuaded their friends to arrange to let us get there by swapping positions with us, but who even at one point gave us their own hard-won position right at Bob's feet.

After the shows I talked to friends from home and previous Dylan concerts. Somewhat surreally I was surrounded by the same people in New York that I met every fortnight at Camden. I also met some American fans that I either didn't know at all or had only met briefly before. A nicer group of people would be hard to imagine, friendly, helpful, and well into Dylan. What a shame that they seemed to be in such a small minority when it comes to the shows.

I had had a fantastic week in New York. The people I met were far friendlier than you'd find in the streets of London – but at a concert? Forget it!

***

This year's fall tour drew to a close on November the 13th. It was followed by Dylan rehearsing for, and performing in, MTV's hugely successful "Unplugged" show. This was a show that presented acoustic performances by leading artists from the electrified fields of Rock music. It had rejuvenated or boosted the careers of many artists and it afforded Dylan a chance to build on his Wood-stock success, especially among the younger generation of concert-goers and album buyers.

Dylan fans, with memories of the greatness of the Supper Club and the suc-cessful TV appearances from Nara and Woodstock, thought they were in for a sublime treat. MTV Unplugged must have thought that they too were onto a winner. After all, "Unplugged" had proved a commercial and artistic suc-cess for Nirvana, Neil Young and REM, to mention only three who had per-formed fine sets. Here, at last, was the most famous unplugged person in popu-lar music history. The scene seemed set for an out-and-out triumph.

This was not what we got. Instead, the discomfort Dylan often feels about being on TV was much to the fore. The dark glasses he kept on for most of the show kept his eyes well hidden though not as occluded as his talent. The rehearsals were much better because Dylan was more relaxed, but even they are not a patch on what could rightly have been expected. Nonetheless they would have been vastly preferable to the broadcast show itself. So what went wrong? Nearly everything. Who was to blame? Both MTV and Dylan, with the latter taking the lion's share.

MTV can certainly be faulted for their ridiculous insistence on putting the most photogenic youthful fans at front, and, even more damagingly, in inter-fering with Dylan's proposed set list. Dylan going along with these against his better judgement seems even more reprehensible. Unlike MTV, he knew better but just did not care enough. Edna Gundersen, interviewing him for *USA Today,* elicited revealing confessions:

Q: "Was the studio audience a typical Dylan crowd? "

A: "I'd never seen them before. [Laughs] As I recall, they were in the polite category...."

Q: "How did you plan this Unplugged project? "

A: "I wasn't quite sure how to do it and what material to use. I would have liked to do old folk songs with acoustic instruments, but there was a lot of input from other sources as to what would be right for the [MTV] audience. The record company said, "You can't do that, it's too obscure." At one time, I would have argued, but there's no point. OK, so what's not obscure? They said "'Knockin' on Heaven's Door'"."

Both MTV and Dylan are to blame for allowing the TV special to omit the best of the songs played. The same could be said for the track selection on the album release. Since it is his work, though, Dylan's lack of care seems the greater fault, especially in the light of his decision not to release the vastly superior "Unplugged"-like Supper Club shows. His lack of commitment was further underlined in the following exchanges from the same interview:

Q: "Was performing before TV cameras difficult? "

A: "It's hard to rise above some lukewarm attitude toward (TV). I've never catered to that medium. It doesn't really pay off for me...."

Q: "Did you approve of the finished show? "

A: "I can't say. I didn't see it. "

Bob didn't miss much. The MTV special was suffocatingly bland, there was nothing special about Dylan, no feeling that here was a major artist or performer; no excitement or invention.

Depressingly, if predictably, this safe, bland Dylan drew some positive reviews. The most misguided of which went as far as to favourably compare it to 1976's *Hard Rain* – a bit like preferring *A Comedy of Errors* to *King Lear*.

Even the one moment of the show as broadcast that looked natural – a bungled opening to "Like a Rolling Stone", that led Dylan to joke with the audience that the band had got ahead of him – was not natural at all. Instead this attempt to make Dylan look like a cuddly old fogey to the TV audience was the result of some trick editing. This lamentable act stands as a fitting metaphor for a programme that presented such a castrated version of the live Dylan experience. It was a poor end to 1994.

Thankfully, the opening show of 1995 would take us from this ridiculous low to a sublime high.

Chapter Eleven: 1995

Hey Chop!

"He just likes to be out there because he likes to feel young and he likes to feel that he can still do it. And out of all the people I have toured with or met, he's definitely the most constant one. He's definitely a road-type person."

Cesar Diaz, from *A&E TV* Dylan Biography

Nineteen ninety-five was to turn out a busy year for Dylan. He played 116 shows, more than he had ever done in a year before. By the year's end he had had a CD and video released (*MTV Unplugged*) and had made forays in to the computer age with an interactive CD-ROM "Highway 61 Interactive", and *Greatest Hits Volume 3* produced as an enhanced music CD, which, when played on a computer, brought up a variety of on-screen information.

Fans may have started the year pining for an album of new Dylan material, but the opening dates of this year's N.E.T. offerings soon drove all other thoughts out of their minds.

The touring started on March 11th, a day later than scheduled, in Prague. Prague 1994 had been one of the better European shows of that year, but Prague 1995 was to prove something else altogether.

As usual a bus was going from London, but, reeling from the expense of European and New York shows in 1994, hassled at work and not wishing ever again to be trapped on a bus for hours on end, I decided to skip the opening jaunt. And what a one to miss!

Not that it seemed such a bad choice on the 10th as Dylan and the band were so ill from the flu that the first date was cancelled/rescheduled. In Dylan's case this is a once-in-a-decade occurrence, but there was serious danger of the next night being an unheard of double postponement. Dylan and the band members were still ill, but proceeded to pull a performance of majestic splendour out of this adversity.

Anyone who has watched a sunrise over the ancient city of Prague will feel they have visited a city of magic and wonder. Anyone who has heard Dylan's performance on the 11th will have felt a similar sense of awe.

Prague 1995
Palác kultury, Prague, Czech Republic, 11th March 1995

1	Down In The Flood
2	If Not For You
3	All Along The Watchtower
4	Just Like A Woman
5	Tangled Up In Blue
6	Watching The River Flow
7	Mr. Tambourine Man (Acoustic)
8	Boots Of Spanish Leather (Acoustic)
9	It's All Over Now, Baby Blue (Acoustic)
10	Man In The Long Black Coat
11	God Knows
12	Maggie's Farm

*

13	Shelter From The Storm
14	It Ain't Me, Babe (Acoustic)

Dylan was so weak after his illness that he forsook his guitars and crooned his way through the night at the microphone. By all accounts this was a late decision and surprised the band, so it would seem that the inspired change in performance style came about due to the flu! It seemed to work so well, though, that you feel Dylan must have been giving a lot of thought as to how he would present a show, guitarless. Perhaps Dylan had been contemplating trying this approach on some songs, and the illness had propelled him into playing all but a few minutes of the 11th March without one.

The shock of seeing Dylan open without a guitar might have taken some time to register on the audience, as the opening song was a huge surprise in itself; a live debut of "Down In The Flood" from *The Basement Tapes* [71].

This was a great song to resurrect and stayed as the opener for many shows. Later it became a bit of a tub-thumping opener, but back in March, he performed a loud, deep, bassy bluesy version with powerful vocals and a bold harp. It was a good ballsy start.

The second song was a much mellower number, "If Not For You". It was quite faithful to the original arrangement, though more dynamic. It featured some appealing country playing and effective, if somewhat hoarse, vocals.

The audience were also being served up a visual display that was completely new to a Dylan show. Without a guitar as a prop, far less a musical instrument, Dylan stood for much of the time with knees partly bent, holding the microphone to his mouth while his other arm was outstretched, pointing outward and upwards, holding the microphone cable. Apart from pain-induced doubling over, his movements included strange, staggering dance steps and what looked suspiciously like slowed-down shadow-boxing routines.

"All Along The Watchtower" had the same basic arrangement as usual, but Dylan could fully concentrate on his vocals. In turn, John Jackson was given leeway to express himself without worrying about Dylan's guitar lines. Dylan really opened up, changing emphasis all over the place, riding the song like a bucking half-tamed mustang. It was magnificent stuff.

And then the concert really took off and soared. "Just Like A Woman" opened with a sensuous, passionate harp while Dylan's singing saw him feeling out a new expression of the song as he went along. The band were unable to keep up as Dylan created something new live on stage. For a few lines his vocals seemed cut adrift from the backing, but he continued anyway and resolved it all in a beautiful harmonica passage. It was a stunning tour-de-force.

"Tangled Up In Blue" was not quite so successful, but it featured a pointed harmonica ending and Bob followed it with a nice piece of audience interaction.

"Thanks. I was sick here last night," Dylan told the crowd, "Got the flu. This is a really good place to recover from the flu."

As he finished speaking, Dylan was heading back to his rack of harmonicas, when a shout rang out above the normal between-song hubbub:

"Bobby, I love you!"

Dylan paused in mid-step, smiled and asked:

"Oh, could you say that again?"

No-one did, but Dylan continued:

"This is called, um, my ecology song here," and launched into "Watching The River Flow", which chugged along very pleasantly. It ended in an instrumental jam that brought in Dylan on guitar. He raised a cheer from someone simply for picking up the instrument – and performed a pleasing enough exchange of riffs with John Jackson. Dylan relinquished his guitar again in time for "Mr. Tambourine Man". Prague began a Spring season full of superlative versions of this vintage song.[72] It is hard to understand how even Dylan can keep re-arranging a song so dramatically, constantly investing it with new meaning and emotion. This version had a genuine warmth to it, there was a lovely "echoe-y" sound to his voice, while the deftness and depth of the harmonica playing was quite transcendent. It was as though a Dylan of yore, the maestro harmonica player opening up our dreams and visions, had returned from a long absence.[73] The crowd were understandably delirious.

"Boots of Spanish Leather" was simultaneously a prayer-like plea and an emotional statement of intent. "It's All Over Now, Baby Blue" was even better than at Woodstock II, and stands with anything Dylan has ever done. Lyrics that were deeply profound to begin with took on new resonance and meaning through delivery. It was like seeing a precious diamond being held at an unfamiliar angle under a new light, revealing yet more depth and beauty to an already treasured gemstone. Dylan then followed the lyrics with a harmonica break from heaven, evoking memories of his killer acoustic sets from 1966. Like much of this show, Dylan fans ache for this version to be released officially.

There was hardly time to take all this in before the darkly menacing introduction to "Man In The Long Black Coat" found Dylan in the voice of a master-story teller; a wise old prophet of the ages. A splendid version of "God Knows" followed, exploding into a rock-based rave up about half-way through. The full-on rock sound was carried forward into the perennial "Maggie's Farm", which brought the main set to an upbeat close.

To close a remarkable evening, instead of running through a couple of stand-ard encores, Dylan returned for a magnificent "Shelter From The Storm". The song started quietly, with phenomenal care taken over the vocals, before build-ing up to a climax infused with extensive and intensive harmonica playing. It was another performance of epic stature, standing near the top of a list of performances – "Just Like A Woman", "Mr. Tambourine Man", "It's All Over Now, Baby Blue" and "Man In The Long Black Coat" – that were amongst the best the N.E.T., or in a couple of cases, Dylan's entire career, has offered us so far.

The closing "It Ain't Me, Babe" found his vocals still in stellar form and even the crowd's clap-a-long seemed not so much an intrusion, as a joyful interaction. This was the kind of show where even describing the way Dylan rolled his "r"s would get one into *Private Eye*'s "Pseud's Corner" for waxing too lyrical.

I still have tapes of the hysterical phone calls backs to my Information Line; mind you, they betray more happiness at my non-presence than at Dylan's magnificent performance! I remember being told how well I was taking all the ribbing. I would be the first to admit that a year earlier I'd have been devas-tated. But now, having given up on my commitment to my magazine, I wasn't as bothered.

I'd decided that the magazine had become too important to me. I was react-ing to events in the Dylan world with the 'zine in mind. I was constantly agi-tated about getting news on the information line as fast as possible. I was actu-ally irritated that *Good As I Been To You* was released at such an awkward time for *Homer, the slut* that I had to delay sending out an issue. Eventually it became so important it stopped being fun, which was ridiculous. Dylan's work was the important thing and Dylan fandom should only be a fun adjunct to that. The minute it stops being fun is the time to change your attachment to it. I suspect too that meeting Dylan in Camden had a lot to do with it – there wasn't much further fan life could go than that.

So, I was once again back in the real world where pleasure in hearing Dylan had performed well was the important thing and one's personal involvement was incidental. If that sounds too altruistic – well it was totally dependent on the certainty of getting tapes of the said shows. As long as I can hear the shows whenever I want, I can have the resolve not to go to so many!

As the following years were to show, I was going through a temporary period of distancing myself from the obsessive life-encompassing demands of the N.E.T. This would probably have started in 1995 if that year had not been so good that I could not pull any freer until the following years.

It was, as you will have guessed, another of those occasions when a great current Dylan performance sparked off an abundance of extravagant claims of it being as good as the best of '66, '79, '78, '81 (name your year). Unlike most times when this happens, on this occasion you could see the point.

Even more remarkably, some of those who continued on the tour thought some of the immediately subsequent shows were even better. Paul Williams picked Brussels as his favourite, while others extolled the virtues of some German shows. Then there were the other two nights at Prague itself. The 12th March show is often overlooked because of the shock and splendour of the 11th. The previous day aside though it was surely the best N.E.T. show since at least 1992. Then on the final day at Prague another show of almost similar standing showcased a marvellous – probably best ever – version of "Licence To Kill" that liberated the great song I always have maintained lurked underneath the arrangement and production on *Infidels*.

Tapes and news of the opening shows flooded into the UK. Gavin Martin had gone to Prague to report for the *NME* and based his extended Dylan feature around an interview with Lambchop in splendid "Lambchop" form. Mr. Martin pointedly compared the "heroic and brazen, masterful interpretative singer honing in on his own canon" of Prague's opening night with the "polar opposite" of the *MTV Unplugged* debacle.

"In Prague," Martin continued, "Dylan took pleasure in stretching his lyrics into new territory, making the words zing and sting again, staking his claim to greatness, laying down the gauntlet, savouring the dark truths, apocalyptic intent and visions of fiery wonder swirling in his songs. This was like no other Dylan anyone had ever seen."

So, once again, UK Dylan fans were buzzing with eager anticipation of a 14-date British Isles tour that began in Brighton on 26th March.

Although I enjoyed the show well enough, I was struck by the self-inflicted curse of listening to too many tapes. I spoke to people who had heard nothing from the year so far and they were in raptures. Still, it was my first live view of the the "guitarless" Dylan. I liked what I saw and heard, but felt that it was not up to the standard of the earlier shows. It is only fair to point out though, that there were some of the all-tape- listening Dylan fraternity who rated Brighton very highly despite their exposure to earlier 1995 treats. I preferred the following night at Cardiff with a fabulous near 10 minute "Desolation Row".

After a day's break we had three shows on successive nights in London. It was no longer at the Apollo (née Odeon) – this time we were at the Brixton Academy. I used to live only a mile or so from this venue, back in pre N.E.T. days and it would never have occurred to me that I would one day see Dylan there. Brixton was usually the territory of Goths, Punks, Rastas and other tribes of the disenfranchised (or those playing at being so). The Dylan crowd included a much higher percentage of the professional classes, illustrating how far Dylan's audience had moved from being anti-establishment to themselves being the establishment.

The Brixton shows got off to a poor start. The Academy is not the best of places either physically or acoustically, but there was more amiss than that. Dylan seemed distant, a spark was missing and it all became a bit of a dull, flat night. I was beginning to worry that the early glory of the year's touring was a fast-fading flame.

Interestingly enough, on re-listening to the show I discovered a "Dignity" that was one of my favourite performances of the year; I hadn't really noticed it on the night! This visceral live version trashes all the officially released takes.

The second night dispelled all my fears of a tapering off in 1995 quality. Dylan played like a man re-energised, re-connected with his performing art, prowling the stage with genuine purpose and conviction.

The set-list was shaken up for the first time in the year, as Dylan stretched himself in front of an ecstatic crowd. "Mr. Tambourine Man" was again exceptional and "Masters Of War" was close to the heights of Hiroshima. A flawless "Love Minus Zero/No Limit" rounded off an exquisite acoustic set. Oh, and the electric songs really rocked too, and "Jokerman" followed by "Every Grain Of Sand" was a perfect pairing, particularly since "Every Grain Of Sand" replaced "Tangled Up In Blue", which previously had seemed as locked in to the fifth slot as "All Along The Watchtower" still was to the third slot. It was quite a night, as was the next, when a show much closer to the quality of the 30th than the 29th, was rounded off with guest appearances by support acts Elvis Costello, Carole King and Chrissie Hynde.

After one night off, it was on to Birmingham where we had another tremendous set list[74] and many highs, including a mesmerising "To Ramona". From there it was straight on to three nights in Manchester, the first of which featured a particularly masterful acoustic set. Magnificent though these acoustic segments were most nights, none could surpass the extraordinary one that night.

As was customary, "Mr. Tambourine Man" opened the acoustic segment, and while as usual this year it was outstanding, this version was even more so. There was such a sense of time, space and movement and an awareness of matters of immense import that it seemed that all of European history was echoing through the hall. Here in Manchester, on the third of April, Dylan completely nailed his spellbinding 1995 arrangement of one of his great masterpieces.

There was no way that Dylan would lose his way having sung so expressively. The second song of this acoustic set, "Spanish Boots Of Spanish Leather", was graced with a gorgeous burr on his voice plus enunciation and phrasing of the highest order.

The third in this acoustic trio was "Gates Of Eden" and it seemed many, many years since Dylan had given it a perfect reading. There were good ones, but not sustained in every verse – usually lyrics or music or both collapsed somewhere along the line. Not here though, he's got it dead on. The overly-long instrumental ending would usually detract from the whole for me but here it worked, as though Dylan knew he had grasped a precious range of expression in the acoustic set and did not want to let it go.

All three shows in Manchester had much to commend them and it was perhaps understandable that a dip in standards had to come. Edinburgh's two shows were much lower key; the performers seemed drained. For those following the tour the most notable thing was that, on the second night there, Dylan spoke to Lambchop, making our friend's day (life?) by calling out from the stage:

"Hey Chop! How you doin' tonight? Where's your hat man? Hey, better put your hat back on!"

I should also point out that I met friends after Edinburgh shows who had not seen Dylan live since 1991 or 1993, and they were completely blown away with these 1995 shows. So much so that they were highly suspicious of any reports that these were poor compared to so many others that Spring. Again the importance of context was made clear to me; a "poor" 1995 show could well be the best in half a decade even for someone who had seen the last dozen or more shows in the UK up to that year.

Edinburgh was a mere blip; Glasgow and Dublin saw fantastic shows, played to wildly enthusiastic audiences and rewarded with rave reviews. Glasgow was the last night for me, another special night. Paul Williams called the 15-song set – which included unforgettable performances of "Shelter From The Storm", "Tears of Rage"', "Lenny Bruce", "Mr. Tambourine Man" and "Lay Lady Lay" – "a doorway to knowledge." Williams considered the cassette tape of the show to be, "Intended or not,... an extraordinary and durable, repeatable work of art... full of beauty and intelligence. Communicative in those very special ways reserved for great works of art... John Coltrane's *Impressions*. Monet's *Water Lilies*. Dylan's *Glasgow '95*."

Tapes, CD-Rs, whatever, yes, as this book testifies they transport us through time and space, and, much as it was great fun to be at the Glasgow show – now I was sated. I couldn't take much more. I didn't need to see Dylan again for a long time really, did I? Well, we will see about that later.

This European leg came to a suitably high energy close with a top quality extended show in Dublin on April the 11th, where Dylan and the band were joined on the encores by Elvis Costello, Van Morrison, and Carole King.

Dylan took the next month off before taking his 1995 show to the U.S. West Coast. The US audiences were ecstatic at these performances. Those who had followed on from Europe were quite *blasé* by comparison, having witnessed greater glories already. These were very strong shows in their own right even if not quite up to the European standard – and especially not Prague's. Individual songs, on the other hand, were still scaling similar peaks: there was at least one "Man In A Long Black Coat", for example, that was right up there with Prague. Dylan's magnificent vocals, brooding over an oppressive backing, combining to create an atmosphere that was downright scary. Also, one could easily choose US shows that were far superior to the "poorer" UK nights like the first Brixton and two Edinburgh ones. Another boon for the US audiences was that there was a greater looseness to the set lists. Something like the May 22nd one, below, would have been unthinkable at the beginning of the year:

22nd May, 1995
The Warfield, San Francisco, California
Down In The Flood
Man In The Long Black Coat
All Along The Watchtower

Most Likely You Go Your Way (And I'll Go Mine)
Tears Of Rage (Dylan/Manuel)
Tombstone Blues
Mr. Tambourine Man (Acoustic)
Desolation Row (Acoustic)
It's All Over Now, Baby Blue (Acoustic)
Seeing The Real You At Last
She Belongs To Me
Obviously Five Believers
*

Lenny Bruce
My Back Pages (Acoustic)

You may have noticed here some songs not discussed so far, in particular "Obviously Five Believers" from *Blonde On Blonde*. This song had finally made its live debut, after tantalizingly appearing as a setlist possibility and at soundchecks (minus Dylan, alas) at various shows on May 15th at the McCallum Theater in Palm Desert, California.

During its first outing, it stood up so well to live treatment you were surprised it had not appeared before, though grateful as ever for a fresh treat.

Another treat that same night, though a more dubious one, was a slowed down "Never Gonna Be The Same Again", appearing for only the second time, and the first in nine years. "Seeing the Real You At Last" had been a regular in these US shows, so perhaps *Empire Burlesque* was on his mind. *Blonde On Blonde* seemed to be too as, in addition to "Obviously 5 Believers" being unveiled on the 15th, the 17th saw the first "Pledging My Time" since September 1990.

Sheryl Crow, in May, was the latest in a long line of support acts on Dylan's N.E.T. to go on to become a star in their own right. All in all, 1995 was going along splendidly. You just knew that Dylan was going to do something to buck the trend.

It happened in June, beginning on the 15th, when Dylan opened for the Grateful Dead for the first of five shows. Yet another ill-fated attempt to grab some of the Deadhead dollars found Dylan playing to a handful of Dylan fans swamped by the tiny percentage of the huge Dead following who came along prior to seeing the headliners. They used the time to throw frisbees and get the joints and the hamburgers in while Dylan went largely ignored and played as though that was all he deserved to be.

As though he knew that what he was doing in those huge arenas was a farce, Dylan played two shows at Philadelphia's tiny (800 capacity), standing room only Theatre of The Living Arts, on June 21 and 22nd, in the middle of these Dead outings. The first of these theatre dates has gone down in Dylan folklore as one of the very best nights of the N.E.T..

Certainly it was an excellent show. Dylan was clearly on top form from the opening moments, ripping into "Down In The Flood" like a man on a mission. There were also great takes on "Licence to Kill" and "Knocking On Heaven's

Door", and Dylan's warm and affectionate band member introductions give you an idea of how much he was enjoying the night:

"Thank you, thank you. Playing guitar tonight, I'm not gonna tell you how old he is though. He's from Memphis, that ought to give you some clue, J. J. Jackson. On the drums Winston Watson. I thought his name was Ice T when I hired him. Anyway it doesn't matter, he's so good we forgot about it. On the steel guitar and a bunch of other stuff, former mayor of Bluesville, West Virginia, Bucky Baxter. He was a fine looking young man when he joined me. Got a lot of years on him now. On bass guitar tonight, Tony Garnier. I'm not gonna tell you anything about Tony either. I don't know anything about him. I know he once tried to milk a cow with a monkey wrench."

In spite of all this, for me the show doesn't quite live up to its reputation among the fan fraternity. The show's acclaim mostly rests on the performance of two songs that have powerful claims to be Dylan's finest. The first of these was "Visions Of Johanna" in the acoustic set. It is undoubtedly a song that means a great deal to any Dylan fan. However, unlike the reinventive Prague performances of other classic songs, this version does not add much to the original.

The second surprise appearance was "Tangled Up In Blue" – as the acoustic encore. It was an extraordinary place for such an important song and the thought of it being played acoustically had Dylan fans around the globe salivating. Once heard, however, it was not so overwhelming, sounding a bit forced and strained.

It was a very powerful show overall, if not as outstanding as is often claimed. However, given that they came in the middle of the lamentable support slots with the Dead, the two shows must have seemed "Prague-like" to those attending a mixture of the soulless stadiums and the intimate theatre.

The second Living Arts Theatre show was pretty good too. It began with "Drifter's Escape", which turned out to be a fairly common alternative to "Down In The Flood" as opener as the year progressed. ("Drifter's Escape" had not been played since November 12th, 1992, in Clearwater, Florida.)

Dylan's ill-fated stint with the Dead ended on June 25th at the Robert F. Kennedy stadium in Washington DC. Jerry Garcia joined Dylan and his band to add guitar to their last two songs, "It Takes A Lot to Laugh, It Takes A Train To Cry" and "Rainy Day Women # 12 & 35". It was to be the last time the two friends were on stage together.

It was a sad setting for such a partnership to bow out. I always thought that the best time for Garcia and Dylan to play together would be sitting on a porch late one night swapping songs. It would nice to dream that maybe they grabbed a chance to do that far from the madding crowds before Jerry Garcia died on August 9th from a heart attack while attending a drug rehabilitation centre in California.

The next day Dylan issued a moving statement through his press office. It gave an insight into how much Garcia had meant to Dylan:

"There's no way to measure his greatness or magnitude as a person or as a player... He really had no equal. To me he wasn't only a musician and friend, he was more like a big brother who taught and showed me more than he'll ever know.... There's no way to convey the loss. It just digs down really deep."

It was not to be the last intimation of mortality that year. In November Dylan would be a performing guest at Frank Sinatra's 80th birthday celebration. It was clear from that night that Mr. Sinatra would not be enjoying many more birthdays. In December, Robert Shelton, Dylan biographer and one time New York critic who helped bring Dylan to the public's notice back in the Greenwich folk club days, died of a stroke.

Back on June 25th, Dylan enjoyed a few days rest before returning to Europe for his customary summer tour. So, although I was previously writing (after the Glasgow show on April 9th) with a certain smug sureness that I'd overcome the extreme levels of behaviour that Bob Dylan inspires; that I was comfortable in the feeling that the UK shows were easily enough for me... come July, Dylan was playing in Germany and I felt I had to go, it seemed like ages since I had last seen him.

So I headed out to Germany on July 1st. Dylan was playing in Roskilde that night but I wouldn't see him until Hamburg, the next day. Instead I flew to Frankfurt and met up with my good friends and travelling companions; (already stretching to Germany '94, UK and Germany '95 with many more to come) Stephan, Chris and Daniel. They lived nearby, and after the obligatory swapping of, and listening to, recent Dylan tapes, we headed off for a pleasant day walking on the hills over-looking the Rhine. The weather was glorious and I was taken to the picturesque tourist village of Rudesheim which just happens to be the home of a famous – and utterly adorable – brandy coffee. This coffee is the highlight of the meal at an obscure country restaurant in Scotland that was the celebratory place for major events in my family's life (engagements, graduations etc.). I was taken with this coincidence and trusted it was a good omen for the days ahead. The evening was perfectly rounded off with a visit to a Straussenwirtschaft, run by Daniel's girlfriends Moni, and her parents. Why am I telling you all this? Because it's part of the fans' N.E.T. – the socialising, the travelling to new places. The fan's N.E.T. is not just about the shows.

Nonetheless, when we rose early the next morning, July 2nd, for the seven hour drive to Hamburg, I was full of intense excitement as the experience of seeing Dylan again drew ever nearer. Hamburg's Stadtpark is the perfect outdoor venue: a picturesque area enclosed by cultivated hedges and trees. On this day the sun was shining brightly throughout the evening. Dylan was due to start at 19:00 hrs, as there was a strict curfew at 22:00.

After soaking in the ambience, the great moment arrived. "Ladies and gentlemen, will you please... " My stomach muscles clenched in painful anticipation, and then there he was, the centre of all our attention. Looking cool, looking great, wearing shades to protect his eyes from the glare, Dylan then tore straight into "Crash On The Levee". It was the first time I had seen him do it with a guitar in his hands and I liked it. Suddenly I was conscious of my tense anticipation melting away. I was back in the presence of our Bob!

Next up was "If Not For You" with its pleasant country-ish backing. The acoustics were superb and Bob was in good voice. I have no idea if he per-

MANCHESTER 1

DOWN IN THE FLOOD
TEARDROPS
WATCHTOWER
WHAT GOOD AM I
MEMPHIS
LONG BLACK COAT

TAMBOURINE
BOOTS
GATES/DESOLATION(G)

JOKERMAN/TOMBSTONE/DIGNITY
RED SKY
MR. JONES

PILLBOX
AIN'T ME BABE
HEAVEN'S DOOR

EDINBURGH 2

DOWN IN THE FLOOD
TOM THUMB
WATCHTOWER
WOMAN
PLEDGING MY TIME/TOMBSTONE
   HIGHWAY 61
BIG GIRL/I DON'T BELIEVE

TAMBOURINE
HARD RAIN
LOVE MINUS ZERO

PILLBOX/TOMBSTONE
LENNY BRUCE/WHAT GOOD AM I
YOU GO YOUR WAY

MR. JONES
WIND/TIMES/BACK PAGES

BIELEFELD

DOWN IN THE FLOOD
IF NOT FOR YOU
WATCHTOWER
JUST LIKE A WOMAN
TANGLED
4TH STREET

TAMBOURINE
MASTERS
BOOTS/DON'T THINK/MAMA

DIGNITY
LONG BLACK COAT/SHE BELI
MAGGIE'S

ROLLING STONE

MANCHESTER 2

DOWN IN THE FLOOD
I WANT YOU
WATCHTOWER
SHOOTING STAR
YOU GO YOUR WAY
SIMPLE TWIST/RIVER FLOW

TAMBOURINE
MASTERS
ONE TOO MANY MORNINGS

DIGNITY
I&I
I'LL REMEMBER YOU

ROLLING STONE
TIMES/BLOWIN'
HEAVEN'S DOOR

EDINBURGH

DOWN IN THE FLOOD
I WANT YOU/WHAT WAS IT
WATCHTOWER
DISEASE/WOMAN
MEMPHIS
SIMPLE TWIST/RELEASED

TAMBOURINE
GATES/MASTERS
TWICE/BABY BLUE

GOD KNOWS
LENNY BRUCE
JOKERMAN

ROLLING STONE/WHAT GOOD AM I
AIN'T ME BABE
RELEASED

GLASGOW

DOWN IN THE FLOOD
LAY LADY LAY
WATCHTOWER
SHELTER
QUEEN JANE/TEARS OF RAGE
BROKEN

TAMBOURINE
DESOLATION(A)
BABY BLUE

GOD KNOWS
LENNY BRUCE/TOMBSTONE
TOMBSTONE/LENNY BRUCE

HIGHWAY 61
BACK PAGES/AIN'T ME BABE

FURTH

DOWN IN THE FLOOD
IF YOU SEE HER
WATCHTOWER
WOMAN
UNBELIEVABLE
4TH STREET/I'LL BE YOUR BABY

TAMBOURINE
MASTERS/BOOTS
DESOLATION A

MEMPHIS
LONG BLACK COAT
MAGGIE'S

ROLLING STONE

MANCHESTER 3

DOWN IN THE FLOOD
IF NOT FOR YOU
WATCHTOWER
QUEEN JANE/LICENSE TO KILL
   I DON'T BELIEVE YOU
RIVER FLOW
HEAVEN'S DOOR

TAMBOURINE
BOOTS
HARD RAIN(D)

TOMBSTONE
IN THE GARDEN
BORN IN TIME

MR. JONES/ROLLING STONE
BACK PAGES

A selection of set lists from
the 1995 era

formed "All Along The Watchtower" well or not, and until it would be given a long rest, or at the very least moved from the third spot, would never really care to know again. (Even obsessives have their limits.)

Fortunately, the fourth song, the majestic "Queen Jane Approximately", raised everything to a whole new level. The subsequent song sounded very like it was going to be "Watching The River Flow", but then became "I'll Be Your Baby, Tonight". After which, Dylan had greater things on his mind and went into "Pledging My Time". This was turning into a very fine show indeed. "Silvio" then brought the first electric set to an ear-shattering close, the song building to a crescendo on wave after wave of guitar attacks.

The acoustic set began with "Tangled Up In Blue". It would be my dearest wish to report to you that Dylan reclaimed this masterpiece from the trashing he's given it in recent years, alas it was not to be. Though Dylan carefully enunciated each word, he just didn't inhabit the song. Even the first appearance, to predictable applause, of the harmonica at its climax failed to hide the fact that this just hadn't worked.

I don't think it was a particularly strong "Masters of War", but Dylan was clearly projecting it better than "Tangled Up In Blue". Suddenly, with a heartrending "It's All Over Now Baby Blue" the whole evening warped into another universe (where Bob is in our heaven and all seems well on Earth). This lovely, slow version, first unveiled just before Woodstock II, was to prove my favourite single performance of this particular trip. You could have heard a pin drop, in fact the only interruption was the singing of the birds above in the tree tops, as Dylan poured himself into a glorious rendition of a magnificent song in a balmy evening in Northern Germany. It was a transcendent moment. Then slam, bang, thank you ma'am guitars led into the second electric set with "Stuck Inside Of Mobile With The Memphis Blues Again". For me this song peaked at the Hammersmith Odeon in 1990, one of my favourite memories. By 1993, after countless turgid renditions, I was completely fed up with it. Fortunately, he followed it here with an excellent "She Belongs To Me."

The highlight of the encores – and the second best performance of the night for me – was a gorgeous, acoustic "My Back Pages". After the closing strains of "Rainy Day Women # 12 & 35", I wandered around the park, meeting lots of friends from Germany and the UK. Then it was time to find a 'phone to call Lambchop and get him to update my information line.

After a few hours sightseeing in Hamburg, 3rd July found us in Hanover in plenty of time, 18:30hrs or so. Dylan was back to the more customary 20:00 starting time. We drove in circles. We stopped to ask directions. We drove in circles. Time passed. We stopped to ask directions. We drove in circles. It was approaching 19:30. We were told to follow the signs. We couldn't see any signs to follow. We looked in increasing desperation. At 19:48, we saw a half obscured sign. This led to our discovery that all "Music Hall" signs had been covered by a poster campaign; thankfully, not quite 100% successfully.

Ten minutes later we caught sight of the venue. Bob was due on in two minutes. All three of us bravely waited in the ante room as Stephan parked the car. Meanwhile, the band struck up the opening to "Down In The Flood". Stephan was astonished to find us all waiting for him. We had missed all of 34 seconds of Dylan. I explained later that it was a sacrifice worth making for a friend, though if the opening song had been "Drifter's Escape" (which I had yet to witness live) he wouldn't have seen me for dust!

Dylan's relentless touring schedule, and the resulting effect of supply and demand forces, meant that there was no problem walking straight down to the front, even when arriving so late. I had a perfect view from about the third row. What a contrast to the pre-N.E.T. days.

It was another excellent show, 1995 was full of them. My highlights from the first set were "Positively 4th Street" and "Jokerman". The majority of the audience – as at the other two shows – were far more enthusiastic about "All Along The Watchtower" and "Silvio". The acoustic set was the usual delight, with "Mr. Tambourine Man" absolutely stunning yet again. From the remainder of the set, "Tombstone Blues", "Leopard Skin Pill-Box-Hat" and "Rainy Day Women # 12 & 35" were real pile-driver party pieces.

Then it was an overnight drive to Berlin. We stopped at the first opportunity for refreshments. Later that night we discovered that we had missed Dylan and his entourage at the same stop by a matter of minutes. Mmm.

We made the most of the day in Berlin. It was my first visit and the centres of the old West and East formed our forward path. There was a fascinating exhibition of the proposed reconstruction of Berlin centre. "Berlin 2005" said the poster, "2005? – the acoustic tour", I murmured. It was as we left this exhibition that major concert-goer and Internet tour agent, Ray Webster came out with a comment that I think sums up all of the more besotted Dylan fans, and illuminates the way the N.E.T. has come to dominate their lives. Ray was deep in discussion with Stephan about previous German Dylan dates he'd attended, and made a slip of memory by calling Frankfurt '87, "Frankfurt '89". When Stephan pointed this out, Ray said, straight-faced and with due gravitas, "Ah, yes, of course, the Berlin Wall came down in '89, Dylan in Frankfurt was '87". Honestly – we measure our history in N.E.T. years!

After a visit to the Reichstag, we took a bus back to the venue, still with plenty of time before the doors were due to open. We alighted to hear the strains of "The Lonesome Death Of Hattie Carroll" being sound-checked. We followed the sounds: "It is alright, it isn't Bob singing..." I began to say, but Stephan was over the road and far away already.

We stood outside the gates. There were intermittent breaks in the soundcheck, so during one I shouted greetings to John Jackson. Ever-accommodating, he returned them with a big smile. We saw Winston and Tony too. The soundcheck, since we first heard it, had consisted solely of different versions of "The Lonesome Death Of Hattie Carroll".

We were having a pleasant time, particularly as we were standing where Bob's bus must almost certainly be arriving. Dylan's road manager Victor Maimudes, a man whose features are carved out of a material even older and more experienced than those of Keith Richards', walked up to the security gates – which had remained unlocked but under close surveillance all this time. He could not find his pass and fumbled for it in every pocket, "just like me at work on a Monday morning", I thought. He eventually found it – not that anyone was waiting on it as he was immediately recognised anyway.

The only person who had more trouble with his pass was Bucky. He had his Bob Dylan access badge round his neck and walked through the guards showing his card to each one. They all completely ignored him, (because he's recognised too, I supposed.)

Bucky clearly felt that someone should nod to him or open the gates or give some acknowledgement of his status, so he made a very firm point of show-ing his pass to the last person at the gates. This was our companion Daniel, who was intently reading the sports pages in his German paper and would only lift his head when Dylan himself arrived. So, Daniel also completely ignored Bucky who was left to wander inside in a rather aimless fashion.

Minutes later the German paper – which included the great line: "Watching Dylan perform "Like A Rolling Stone" is like hearing Goethe reading Faust" – was discarded as THE (pronounced theee) bus arrived. It was only now that anyone paid attention to us and we were asked to move, asked quite firmly as it happened. However, there was no way we were going to miss Dylan's appear-ance, so we ignored the requests and surrounded the bus.

Dylan emerged pretty quickly, but I got a lovely glimpse of him, dressed in a hooded sweatshirt with jacket on top in the height of summer. When I returned to the UK I was asked more questions about this brief glimpse than about all three shows combined, which is a slightly worrying indicator of what Dylan fans can be like. Then again, as fan David Bristow remarked to me, "Those are the moments we live for."

So, with Bob in place, it was time for us to join the queue at the doors to the Berlin Tempodrome. Strange venue, really, like a big circus tent; it turned out to be a pretty good way to see Dylan, with the massed foot-soldiers at the front and well-raised seats around. Highlights included "I Want You", "Under The Red Sky", "Girl From The North Country", driving versions of "Lenny Bruce" and "Cat's In The Well". "Knockin' On Heaven's Door" and "The Times They Are A Changin'" were pretty special too. During the latter's magnificent har-monica climax, I felt overwhelmed with sadness that I would not be seeing Bob again properly for months. If it wasn't for his scheduled appearance at The Phoenix Festival at Stratford-Upon-Avon still to come, I'd probably have been feeling a lot worse. I was even closer to tears when I saw the original set list with acoustic alternatives which included "Visions Of Johanna" and "Desola-tion Row", plus "Tears Of Rage" as an electric alternative.

Of my fellow travellers, Marion and Giovanna had Glaucha to look forward to, Chris, Daniel and Stephan had Dortmund and Stuttgart, Ray had Stratford and Spain. I only had Stratford; it did not seem enough! Worse still, the Strat-ford show was a low point in a year of high points.

***

The Phoenix experience began when we arrive at an airfield packed with thou-sands of Suede fans. After an unsavoury spat between Dylan and Suede, Dylan was billed as the headline act, while Suede were to close the show.

Dylan is out of place and so are we. There is even a rumour Dylan won't appear but he does, and he looks fantastic when he takes the stage: Supper Club jacket, shades, *that* hair. Unfortunately, the giant video screen that showed previous acts such as Van Morrison and Tricky in close-up is switched off for the duration of Bob's set.

At least I finally get to hear "Drifter's Escape", though that claim is more in theory than practice. This opening thrash bears virtually no resemblance to the song. "I Want You" makes an overwhelmingly, joyous contrast. However, during another unwelcome "All Along The Watchtower", throughout which my view is obscured by a steward, I am left to wonder at the manic security that tries to block videos and photographs of our man. The giant, blank screens bear mute witness to this nonsense.

After a solid "Tears Of Rage" and another unsuccessful "Tangled Up In Blue", things look up with "Mama, You've Been On My Mind", and really take off with its climactic harmonica playing. The highlight of the night is a beautifully paced, vocally rich, "One Too Many Mornings". It is all over far, far too soon though, and "Seeing The Real You At Last" and "Rainy Day Women # 12 & 35" finish off what seems a let-down of a set after the three German shows. Bad sound; horrific venue; a shortened set and, finally, the heavens open and torrential rain lashes us as we leave. There is no shelter from this storm. It didn't seem a fitting farewell to my July stint on the Bobwatch campaign.

***

I might have finished attending shows, but Dylan was only in the middle of his busiest touring year ever. The European trek ended on July 30th, but the end of September found Dylan out on the road in the States, yet again. The shows, while not reaching the heights of the Spring, were enthusiastically received by fans and press alike. In addition, they were bookended by two more events that were broadcast on TV.

The first of these was on September 2nd when Dylan made a high profile, though musically merely competent, five song appearance at the opening of the Rock And Roll Hall Of Fame Museum in Cleveland. Bruce Springsteen joined him for the final song, "Forever Young".

The TV episode at the other end of this leg was at the previously mentioned Frank Sinatra 80th Birthday Tribute on November 19th. All the guests were to perform one song associated with Sinatra. Dylan however, allegedly at Sinatra's request, sang one of his own songs, the long neglected "Restless Farewell".

Intriguingly, the quintessentially Dylan ending we have to this song, which signalled the end of both an album and an entire phase of his career, echoes the sentiments of Sinatra's signature tune. "So I'll make my stand", sings Bob, "And remain as I am/ And bid farewell and not give a damn". It's a far greater "My Way" from a near-forgotten, half-formed back page.

I should not leave the autumn of 1995 without remarking on a special show on September the 23rd at a tiny club called The Edge in Fort Lauderdale, Florida. Another "live rehearsal" in an intimate setting, the show stirred memories

135

of 1990's Toad's appearance. No four hour marathon here however, but the normal-length set was dominated by eight covers:

Fort Lauderdale, 23rd September 1995
The Edge Club, Fort Lauderdale, Florida
1   Real Real Gone (Van Morrison)
2   Friend Of The Devil (Hunter/Garcia/Dawson)
3   Maggie's Farm
4   It's Too Late (Chuck Wills)
5   Silvio (Dylan/Hunter)
6   Confidential (Dorinda Morgan)
7   Willin' (Lowell George)
8   Lucky Old Sun (Haven Gillespie/Beasley Smith)
9   West LA Fadeaway (Garcia/Hunter)
10   When I Paint My Masterpiece
11   Key To The Highway (C Segar/Big Bill Broonzy)
12   Tangled Up In Blue
13   With God On Our Side
14   Highway 61 Revisited

After one of the covers Dylan is clearly heard to say that he is tired of trying to "turn bullshit into gold". This is one of his most peculiar remarks, considering that he has spent nearly every night of the N.E.T. making "gold" from his cover versions. We also know, from many interviews, just how important these songs are to him, which makes the "bullshit" comment even more mysterious.

John Dolen of *The Sun Sentinel* managed to get a telephone interview with Dylan soon after and tried to prise an explanation out of Dylan, but the response raises more questions than it answers.[75]

John Dolen: "At the Edge show Saturday, you did a lot of covers, including some old stuff, like 'Confidential'. Was that a Johnny Ray song?"
Bob Dylan: "It's by Sonny Knight. You won't hear that again."
John Dolen: "Oh, was that the reason for your 'trying to turn bullshit into gold' comment at the show? Were these covers just something for folks at the Edge? Does that mean you aren't going to be doing more material like that on your tour, including the Sunrise shows?"
Bob Dylan: "It will be the usual show we're used to doing on this tour now, songs most people will have heard already."

1995 had a most surprising ending as Dylan broke with his own tradition of not touring through the Thanksgiving-Xmas-New Year holidays. This year, rather than spend all that time – as was customary – with family members, he lined up ten dates in December. This was a special tour with the particular purpose of helping Patti Smith get back on the road and her career on track. It worked very well for Patti, but as far as Dylan was concerned, it was a depressing end to a great touring year. Dylan's voice was wasted and he and the band sounded like they needed a well-deserved break. The shows were high energy enough – a blanket of live, loud rock to cover a poverty of quality – and, to my surprise and dismay, as warmly greeted by some fans as those earlier in the year. The more discerning wrote them off as a good thing for Patti, forgettable for Dylan.

There were some highlights though; Dylan chronicler Clinton Heylin is particularly fond of "Desolation Row" at Bethlehem on December 13th. By the time you got to the same song on the last night at Philadelphia on the 17th, Dylan's voice was so strained that it is painful to listen to. Which is something it shares with the appalling performance of "Tangled Up In Blue" before it. The gulf between these pitiful acoustic set openers and the repeated vocal splendour of the Spring sets was too vast to comprehend. Redeeming features were a fine "Every Grain Of Sand", a burst of stellar harmonica on "It's All Over Now, Baby Blue" and, of course the big talking point of this mini-tour, Bob and Patti duetting on "Dark Eyes". Patti was the one who had brought this magnificent song back into circulation.

Unfortunately, the first time Bob and Patti attempted the duet her talents were all one could admire. Dylan's memory of the lyrics seemed to stretch only as far as the title phrase. Given the wretched state his vocal chords were in, one could be forgiven for wishing that had eluded him too. Suitably chastened, Dylan relearned the words from his own lyric book and his performance of it improved.

A final footnote to 1995 is to mention that our old friend G.E. Smith joined Dylan on stage for the final song on December 14th. Many shows had passed since G.E. had departed; the current line-up had lasted 300 or so shows unchanged.

Would 1996 bring any line-up changes? Would there be new Dylan material? These were the questions that dominated Dylan fans' minds that Xmas – as well as the perennial "When's the first show next year that I can see him at going to be"?

Chapter Twelve: 1996

...It Looks Like I'm Moving,
But I'm Standing Still

"I was born here and I'll die here against my will
I know it looks like I'm moving, but I'm standing still
Every nerve in my body is so vacant and numb
I can't even remember what it was I came here to get away from. "

From "Not Dark Yet", released 1997

Nineteen ninety-six was a strange year. There were about 30 less shows in 1996 than 1995's record busting 116. However, after 1995's surprising December tour 1996's did not start until April, so it seemed hectic enough once it had begun. Apart from one-offs, the 1996 shows took place in three bursts: April-May saw 27 shows in the USA and Canada, then it was European summer time again with 28 shows through June and July, followed by the same amount in the USA in October and November.

It is not a year remembered with great fondness by most long-term fans. In contrast to the innovation and performing levels of most of 1995, it was all too predictable; same band, same set structure, and not many song debuts. Overall, the shows were solid enough, as in late '93 and periods of '94, just not particularly special. More alarmingly, some of the overlong, and uninspired, unproductive guitar instrumentals were reappearing too.

By 1996 there was a change in my own situation. I had started to catch up on other people's music again, and started to catch on up reading about subjects other than Dylan. I was still "obsessive" by "normal standards" and I still went to shows in both the UK and Germany and I followed the news daily, collected tapes and CDs and videos. Nonetheless, there was a palpable lessening of intensity.

It is inevitable that there will be such 'peaks and troughs' within one's own personal energy, time and enthusiasm. Perhaps too, there was still an after effect of having met Dylan in Camden. It's not as though I would ever get that close again; nothing was going to top that. Also, the sheer longevity of the Never Ending Tour was energy-sapping for a dedicated fan, so goodness only knows how much more so for the band and their singer. However my diminished obsession with the N.E.T. was also partly down to the fact that so many shows by now had featured the same personnel and utilised the same basic set structure. How I longed for a return to a half acoustic/-half electric show. Or more keyboard playing, or a saxophone or a violin...

After I stopped running my Dylan fanzine, I found myself able to gain a better perspective on the N.E.T., just as I pulled away from my all embracing involvement with it. Although I went to six consecutive shows in June and July 1996, my interest was not as intense as it had been, especially when I eventually stopped my telephone information service later in the year.[76]

By now I was going to Germany primarily to see my friends and if that could be made to coincide with Dylan shows that was all to the good – rather than the other way round.

Not going to so many shows did not, however, mean that I was unable to follow the tour in other ways. The beginnings of what was to be an explosive growth in the availability of CD-Rs aided me in overcoming a palate jaded by tape after tape of similar sounding shows, and the rise of the Internet was playing a larger and larger role in my experience of the N.E.T.. With its swift dissemination of information and unparalleled global communication capability, the Net seemed tailor made for the N.E.T..

Much as fanzines had helped to create communities out of disparate and geographically separated Dylan fans in the 1980s, so the Internet facilitated this – at an exponential growth rate – in the 1990s.

Apart from the ease and speed of e-mail itself, the 'Net soon furnished Dylan focussed Newgroups, chat rooms and Web pages. Back in 1996, the only newsgroup was rec.music.dylan. It had started at the turn of the decade, and I had been participating in it for around four years. However, even in 1996, there were hundreds of messages daily and I could not keep up. The newsgroup – for me – was becoming a victim of its own success.

It was however, both great fun and very informative over those years and led to me making many friends. The newsgroup had many spin-offs where people would help others get to shows, upgrade tickets, and even spawned a dedicated team of "agents" who one could write to for help and information on their specialist subjects. These covered everything from tickets and civil rights to tape decks and tour parties.

Like all popular internet newsgroups the postings varied: from someone dropping in to ask "what album is 'Blowin' In the Wind' on?" to long, erudite lyrical analysis and in-depth concert reports. Unfortunately, too, like all unmoderated newsgroups the occasional "nutter" would be attracted to the site and try to spoil it for everyone else.

One of the reasons I could afford to let go of the newsgroup was that a number of dedicated Web pages had sprung up around Dylan, including one begun in Autumn 1995 and run by Bill Pagel which includes an entire area dedicated to the Never Ending Tour.

After the show, as soon as possible, the set list is posted along with (usually) a picture of the set-list that had been pinned up on the stage, and (sometimes) photos of Dylan on-stage. Reviews are posted too, though these are nearly always written from the point of view of a fan in full flush of joy at having been at a show so one tends to get a large proportion of "best he's ever been" raves.

So it was easy to stay well and truly informed of all that was going on in the N.E.T. even without waiting for one of the Dylan fanzines to pop through the letterbox.

My touring for 1996 was restricted to the following dates: June 26th and 27th, Liverpool, June 29th (shortened set) Hyde Park and July 1st-3rd in Germany at Munster, Mannheim, and Konstanz.

I had found the two nights at Liverpool to be contrasting. I disliked the first Liverpool date – competent without being exciting. The second was much improved – including a fine acoustic set – without being sensational. Still, it's quite a testament to Bob's pulling power that he could draw a crowd on the night when the English football team were playing Germany in the European Championships.

For these dates, Dylan was joined by Al Kooper. As Michael Gray picked up on in an article for U.S. Dylan fanzine *On The Tracks*, this evoked thoughts of the mid-60s and the contrast with the last time he played in Liverpool, 30 years before. Unsurprisingly, the 1996 shows did not do well in the comparison:

"The band is 1/10th as good as The Band; Bob Dylan isn't 1/10th as energetic or innovative or communicative or accurate or acute; only the ragged rapture that greets him is greater than it was.

"Ironically, now that Dylan has got so much less to say, and cares even less how he says it, he's knee deep in Lifetime Achievement Awards and disproportionate adoration. This time half the audience comes to both shows, and the Bobcats who descended from all corners of the land occupy all the front rows; the usual 18 faces peering up at Bob's (how very dispiriting is must be for him). They spend the whole show on their feet, whooping at every number in the usual ritual way, regardless of how well or badly Dylan sings it.

"There is nothing healthy in this ballyhoo of over-reaction; nothing to tell the Bob Dylan of the 1990s what he knew instinctively 30 years ago; that just one new, thoughtful song, with words unfamiliar to the audience – but fresh and invigorating for their creator – and delivered directly from the calm centre of the artist, would be an infinitely greater treasure and thrill than any number of patchy re-visits to the obvious hits of the past."

Yet for all the Bobcats' whooping on the night, and in spite of Liverpool's local papers praising Dylan for his professionalism and his inspirational performing art, for the jaundiced regular N.E.T.-goers, it was inevitably "just another show".

The very title for the Hyde Park event showed it not to be "just another show" but something far less worthy. June the 29th was the date for Dylan to play at "The MasterCard Masters of Music Concert for The Prince's Trust" which probably tells you all you need to know about the event. Also on the bill was the hugely successful newcomer, Alanis Morrissette, plus Eric Clapton, The Who and for some strange reason, the subsequently disgraced Gary Glitter. Most of the crowd were there to see the Who. Dylan performed only nine songs. Al Kooper was still on board and was now joined by Ron Wood. Depending on where you lived you would get either three or five of Dylan songs shown on a TV broadcast of the event.

In the end, Dylan at Hyde Park was not as bad as I had feared, though the day itself was as gruesome as its title and location imply.

"The Who plus Bob plus Eric Clapton plus no booze in a bleak, midsummer Hyde Park equals one damp squib," *The Independent*'s Andy Gill quipped in his review, continuing:[77]

"It was all dismayingly corporate, and the only way around the Royal Parks' alcohol ban was to pay £200 to enter the VIP area, where Royal tradition was washed away in a sea of free champers. From my windswept eyrie in row ZZ of the seats, I could see the VIP tent, over whose entrance was strung a banner bearing the corporate sponsor's logo and the mystifying claim 'Palace of Rock', wherein slavering rock beasts like Virginia Bottomley and the charity's distinguished patron – to whom I overheard one plummy voice refer, with overweening familiarity, simply as 'Wales' – could refresh themselves and rattle their jewellery away from the hoi-polloi. With no equivalent means of warming up from the inside out, the bulk of the crowd was dependent on the show itself raising the temperature, and this remained steadfastly tepid."

While Dylan was better than I feared, his set was far from inspired. As Andy Gill pointed out, Dylan spent "much of his time onstage subverting his own material, rendering some of the most well known of rock anthems virtually unrecognisable, both to the audience and, at times, to his own musicians, who follow gamely wherever Bob's boot-heels may be a-wanderin'."

Gill sympathised with an audience stuck playing "Spot the Intro". "Even spotted correctly," he continued, "the songs were impossible to sing along with, Dylan twisting his delivery in the most tortuous fashion, flattening most of the melodies in a manner that sounded utterly dismissive of the songs."

However three less than special shows was enough to deter even my new less obsessive self from continuing on to Europe for another Dylan-led visit to my good friends Chris, Stephan and Daniel.

Munster, 1st July, 1996
Halle Munsterland, Munster, Germany

1	Drifter's Escape
2	Shake Sugaree
3	All Along The Watchtower
4	Simple Twist Of Fate
5	It Takes A Lot To Laugh, It Takes A Train To Cry
6	Silvio
7	Boots Of Spanish Leather (acoustic)
8	John Brown (acoustic)
9	Mama, You Been On My Mind (acoustic)
10	Maggie's Farm

11	Ballad Of A Thin Man
12	Obviously Five Believers
13	Alabama Getaway
14	It Ain't Me Babe (acoustic)
15	Rainy Day Women # 12 & 35

Some people seemed to love this show; I was less impressed, placing it somewhere between the first and last Liverpool shows. It kicked off with a chaotic "Drifter's Escape", cocked-up as only Bob can cock things up. He was all over the place, beginning verses just as Jackson's guitar was ending them! I really liked "Shake Sugaree" though, and not just because I'd never heard him sing it before. It was entrancing, but the mood it engendered quickly passed as the concert continued. I knew, though, that it would be a song I'd return to.

I can't remember anything about "All Along The Watchtower" or "Silvio" (thankfully) but in-between them we had a tender "Simple Twist Of Fate" and a fine, rocking "It Takes A Lot To Laugh, It Takes A Train To Cry". Although these were very good indeed, this was as good as it got.

The acoustic set was OK, they are never less than that. Dylan usually does "Mama, You Been On My Mind" better, however, and it now had the identical tune to "Don't Think Twice, It's All Right". In fact, I was starting to think that Bob was gravitating towards having one acoustic and one electric song and just giving them different names:

The acoustic song could have the same melody and still be any one of: "Mama, You Been On My Mind"/ "Don't Think Twice, It's Alright"/ "It Ain't Me, Babe"/ "Girl From The North Country" etc.

And the electric could be a standard live run through one of: "Maggie's Farm"/ "Ballad Of A Thin Man"/ "Leopard Skin Pill Box Hat"/ "Tombstone Blues"/ "Highway 61 Revisited", the encore then would be an amalgam of "Silvio" / "Alabama Getaway" and then the acoustic song again. The disappointments of many repetitive shows had made me paranoid. I was getting N.E.T. stir crazy.

"Maggie's Farm" passed by and then Bob started "Ballad Of A Thin Man" which I thought had been one of the few electric successes in Liverpool, where he seemed to be inventing a whole new version as he went along. I was sure he was going to attempt that same version but, unfortunately, he lost the words and went into a sulk. It was dire.

"Obviously Five Believers" picked things up slightly before the all too predictable encores. I felt like the year since I'd been in Germany had not passed for Bob, it was more or less the same stuff except that now it had lost its sparkle. What had been fresh and innovative the year before was now merely a show he could put on, professionally, night after night.

It was certainly not unenjoyable, but that special spark, that great rush of mental and emotional exploration Dylan can inspire, was missing.

Mannheim, 2nd July, 1996
Mozartsaal im Rosengarten, Mannheim, Germany

1	Down In The Flood
2	Pretty Peggy-O
3	All Along The Watchtower
4	I'll Be Your Baby Tonight
5	Man In The Long Black Coat
6	Silvio
7	Ballad Of Hollis Brown (acoustic)
8	Gates Of Eden (acoustic)
9	To Ramona (acoustic)
10	Everything Is Broken
11	What Good Am I?
12	Seeing The Real You At Last

*

13	Alabama Getaway
14	My Back Pages (acoustic)
15	Rainy Day Women #12 & 35

Designed for Opera and Ballet, this hall is magnificent both acoustically and for ease of viewing the stage. Thankfully Dylan made the most of this opportunity. It was great to hear so many variations from the night before, it took someone as churlish as myself to pine for the as-yet-unheard "This Wheel's On Fire".

A chaotic opening song was again followed by a great choice for the second: "Pretty Peggy-O". There were many other highlights: principally a magnificent acoustic set (even though "Gates Of Eden's" last verse began with "the motor-cycle Black Madonna" lines) and a moving "What Good Am I?". "Everything Is Broken" was instantly forgettable and I only wish "Seeing The Real You At Last" had been too. Still, it was my favourite show so far that I had attended in 1996. A strong "My Back Pages" redeemed the usual uninspiring encores. (It also featured the only harp solo of the night – a good one too, so much more effective than just throwing them in all over the place.)

Konstanz, 3rd July, 1996
Zeltfestival (Tent Festival), Konstanz, Germany

1	Down In The Flood
2	I Want You
3	All Along The Watchtower
4	Shelter From The Storm
5	Watching The River Flow
6	Silvio
7	Mr. Tambourine Man (acoustic)
8	Masters Of War (acoustic)
9	One Too Many Mornings (acoustic)
10	Maggie's Farm (dma)
11	I'll Remember You
12	Everything Is Broken (dma, dmb)

*

13	Alabama Getaway
14	The Times They Are A-Changin' (acoustic) (dma)

15   Rainy Day Women #12 & 35 (dma,dmb,dmc)

(dma) Dave Matthew's violinist played on this song
(dmb) Dave Matthews on guitar
(dmc) Dave Matthew's horn player played saxophone on this song

In the intimate setting of a tiny tent perched on a beautiful lakeside, this was one of the strangest Dylan shows I've been to: a boring set list, a very indifferent performance from Dylan for most of the show, but immensely entertaining and fun by the end.

Back to the beginning, though, and there was a promising start as Dylan and the band actually played the same song for the opener. This was followed by a very pleasant "I Want You" and an as-good-as-it-can-get-under-the-circumstances "All Along The Watchtower". All this augured well, but there was something wrong with his voice. I'm not sure if he had a cold or was hoarse from over-touring, but he couldn't pull off the tender version of "Shelter From The Storm" that he was attempting. Then the show dipped alarmingly with a turgid "Watching The River Flow" and a worse-than-normal (if that is possible) "Silvio".

The weakest "Mr. Tambourine Man" I could ever remember hearing (making such a depressing contrast to the year before) was followed by the most boring "Masters Of War". I was glumly thinking that it would probably be my last show for about a year and I hadn't liked anything apart from the second song.

Fortunately, Dylan finally began stretching his voice – hesitantly at first, then with more confidence – on "One Too Many Mornings". Things were looking up, though my interest was dimmed by the opening chords of "Maggie's Farm". I should not have despaired, help was at hand – from an unlikely source.

I am as anti guests-on-stage with Bob as it's possible to be. I was even furious when Dylan fans cheered George Harrison when joined Bob on stage at Wembley Arena in 1987. I thought he should have been booed for causing a distraction from Dylan. Nonetheless, it was a guest who saved this show, someone I did not even know the name of: the electric violin player from the supporting Dave Matthews Band.[78] This tall, muscular, distinctly cool coloured man bounded on stage with a huge grin and a presence to match, and suddenly Bob had to wake up.

Here was someone on stage who was not only drawing the audience's eyes away from Dylan, but who could also play like fury and had no inhibitions in showing it. "Maggie's Farm" really took off and ended in a duet/duel between Dylan's guitar and the tall Dude's manic violin. The sheer joy on Dylan's face was something to behold. The audience went potty.

At the song's conclusion Dylan high-fived the violinist and we were into a run of the mill "I'll Remember You". A grim "Everything Is Broken" followed, with Dave Matthews himself now on guitar but probably as unfamiliar with the song as Dylan appeared to be. However, half-way through it was transformed when the violinist returned to the stage. A huge grin split Dylan's face and they were off again, Dylan revelling in having a musician on-stage who played for playing's sake and, although clearly admiring Bob, deferred to no-one.

A typically God-awful "Alabama Getaway" was played next; but was then succeeded by the highlight of the night as the violinist re-appeared for a stunning "The Times they Are A-Changin'".

After a verse or so to familiarise himself with the arrangement the violinist upped the ante. Dylan responded with vocals and guitar; the two of them egging each other on. Then Dylan grabbed a harmonica and started his walk around the centre stage. The violinist took this as a cue to circle Dylan, playing ever louder and faster. Dylan responded by re-doubling his harp playing while moving to the violinist's (previously John Jackson's) microphone as the demented violinist took centre stage. The two then came together, warily at first, like two nervous fencers, before meeting up again at the centre microphone for a blistering end to the song. By this time the crowd could probably be heard in about five central European countries and the whole thing ended with a completely over-the-top "Rainy Day Women # 12 and 35" with both bands on stage and crashing guitars competing with sax, violin and Dylan's voice in a wild orgy of sound.

Never have I seen Dylan so happy on stage. More hugs and high fives followed for the guests. It was a fun end to my little trip and a show that was at best mediocre in the grand Dylan scheme of things ended up leaving me smiling. All I could think was: "Until next time, thanks again, Bob".

I mentioned above that it was a shame that the visual spectacle of Bob duelling with Dave Matthews' violinist wasn't preserved on video. However, in 1996 two N.E.T shows were captured on film: the previously discussed Hyde Park show and a gig at the so-called House of Blues – a temporary venue set up in the Olympic Village as part of the Olympic Games' celebrations at Atlanta, Georgia.[79] Sadly, both turned out to be wasted opportunities: Dylan is just going through the motions, and his voice is extremely the worse for wear – typical of the N.E.T. at its worst. Still, for a nine song festival set, Hyde Park was okay – in a bland kind of way – but there was very little on stage worth preserving on celluloid.

The House of Blues, which is not yet on general release, was little better. What you won't see or feel is any sense of Dylan's presence – not because of the limitations of the video medium – but because he simply was not present to any meaningful degree. There was no fire, no passion, no engagement with the songs. It was "just another show". Of which there were becoming far too many that could be referred to so dismissively.

A measure of how poor the House of the Blues show was came when even "Under The Red Sky" sounded dull and, in the acoustic set, "Love Minus Zero/No Limit" – a song Dylan usually performs at the very least to a high standard and often raises to an exquisite level – just passed by in a blur. As for the long guitar jams on "Watching The River Flow", I don't know what this inoffensive little song had ever done to deserve such a fate. I think the closing guitar instrumental was probably longer than the original song itself.

Dylan seemed happy enough though; nodding and waving to the audience who as usual loved "Silvio".

If little of value was preserved by the professional television crews, the dedicated tapers provided high quality tapes of most shows. As I mentioned at the beginning of this chapter, however, I (and many others) had grown weary of listening to whole shows in 1996. The same band (until October), the same format and the perpetual re-occurrence of songs that had been done to death caused this weariness. Fortunately, bootleg-industry transforming technology meant that by 1996, one could get a show on CD-r rather than on tape, with all the convenience that brings. Heard "All Along The Watchtower" too many times? Simply press the "skip" button. Want to locate the new song played for the first time? Press the requisite track number.

Then there were compilations. Fans have always made and shared compilation tapes. "My favourite acoustic songs in 1988"; "Best of 1992", "15 N.E.T. versions of Maggie's Farm" (no, I am only kidding with that one) and so forth. The same concept on CD-r was even more attractive given that format's flexibility and programmability. Stack a number on a multi-player and you could programme all kinds of tailored N.E.T. experiences.

While something is certainly lost when one is listening to a song without the proper context of an evolving show, needs must! With less time to listen to shows this was a marvellous way to keep some kind of track on over 80 shows in three two-month bursts. In addition, if certain performances sounded particularly fine I could always then listen to the whole show. Just because I had stopped listening to all the tapes didn't mean I had stopped collecting them. Hell, what are shelves for anyway?

So, via CD-Rs and tapes and so forth, I heard much to enjoy in 1996. Some of the highlights are worth pointing out to balance the rather jaundiced overall impression the year gave off.

Far and away the finest performed song of the year was the N.E.T. debut in Berlin of "Shake Sugaree". This is credited to Elizabeth Cotton, but this version came via Fred Neill.

I was entranced by this at the Munster show. I didn't know what the words meant, but I felt their poetic depth when Dylan sang them. It is a sumptuous song and if Dylan didn't write it, it feels like he should have. It has just the right mixture of simplicity, mystery and discontinuity not to be out of place on *The Basement Tapes*. In Berlin, Dylan sang it beautifully.

Speaking of *The Basement Tapes* and song debuts where Dylan got it absolutely right first time, the first show in Madison on April 13th saw the live debut of "This Wheel's On Fire".

"Gonna try something new," Dylan began to audience cheers, "new for us anyway...."

I cannot imagine that anyone would have guessed what it would be, though it seemed an apt follow up to 1995's first show unveiling of the contemporaneous "Down In The Flood".

As with "Shake Sugaree" you feel there must have been some serious rehearsing going on: both debuts of these marvellous songs were given proper readings, and in both cases the first performances have not been bettered since.

Other debuts included an acoustic take of the Grateful Dead's "Friend Of The Devil" – a vast improvement on the electric version, but then the acoustic performances have been the better in much of the N.E.T. Maybe the famous "Judas" shouting guy in 1966 was just ahead of his time by 30-odd years!

The song's lyrics tell a banal tale of absurd macho posturing, yet you find yourself drawn to the old loveable rogue of a narrator rather than despising him. Dylan's voice inhabits the song and makes you side with him, just like he makes you empathise with the protagonists of the old traditional songs he performs so compellingly.

"To me each song is a play, a script," says N.E.T. guitar-technician-cum-guitarist, Cesar Diaz, "and he'll be that guy from the song for that moment, but [then] he'll change back to Bob....It took me a while to realize that. But he actually convinces you that yes, it is me who is talking to you, and I'm being sincere about it." [11]

My favourite version of this, taped in magnificent quality, is part of a CD-R collecting the best performances in the best quality available. Alas, all tracks are undated, so in this case I do not know if the song is representative of a particularly good show, or a standout in an otherwise-ordinary affair. Actually, I quite like the mystery – perhaps there's a really good show out there that I have still to come across.

There was another Dead connection in the debut of a song called "New Minglewood Blues", a version of which Garcia and Co had long been playing under the title "New, New Minglewood Blues". Confusion abounded as to which version Dylan was playing. Unlike "Shake Sugaree", however, once one heard "Minglewood Blues" one didn't really care too much which version it was.

It was not just covers that made their entree during this '96 trek. "Seven Days", had its N.E.T. debut too. This song, a minor hit single for Ron Wood, had previously enjoyed four Dylan live outings – back in 1976. This is not a "great" song, but it is fun, has a strong melody, and is clearly the work of someone who knows what rock and rock'n'roll pop hooks and internal rhymes are. It might be a throwaway, but how I could have done with Dylan writing something like this in the mid '90s.

In addition to debuts and covers, my "Best of N.E.T. 1996" also included such delights as a towering "Disease Of Conceit". Once again Dylan brought out the best of an *Oh Mercy* song on stage. There was also a beautifully paced, wistful "Pretty Peggy-O" showcasing Dylan's wonderfully deep, dark *World Gone Wrong* tones, and a funereal but gripping "Positively 4th Street" from Berlin on June the 17th, where Dylan's magnificent regret-steeped vocals turned this well known piece of vitriol into a whole new song. This was same night that featured the sparkling "Shake Sugaree" and it also boasted a fine "Friend Of The Devil".

In general, in 1996 as in so many years, it was in the acoustic sets that Dylan most regularly pulled out the stops. One compilation I have features a version of "The Lonesome Death Of Hattie Carroll" which is truly dazzling.[12]

Listening to such highlights is both exhilarating and cautionary. It is so easy to get lazy, to write off whole legs of Dylan's touring years because they do not match up to some of his stellar periods. It is important to remember that even the dullest runs on the N.E.T. can harbour such gems.

One of the biggest events for long-term fans was an acoustic "Visions Of Johanna" on June 24th in Luxemburg. As with Philadelphia in 1995, much of the fuss was down to the choice of song rather than the performance, especially among the travelling fans that saw many shows but missed this one. Nonetheless, while the performance may not have been superlative, it was very fine indeed.

Many of the travelling caravans of Bobcats missed Luxembourg, but most were in Utrecht on 21st June to hear Dylan once again address Lambchop. After Edinburgh the year before they were becoming quite chatty:

"Dylan: Thank you. Thanks everybody!"

Lambchop: "Thank you, Bobby. "

Dylan: "On this side, gentleman playing the guitar, from Memphis... J.J. Jackson! Also we wanna say to our good friend the Chopper, who's down here. Hey Chopper, how come you never made it to Cincinnati, you were supposed to come over there, supposed to come down to Atlanta, you never showed up there."

Lambchop: "I didn't know about it, I wasn't invited."

Dylan: "On the drums tonight, Winston Watson, give him a big hand. And on steel guitar, Bucky Baxter, he's playing the mandolin too. On bass guitar tonight, Tony Garnier. We'll be seeing you Chopper. All right! Ha-ha-ha! Hey! We've been missing you. We've been missing you the last hundred shows. Listen to what he is saying..."

Lambchop: "You're the guv'ner – you always have been and you always will be, play what *you* want to play – *You* choose!."

Dylan: "That's it! That's it! Ha-ha-ha. How about giving the Chopper a hand! He's seen more shows than me! He-he-he. He's seen me play more times than me!!"

I have mainly been talking about the first two legs of the tour, as that's where the debut songs appeared and where I saw him myself. The last bout of touring for the year was a return to the Southern States for the Fall.

By now the long absence of original Dylan songs had begun to assume as "endless" a feel as the Never Ending Tour itself. Throughout the year rumours continued to grow that we were indeed about to get a new album of such songs. By September '96 those in the know were telling us that Daniel Lanois was working on a set of Dylan acoustic demos, and that the songs were masterly insights from a mature artist.

The anticipation was now at dangerously high levels and some fans even hoped that the Fall 1996 shows would feature some of these songs. Nothing could have been further from Dylan's track record on such things, and this tour was no exception.

The Southern shows were much of a muchness in what was for Dylan a routine year; the songs themselves might change but you had to pay close attention to notice which mid-sixties "classic rocker" replaced which from the night before or which old folkie he was singing to the tune of "Boots Of Spanish Leather". There were no new songs debuted; the nearest to a surprise was the first appearance of "Man Of Peace" since 1991.

This was no great Fall tour to revive the year – as the same locations had witnessed five years previously – though some seeds of future change were evident. First of all there was a change in band personnel. Drummer Winston Watson was replaced by David Kemper (formerly of the Jerry Garcia Band, keeping the Grateful Dead connection going). Fortunately, unlike the hapless Watson, Kemper did not seem to have been given the same instructions to just keep bashing away, whatever the song. His contributions would be part of a new sound, though this was not noticeable at first. This was partly because Kemper needed time to bed in, and these shows comprised mostly guitar-dominated standard run-throughs of old hits punctuated by longed for and much appreciated acoustic sets.

A very public on-stage falling-out with John Jackson saw him temporarily replaced mid show by the excellent Charlie Sexton. It seemed certain that Jackson's time was running out, and so it would prove early in 1997. Charlie Sexton's appearance on the Never Ending Tour was not to be his last, though.

While Charlie's "guest" appearance was rather out-of-the-ordinary, 1996 was a year full of more conventional such appearances. The roll call of those who joined Bob on-stage during the year included Nils Lofgren, Ray Benson and James Burton, Roger McGuinn, Jewel, Paul James, Al Kooper, Aimee Mann, Ron Wood, Dave Matthews Band, Leroi Moore and, of course, Van Morrison.

Before the year's touring came to a close on November 23rd, the '60s were once again officially pronounced over, when Dylan allowed the Bank of Montreal to use "The Times They Are A-Changin'" in an advert. An unmemorable end to a relatively unmemorable year. "Give us something new", "It's time for a dramatic change" were the wishes of the fans. As the saying goes, you should be careful of what you wish for....

Chapter Thirteen: 1997

I Really Thought I'd Be Seeing Elvis Soon

"When I was a little kid in La Hoya,... we had a parade on the Fourth Of July, and I remember clearly the sight of civil war veterans, marching down the main street, kicking up the dust. The first time I heard Bob Dylan it brought back that memory and I thought of him as something of a civil war type, a kind of 19th Century troubadour, a maverick American spirit. The reediness of his voice and the spareness of his words goes straight to the heart of America."

Gregory Peck, 1997

If 1996 had been a largely uneventful year, 1997 was chock-full of incidents. The three most startling of which sent news scurrying around the world: first, Bob Dylan was hospitalised with a "potentially fatal" illness; second, Dylan met, and performed for, the Pope; third, and not least, "All Along The Watchtower" was moved from the number three slot – and then dropped altogether!

Before these dramas unfolded, January saw Dylan record a new album of original material. The year's touring then began on February 9th in Tokyo. The shows on this short Japanese tour followed on directly from 1996 with few changes in the set lists. There was, however, a one-off version of Noah Lewis's "Viola Lee Blues" at Sapporo on February 24th, – yet another song heavily associated with the Grateful Dead. "Viola Lee Blues" was a delight to hear and its classic blues riffs paved the way for the one-off version of Dylan's own "Pledging My Time" that was to follow a couple of months later.

Japan also saw Elizabeth Cotton's "Oh Babe, It Ain't No Lie" introduced to the set list. It was a perfect melody for Dylan, and he gave lines like "*Stop telling all those lies on me*" an added resonance. This really was a highlight in Japan and through the upcoming Spring shows. It was also reprised twice later in the year, so more people could enjoy the aptness and execution of Dylan plaintively singing: "*Been all around this whole wide world*".

In general, however, Japan 1997 was very much a continuation of the Fall/Winter 1996 shows. It appeared that the relationship between Bob Dylan and

John Jackson had not improved; the atmosphere between the two was reported by concert-goers to be verging on a breakdown. Before the next leg of the tour began, Jackson turned up to rehearsals to discover that Dylan was auditioning new guitarists. Jackson hadn't even been told that he was no longer wanted. It was a shabby and ill-deserved end to six years and near seven hundred shows of service.

By the time Dylan headed off for another bout of touring on March 31st, Larry Campbell was on board as Jackson's replacement. While Campbell was more versatile and could also play violin, he would take some time to settle in, and these Spring '97 shows continued in much the same vein as Japan, and indeed in 1996. There were, though, a number of interesting developments in the band's playing, and a few more set list surprises to augment the impressive "Oh Babe, It Ain't No Lie".

This leg also saw a rare postponement of a couple of shows when a Nova Scotia ferry transporting the band's equipment from the opening night venue – St John's, Newfoundland, Canada – got trapped in packed ice. The shows on April the 3rd and 4th were both put back by two days as a result. With the gear recovered, the leg's rescheduled second show on the 5th began a seven night run without a break during which the new guitarist could properly get his bearings.

April 5th 1997 was also the date that Allen Ginsberg died of a heart attack. He was 70 years old. That night, Dylan dedicated "Desolation Row" to his old friend.

"That was one of his favourite songs, the poet Allen Ginsberg," Dylan told the crowd afterwards, "that's for him".

It was a splendid version that would have made Ginsberg very proud.

***

While the latter half of the '90s saw CD-R technology encroaching on the larger bootleggers' territory, early 1997 saw those nefarious fellows pull out one of the best examples of why fans will search out their illegal wares: the bootleg double CD *Bathed In A Stream Of Pure Heat* showcased the 1997 N.E.T. from Japan right up until a special one-off show on May 22nd. This was obviously the work of fans with an intimate knowledge of the N.E.T., as it not only collects the rarities, the one-offs and the covers but also provides an overview of the best of the shows played during the period.

From it you can hear, amongst many other things, how Dylan continued to spice up his Never Ending Tour sets with covers. From the 19th April in Hartford, Connecticut you can hear the first version of "I'm A Roving Gambler" since the marvellous South Bend show, back in November 1991. This version is effective enough and the song would grow to become a valuable visitor to N.E.T. sets through this and future years.

That same night in Hartford saw Buddy Holly's "Not Fade Away" open the set. While it would take the most besotted fan to actually describe this attempt as "good", it was much better than most of the desecrations that have since been inflicted upon the poor song after it was moved into the "rave-up-

151

encores" slot. It is a pity Dylan has not covered Buddy's songs with the same excellence he has brought to so many other artists' work.

The night before, in Albany, New York, there was a notable "Pretty Peggy-O". Yet another different arrangement for this ever welcome traditional song. Here the lines "caught up" with succeeding ones, almost as though they were running on too fast. Consequently, it was not always the last word of a line that was stressed, resulting in a different, and mixed, pace to the melody. Dylan's semi-wasted voice sounded appropriately like that of a soldier fading away through illness or injury.

Even more welcome, and better performed, was the 28th April appearance of "Long Black Veil"; a perfect song for Dylan to sing during the N.E.T.

Though created in the modern age in a conscious attempt, as lyric writer Danny Dill recalled, "to write an instant folksong", this beautifully-constructed, heartbreaking ballad sounds like one of the great old-time songs, reeking of guilt, crime, punishment, stoicism, bravery, lust, love lost and death. I had wanted Dylan to tackle this for about as long as I could remember, I still semi-dream that there is a *World Gone Wrong* outtake of it (in pristine quality, one Dylan hasn't "re-engineered!). Now I could lay aside the wonderful versions from people like Dylan's one time support act, BR5-49; from his one-time backing band, The Band, from his great fan, Nick Cave, from his friend, Johnny Cash and luxuriate in the definitive article. Like "Delia" and "Stagger Lee", this dark elemental ballad is perfectly suited to Dylan's withered old prophet croaking.

Not every cover was as successful. The trite lyrics of "Friend Of The Devil'" could not carry the burden of the high relief into which Dylan's Spring '97 version had thrown them. Dylan may have sounded genuinely like a man at the end of his tether, but the effect was unsettling rather than satisfying.

If the covers were a mix of the great, the good, the merely curious and the poor; well so was everything else at this time. There were, as this trusty compilation showcases, very splendid versions of Dylan originals like the ultra-bluesy "Pledging My Time" from April the 22nd. Or you could marvel at the mysterious angst of "This Wheel's On Fire", where Dylan's yearning take on the doom-beckoning lyrics became a fearful query by the end of the song. You have to marvel at what an actor Dylan is when presenting us with these compelling visions, for the very second the song ended, he snapped out of the mood and into a laconic "Thanks everybody" followed by jokey band intros. It was as if a switch had been flicked.

Other notable Dylan originals included a brave, if unsuccessful, attempt at "John Brown" featuring understated backing and high emphasis on the words.

Some other songs didn't work at all. A 9th April "Every Grain Of Sand" was hampered by Dylan's "dying voice" – a phrase ironically included in the song's lyrics. Bob's voice was shot. When Dylan debuted "You Ain't Goin' Nowhere" at Portland, Maine on April 10th, the narrator's call for an "easy chair" seemed imperative considering the pinched, strained voice the demand was sung in. Meanwhile, a few days after, "All Along The Watchtower" was performed live for the 1000th time.

Yet, in the same leg of the tour, there were times when Dylan's vocals were not only strong enough to carry "Shooting Star" and "Born In Time" but his lungs would also ably propel the harmonica in heartfelt versions of "You're A Big Girl Now" and "Love Minus Zero/No Limit".

The *Bathed In A Stream Of Pure Heat* bootleg was obviously intended to show this N.E.T. leg in the best light, and this it does. It successfully interspersed the nightly routine of croaked vocals and rock guitar work-outs with short bursts where his voice and lungs seemed to find renewed power. As it happens, the capabilities or otherwise of Dylan's lungs were about to become the main talking point of the year.

Meanwhile, this leg of touring came to a halt on May 3rd. On May 22nd Dylan and his band, excepting Kemper, played three songs as the headline act at the Simon Wiesenthal Center benefit dinner at the Beverly Hilton Hotel in Los Angeles. Jonathan Dolgen, chairman of Viacom Entertainment Group, received the Center's Humanitarian Award and requested Dylan as the main entertainment.

"He's the poet of my generation without question," Dolgen told the press.

Dylan played three songs, all in band-backed acoustic mode. The last two, "Masters Of War" and "Forever Young" were both relevant to the extremely worthy occasion. The opener, Ray Pennington and Ray Marcum's "Stone Walls And Steel Bars", was completely surprising. Like the sublime "Long Black Veil", this is a carefully crafted ballad about the tragic consequences of pursuing "the love of another man's wife."

After the show, Dylan took a break to celebrate his 56th birthday at home in Malibu.

Everything seemed to be going along as normal when Dylan announced a joint UK tour with Van Morrison for June. Dylan fans groaned in anticipation of the shorter sets dictated by a double-header. However, such mild complaints soon became irrelevant when on May 25th, the day after his birthday, Dylan was admitted to hospital in Los Angeles with chest pains. The papers were quick to print scare stories of heart attack and near death. The truth was, Dylan had contracted "histoplasmosis" – an infection of the sac surrounding the heart – which, though potentially serious, is rarely fatal. Dylan was released from hospital on June 2nd.

"Doctors are continuing to treat him," a record company statement informed the world's media, "and are confident that Mr. Dylan will make a full recovery in four to six weeks."

When asked about his plans for his recovery period, Dylan was quoted as saying, "I don't know what I'm going to do. I'm just glad to be feeling better. I really thought I'd be seeing Elvis soon".

The record company also announced that Dylan had cancelled a European tour scheduled to begin on June 1st in Cork, Ireland, though he planned to fulfil his US concert commitments.

From worrying about set lists and set lengths, Dylan fans were suddenly faced with the prospect of the Never Ending Tour actually ending, and for the worst of reasons. I remembered fellow N.E.T. traveller Ray Webster asking me in Germany once what I would do if "anything happened" to Dylan. I hadn't been able to answer; I found the concept of the N.E.T. finishing difficult enough to imagine, never mind Bob's demise. And I was sure I wasn't alone. That Spring there were many worried Dylan fans around the globe, though the more news that came out the better the situation became. The main thing was that Dylan was going to be all right. Dylan later recalled, "The pain stopped me in my tracks and fried my brain." There were "no illuminations", just six weeks of being bed-bound and staring at the ceiling as his body struggled to overcome the sickness.

However, nothing seems to stop Dylan in his tracks for long. Amazingly he resumed the Never Ending Tour on August 3rd and kept going all the way to the end of the year, to complete ten more shows than 1996 and, once again, play almost 100 shows in a year.

August 3rd's "comeback" show at Lune Mountain in Lincoln, New Hampshire, will always retain a special place in fans' hearts. It took place. Press attention centred on Dylan in a way it had not been for years. The media interest was nothing, however, compared to the ferment the fans were in. My friends from Germany were among the large number of people who flew over from Europe. I got a phone call straight after the show from Stephan to tell me that Dylan was in fine voice though looking, understandably, very tired and a little bit shaky. It was great to hear that he was back on the road and well enough to do a show. There was, though, a genuine fear that he was pushing himself back too soon, a fear not allayed by his need to sit down for a rest between songs nor by the fact that his latest touring leg started with shows on the 3rd, 4th, 5th, 7th and 8th. Dylan assured Edna Gundersen in her interview for *USA Today* that the doctors had told him it was fine to proceed with the tour. More than one night off in the opening six might have been more prudent, but Dylan was not in a cautious mood. Running at about 20 minutes shorter than the spring tour, and without any harmonica, Dylan managed his 22-date stint between the 3rd and 31st August with aplomb and no little daring. Not only was he on the road again, but he was also still experimenting with the set list.

He opened with an infectious, good-time "Absolutely Sweet Marie", the mood of which quite belied its cynical lyrics, the gorgeous upbeat pop melody seeming to be a celebration of Dylan being back on the road. Then came "I Want You", with the "took his flute" verse restored. You could hear Dylan forcing himself, you could almost *feel* his physical exertion, in his determination to ensure he put on a good show for this "return" gig.

Dylan, though, is a man of surprises and the next song was, astonishingly, "Tough Mama" which had not been played since the year of its release on 1974's *Planet Waves* album. The melody was faithful to the original and if Dylan's vocal and lung power were sadly diminished in the interim and by his illness, he gamely carried it as best he could.

For those who haven't noticed, "Tough Mama" was the *third* song of the night. Its selection would have been remarkable in itself, but Dylan's illness had clearly caused a rip in the space-time continuum. For the first time in hundreds and hundreds of shows and many, many years "All Along The Watchtower" was not at number three in the set list. Planets did not fall out of orbit, however, as it was played as the next number. Nonetheless, it was the first thing that was reported to me after the fact that Dylan was "looking alright if a little tired" – mentioned before "Tough Mama" or the introduction of the wonderful "Cocaine Blues" in the acoustic set, a traditional song Dylan had last played in 1962, and one which was to become a welcome addition to many an N.E.T. set-list.

The next day, August 4th, saw this rip in the space time continuum became a tear that threatened existence throughout the galaxy. For the first time in seven years and approximately 700 shows, "All Along The Watchtower" was nowhere on the set list. Having earlier that year become the first song Dylan had performed live over 1,000 times (April 7th was the one-thousandth) it was gone. Worldwide, Dylan fans receiving tapes of the show must have thought that they had been given an edited version. "Watchtower" made a brief return about six days later at Montage Mountain and was then dropped for the rest of the year. Fans were delighted to see the back of it, and probably even more elated, if that's possible, with the live debut of "Blind Willie McTell".

"Blind Willie McTell" is one of Dylan's finest-ever songs. While it lay unreleased (officially) in a vault between 1984 and the release of *The Bootleg Series* in 1991 it acquired a mythic stature amongst Dylan fans. If you had asked a group of them which songs they would most like to be played live, "Blind Willie McTell" would have been very high on that list. After all these years, Dylan blessed Montreal on August 5th with this lost touchstone.

It was as if Dylan was going out of his way to make this post-illness return to the stage as memorable as possible, an impression strengthened by the appearance a week later of "One Of Us Must Know" for the first time in 20 years. Dylan's massive back catalogue of songs allowed him to keep the surprises coming, without upsetting the standard set-list construction that had held for so many years of the Never Ending Tour. For example, even that August 3rd set list that caught everyone by surprise had a very predictable "spread" amongst its fifteen songs: ten songs from the 1960s; three from the 1970s; one from the 1980s and one cover.

This was an exciting and rewarding time of the N.E.T. but it was shadowed by one particularly negative development that would have a lasting effect on Dylan's choice of song and style of performance in future years. Dylan's voice was already damaged from years of non-stop touring and his recent illness had clearly further ravaged both his vocal chords and lungs.

At the time this was hardly a fan priority. It was a miracle that Dylan was up and touring so well, so quickly. However, from this point on Dylan has seemed physically unable to sing in certain ways. His vocal range was narrowing, and the possibility of fully expressive vocal inflections night after night, month after month now appeared unattainable.

This is something that an ageing, and only human, Dylan would probably have had to face eventually in any case; it is not as though the difficulties first appeared at this point of the N.E.T. The illness, however, accelerated the inevitable.

Dylan would deal with the problem by choosing songs and arrangements more suited to his restricted vocal range, and by finding a way of performing that was not so taxing night after night. This was to particularly influence shows from late 1997 onwards. On this leg, and for obvious reasons, the vocal problem appeared almost randomly as far as type of song was concerned. You could get a "Man In The Long Black Coat" performed with a despairing whine rather than a yearning keen, or a "Tough Mama" that musically excited you but was painful to listen to, so enfeebled was Dylan's voice.

Even traditional songs that should come comfortably to him at any stage of life, like "Stone Walls and Steel Bars" and "Oh Babe, It Ain't No Lie" were laid to waste by a raw, pinched voice that simply had nothing more to draw on. Oddly, Dylan's vocal strength would return intermittently. On another night, or at a different time in the same show, (especially later in the month) he produced a powerful "One Of Us Must Know (Sooner Or Later)", an assured "Blind Willie McTell" or (as on the 18th August) a masterly, mournful "Pretty Peggy-O". You just never knew what was coming next; a mangled and wheezy "Tangled up In Blue" could be followed by a clear, dramatic reading of "Cocaine Blues". There was even a show where I found "Under The Red Sky" for once unappealing, due to Dylan's vocals and then during the following *bête noir*, "Silvio" of all things, everything changed: though raspy, Dylan was *doing* something with his voice. This was a strange and unique time in the unfolding drama of the N.E.T.

It should be remembered too that, Dylan, on form, can turn even his hoarseness to great communicative effect, as he did on the 23rd of August with "I Want You". A broken and despairing voice was quite fitting, for lines like "Cracked bells and washed out horns". Dylan paced it perfectly that night, growing a bit more defiant by the end of the song.

Dylan's illness meant that both fans and press would feel an extra significance to many of his lyrics that late summer. On the opening night, who did not see special meaning in lines like "*You knew that we would meet again*" from "This Wheel's On Fire" or "*I'm still on the road*" from "Tangled Up In Blue".

Reviewing a Vienna Wolftrap show in *The Washington Post*, Mike Joyce was startled by how during the encore "Don't Think Twice, It's Alright", "...each time [Dylan] sang the chorus, the song seemed transformed, as if it had been inspired not by a lover's farewell but by a friend's recovery."

Indeed, the press responded warmly towards the shows and especially Dylan's performances. The media's former scorn appeared to have dissipated with the realisation that Dylan was a treasure that we might have lost earlier that summer. For the next few years Dylan was to receive, in general, very favourable press. Of course, there would be exceptions to this rule, and an event which would provoke Bob's critics was just around the corner.

The N.E.T.'s first post-illness leg ended in Kansas City on August 31st, but Dylan's restless spirit saw him back on stage again within a month, in truly unexpected circumstances. Dylan's already high press profile went into hyperdrive when it was announced that he was to play the satellite TV-syndicated World Eucharistic Congress in Bologna, Italy on September 27th, sharing an audience with the Pope.

The event was a Vatican attempt to convince Italian youth that the Catholic Church was modern and relevant. However, Dylan aside, the show was a bland mixture of anodyne native pop and watered-down gospel.

The press that seemed so delighted Bob was still with us could not resist weighing in with references to two "tired old spiritual leaders, revered by a multitude of followers". The Pope was not in the best of health, but most writers seemed to think that the 77-year-old Pontiff looked in better shape than his 21-year-younger star turn. Dylan did look frail, and given that he was due to play a very short set and that he normally takes a few songs to warm up, I feared the worst.

Dylan took to the stage in full "riverboat gambler" mode with his embroidered suit, white shirt, crossed leather black tie and cowboy hat proving quite a counterpoint to the Pope's white robes and somewhat smaller headgear. He opened with "Knockin' On Heaven's Door", a song to launch a thousand post-hospital newspaper headlines, playing it straight while Tony Garnier beside him guarded his master like a dutiful spaniel. Even Bucky was concentrating.

During a very short pause before "A Hard Rain's A Gonna Fall" a wide-angle TV shot revealed a distinctly unimpressed Pope on a raised dais. Dylan's performance appeared to have sapped John Paul II's will to live.

After just two songs, the legendary iconoclast of "don't follow leaders" fame, climbed the dais steps to meet the Pope. After stumbling on the first few stairs, an ill at ease Bob recovered his composure in time to remove his hat as he approached the Pontiff. The Pope rose from his seat to greet Dylan and in a touching, if somewhat surreal scene, the two men shook hands.

John Paul II then stepped forward to speak, and in an instant the frail old man came alive in front of the microphone. Eyes that had seemed asleep, were suddenly alert and darting around the audience. Here was someone else who lived for an audience, for putting his message across... His speech went down well and he revelled in making the crowd laugh by saying:

"You say the answer is blowing in the wind my friend...", the Pope said – presumably addressing the audience, rather than the composer of the line – to warm laughter and applause. "....And so it is, but it is not the wind that blows things away, it is the wind that is the breath and the Life of the Holy Spirit...."

The Pope also had an answer to that song's thorny question of "How many roads must a man walk down?"

"One," he told the rapturous audience, "there is only one road for man and it is the road of Jesus Christ."

By now Il Papa was really enjoying himself, though he appeared bemused at the football-terrace style reception he got when he finished his speech and retired from view. It was quite an act to follow. Had even Bob Dylan ever experienced a crowd so in awe of a "performer", one wondered? Indeed, did the same question cross Dylan's mind?

With his hat still off, Dylan played a delicate, heartfelt "Forever Young" – a song that was appropriate for a youth festival and that was alleged to have been requested by the Pope himself. Rumour also had it that the Pope had asked for "Blowin' In The Wind", which had more credence as it tied in with his speech. This song's absence from Dylan's set was rectified – at least in terms of the Pope's oratory – by its performance by a number of local singers. "Forever Young" brought Dylan's performance to an end, his three song-set falling considerably short of the half-hour that had been promised in the press.

Most Dylan fans I know disliked Bob's Papal performance. There were negatives, undeniably, and as I had feared, his voice never fully warmed up. However, Dylan tried hard to do himself and the songs justice in front of a very untypical audience, and I found it quite moving. Nonetheless, nothing Dylan could have done on stage could have competed with the overpoweringly odd symbolism of the whole event. Why did he do it?

When quizzed over his motives, Dylan insisted "You don't say no to the Vatican". He was handsomely rewarded too. Press estimates put the Papal promoter's pay cheque at $350,000. The event also generated a huge amount of publicity, with reports of the event and photos of Dylan shaking the Pope's hand splashed across newspapers around the globe.

Three days later, on 30th September, 1997, the long wait for an album of new Dylan-penned material ended with the release of *Time Out Of Mind*. The massive wait since 1990's *under the red sky*, in addition to Bob's recent brush with mortality, ensured that anticipation among fans and other observers was acute.

For the Never Ending Tour, the implications were profound; a new album was exciting in itself, but one of the greatest joys it brings is watching the development of the new material in live performance. This had been especially true of the first real such album of the Never Ending Tour, *Oh Mercy*. Now that *Time Out Of Mind* was out Dylan would maybe play some tracks at his upcoming four UK shows; then again, being Dylan, having an album so acclaimed might well mean he'd just shun it. We did not have to wait long to find out, as these four shows started in Bournemouth the very next day.

As Dylan took to the Bournemouth venue's smoky-incense-filled stage on 1st October, the day after *Time Out Of Mind*'s release, it was an emotional moment. For most of us it was the first time we had seen him on stage since his illness. In contrast to the Papal audience, Dylan looked completely at ease from the off. His lively expressions of sly humour in the first song, "Absolutely Sweet Marie", were to be repeated throughout this and the following shows. The ovation that greeted this opener was rewarded by the opening chords of "Man In The Long Black Coat". I was present for "Tough Mama" and "Blind Willie McTell" for the first time, as well as for a very affecting, "Cocaine Blues" – a simple song that was nevertheless one of the highlights of the period.

None of this was enough though to detract from fans' greedy need for the new. As the concert progressed without any *Time Out Of Mind* material, it seemed more and more likely we would not hear anything off the new album.

(As usual, tapes of the album had been circulating for some time before the actual release, so most hardcore fans were already familiar with the entire record.) Our hope was finally rewarded, in the encores of all places, with "Love Sick".

Although not one of Time Out Of Mind's "big four", this is unquestionably the track I next most admired on the album. Still, I had two problems with it as released. One was Daniel Lanois' trademark swampy, soupy production. The other was the banal lyrics and obtrusive rhyming of one verse:

"Sometimes the silence can be like thunder.
Sometimes I wanna take to the road and plunder.
Could you ever be true?
I think about you
And I wonder."

I knew my problem with the production would be overcome in live performance, however I was even more delighted when it later appeared even Dylan himself had realised how clumsy that problem verse was. After giving it a straight reading for its debut, Dylan went on to sing the verse with a sheepishness that developed into swallowing the word "plunder" or deliberately singing it off mike. Eventually he took the rather more sensible step of rewriting the words.

Lyrics aside, Dylan sang "Love Sick" so well at Bournemouth that I don't think he has ever improved upon that first performance. Meanwhile, the band were quite menacing. The clock the tormented singer hears ticking is the drums we hear beating, pushing Dylan and all of us towards the end of this love that he is so sick of.

At the sound of the opening chords to "Love Sick", I had spun round in glee only to realise that I was standing right beside two friends, and well known Dylan fans, Phil and Alison Townsend. It was great to have my excitement reflected by the delight on their faces. There was a tangible feeling of being somewhere special, among friends, when Dylan, back from his illness, first debuted a song from his long awaited album.

After another tortuous N.E.T. journey – this time from a badly timed work assignment in Paris – I was back at Bournemouth the next evening. Another mad taxi dash from an airport, Heathrow this time, got me there just in time to catch a very predictable show. The songs that you would think would stand out did, the rest were a routine run through. "Love Sick" appeared in the same place in the set list (it would retain that position throughout the rest of the year) and though it was not as excellent as the previous outing, one could now admire it with more composure than the night before.

I had to miss the Cardiff date but was soon back at Wembley Arena to catch a strong Dylan performance with a rewarding set-list that featured a transfixing "Blind Willie McTell" and a tender "One Too Many Mornings". Yet for all the show's strengths, we still pined for more songs from *Time Out Of Mind*.

A couple of weeks later on October 16th, in New York, Dylan was honoured with yet another award and cheque (for $200,000). This time it was the Dorothy and Lillian Gish Prize. Bob said "Thanks", adding that he "wished [he] had made a movie with her".

Four days later, rehearsals were under way for another bout of touring in America. Showing no signs of weariness, Dylan began another leg of the Never Ending Tour at Humphrey Coliseum, Starkville, Mississippi. The soundcheck tantalizingly included a run through of *Time Out Of Mind*'s epic closing track, "Highlands". Although it was not played that night, three more *Time Out Of Mind* songs were added to "Love Sick": "Cold Irons Bound"; "Can't Wait"; and "'Til I Fell In Love With You". Shortly afterwards, "Make You Feel My Love" was also unveiled so that with the exception of "Million Miles" and the ill-fitting "Dirt Road Blues" all the songs from the new album had been played live – except the four standout pieces.

Not that many in the American audiences were complaining during these auspicious times when the nature of the shows went through a transformation. The set list from 2nd November, at the Township Auditorium, Columbia, South Carolina, for example, went as follows:

1	Maggie's Farm
2	Pretty Peggy-O
3	Cold Irons Bound
4	Born In Time
5	Can't Wait
6	Silvio (Dylan/Hunter)
7	Stone Walls And Steel Bars (Acoustic)
8	Tangled Up In Blue (Acoustic)
9	Tomorrow Is A Long Time (Acoustic)
10	Friend Of The Devil (Hunter/Garcia/Dawson)(Acoustic)
11	Make You Feel My Love
12	'Til I Fell In Love With You
	*
13	Like A Rolling Stone
14	My Back Pages (Acoustic)
15	Love Sick
16	Rainy Day Women Nos. 12 & 35

What a change from what came before! As well as the extra song in the acoustic set, the split of songs was now radically altered. Here we had five songs from the '60s; one from the '70s; two from the '80s (I include "Born In Time" here as although it was released on 1990's *under the red sky* it came from the 1989 *Oh Mercy* sessions); five from the '90s; and three "covers". Quite a contrast to the 1960s based sets that had dominated for so long. Certainly the new songs were all written by a man conscious that his voice had a more restricted range – rooted in a deep baritone. Songs from *Oh Mercy*, under the red sky and *Time Out Of Mind* suit his N.E.T. range. Traditional folk pieces, by their very nature, suit anybody's range. With these kinds of more balanced set lists Dylan can exploit his current voice and limit the amount of times he needs to stretch to hit the notes of his younger days. Experiments with changing set lists would continue over the succeeding dates.

In general terms, the *Time Out Of Mind* songs were still finding their feet. Dylan was working on how best to present them and how they should sit in the set. "Cold Iron Bounds" particularly benefited from escaping the cold, clangy production that drowns it on the album; while "'Til I Fell In Love With You" live implied a deeper meaning than on record. Perhaps most surprising of all, "Make You Feel My Love", a song so mawkish as to make "I'll Remember You" sound like "Visions Of Johanna", became something quite moving. It was to assume the position of "big, overblown ballad" in many a set list in years to come and really it should not have worked. The number had already been recorded by Garth Brooks and Billy Joel – and would soon be by many more – and is exactly the kind of meaningless, cliched pop you hear on a hundred radio stations and never think twice about. How it became so central to Dylan shows is a startling testament to his live powers – I swear there were shows in 1998 where it was the best thing played. More importantly, the majestic "Not Dark Yet" made an appearance on October 30th. It was at the time a one-off, but it hinted at what was to become a major N.E.T. song in the succeeding years.

Having survived his illness, and now touring to acclaim, Dylan suddenly found himself so popular that he could play a private corporate party for the company Applied Materials, without attracting too many cries of "Sell-Out". Dylan and the band played it as a normal N.E.T. set. Closed to the general public it may have been, but you can't stop Dylan fans from getting in to see/tape their man that easily.

Unusually, with the sole exception of 1995 thus far, Dylan decided to tour in December. Not even a long summer illness had deterred this road warrior, and he ended the year with a headline-grabbing so-called "club tour". The thought of Dylan playing to audiences of a few hundred in very small venues caused a rush of excitement for the fans and attracted a lot of publicity. Given all that had happened in 1997, the idea of seeing Dylan in such intimate settings had fans in a ferment for the tickets and the shows sold out almost instantly. On December 1st and 2nd Dylan played at the Roxy theatre in Atlanta and set the scene for this welcome tour by mixing up covers ("Shake Sugaree" and "The White Dove", for example) and originals.

Not all of these December shows were great, but the best were to be savoured and club dates became something Dylan would return to as the N.E.T continued over the next few years in its crazy path, zigzagging between huge stadiums and tiny theatres via soulless arenas and ice rinks.

Dylan ended 1997 with an exhilarating run of five sold-out shows at Los Angeles' El Rey Theatre from 16th to 20th December. The shows also featured notable opening acts each night including Joan Osborne, with whom Dylan recorded a version of "Chimes Of Freedom" for a TV show the following October. Sheryl Crow not only opened on the 19th but joined Dylan onstage for the first two of the "encores". The following year would see her present Dylan with a Grammy Award and delay the release of her new album to include "Mississippi", an outtake from the *Time Out Of Mind* sessions that Dylan thought would suit her.

"Rock's most celebrated songwriter was alternately playful, arbitrary, purposeful and, as always, unpredictable," Robert Hilburn enthused in the *L.A. Times*. "And he only did four songs from the widely hailed new 11-song album – and not the four that most people would agree are the most memorable. Yet, there wasn't a moment in the fast-paced affair that didn't seem like a special occasion."

Support act Beck opened the five-night extravaganza with the words:

"Let the games begin, this is the opening of the Bob Dylan festival."

And the festival proved a great pre-Christmas treat not only for ordinary fans, but also for some of the stars of the neighbourhood including Ringo Starr, Eric Clapton and Andre Agassi. The guest that seemed to most please Dylan though was Gregory Peck.

It was Peck (himself an honouree) who presented Dylan as one of the four Kennedy Center Honourees that December (on the 6th). Dylan was inducted along with Lauren Bacall, Charlton Heston, Jessye Norman and Edward Villella. I'm sure he was pleased to be following in the footsteps of Johnny Cash, who had been similarly honoured the year before. There was not only the Gala event itself but a reception at the White House where President Clinton said of Dylan:

"He probably had more impact on people of my generation than any other creative artist. His voice and lyrics haven't always been easy on the ears, but throughout his career Bob Dylan has never aimed to please."

This presidential recognition came only five days after former President Jimmy Carter and his wife attended the opening show of the "club tour" and witnessed not only "Shake Sugaree" but also the live debut of "Million Miles". Popes and Presidents: Phew! Rock'n'Roll.

"When I was a little kid in La Hoya, California, which is a very small town, we had a parade on the Fourth Of July," Peck told the Kennedy Centre audience. "And I remember clearly the sight of civil war veterans, marching down the main street, kicking up the dust. The first time I heard Bob Dylan it brought back that memory and I thought of him as something of a civil war type, a kind of 19th Century troubadour, a maverick American spirit. The reediness of his voice and the spareness of his words goes straight to the heart of America."

It's an interesting portrait, and it shows how far Dylan's image had come from the fiery, drug-fuelled, verbose *Blonde On Blonde*/1966 tour days. Gregory Peck then recounted how wonderful it was for him to buy a Dylan album years later and hear Bob sing about watching a Gregory Peck western (in "Brownsville Girl" from *Knocked Out Loaded*).

Peck explained that the song referred to the film *The Gunfighter*, and that all through the movie the townspeople kept telling his character to get out of town before the shooting started.

"Bob Dylan's never been about to get out of town before the shooting starts," Peck added, while Dylan looked genuinely moved.

In an attempt to answer his own question, "Who is this fellow 'Bob Dylan'?" Peck concluded:

"He is surprises and disguises; he is a searcher with his songs. In him we hear the echo of old American voices: Whitman and Mark Twain, blues singers, fiddlers and balladeers. Bob Dylan's voice reaches just as high and will linger just as long."

This is the Romantic side of the N.E.T. Bob Dylan – the troubadour who is still out there, still searching, still touring. While so many of his contemporaries have gone to ground, the N.E.T. sees Bob constantly lighting out for the territories, exploring the frontiers both artistically and geographically, changing directions and changing shapes, all the while as contradictory as Whitman's *Leaves of Grass* persona.

Musical tributes followed Peck's opening address, with Bruce Springsteen first on the grid. Springsteen's opening eulogy was the highlight of his performance.

"The yearning for a just society in America just exploded," Bruce told the audience. "Bob Dylan had the courage to stand in that fire and capture the sound of that explosion. This song remains as a beautiful call to arms. The meaning of this song and the echo of that explosion live on in the struggle for social justice in America, that continues so fiercely today."

It was a great pity Bruce hadn't stopped there, instead of proceeding to murder "The Times They Are A-Changin'". Dylan, who gave Bruce the Bob Dylan huge wave at the song's end, spent most of it with a furrowed brow and bitten lip looking worried for him. Indeed poor Bruce seems so lost in later life, so removed from his muse that Dylan's 1980s wanderings from the creative well seem like a momentary blip in comparison. David Ball followed onstage, thanking Bob for writing "Don't Think Twice, It's All Right", calling it "a country classic" and played it as though it was. President Clinton clasped Hilary's hand and sang along. Everyone toe-tapped to this irresistible song.

The best was still to come however, with the final number by Shirley Caesar. Dylan may have liked Bruce just for being Bruce, and enjoyed "Don't Think Twice, It's All Right" because it was so "nice", but his delight at her speech over the opening chords of "Gotta Serve Somebody" was obviously deeper and heartfelt. She gave a fabulous performance, ad-libbing and inserting her own words without detracting from the song – "*I heard Bob Dylan say it,*" she sang as the whole place moved to a full gospel onslaught. Dylan's mother, Beatrice, seemed as into it as Bob was.

So Dylan's segment ended, as the President, First Lady and Lauren Bacall led the applause for a bemused, little-boy-lost Bob with his mother sitting behind him. The entire event ended with all the honourees present on stage as President Clinton gave a speech, the concluding words of which were "America The Beautiful". It was overplayed, I kid you not, with an advert for Continental Airlines! The advert cleared just in time to see Bob standing shoulder to shoulder between Lauren Bacall and President Clinton, singing the anthem for all he was worth.

What a strange old trip, indeed.

Chapter Fourteen: 1998

I've Found A Different Audience

I've found a different audience. I'm not good at reading how old people are, but my audience seems to be livelier than they were 10 years ago. They react immediately to what I do, and they don't come with a lot of preconceived ideas about who they would like me to be, or who they think I am.

Bob Dylan, *Guitar World* interview[80]

You would think that Dylan would want a break and a nice easy start in 1998 after the December tour in 1997, which brought the final tally of N.E.T. shows in the year of Bob's illness to 110, but not a bit of it. He was already playing shows on the 13th and 14th of January, in New London, Connecticut, to warm up for some East Coast U.S. dates with Van Morrison. From January 16th to 21st at New York's Madison Square Garden Theatre, followed by two shows in Boston on 23rd and 24th, Dylan and Van Morrison alternated as headliners, making it difficult for fans to know which bit of the show to avoid.

The press praised Van Morrison and Dylan for still playing in the small, intimate confines of the Madison Square Gardens Theatre, while the Rolling Stones strutted their stuff in front of capacity crowds in the Garden itself. In comparison to the size of the venues The Stones were playing, the Garden Theatre was intimate, but compared to the venues the N.E.T. had become accustomed to in the 1990s, it was a large arena.

Bob's proximity to The Stones led to a plan that Dylan would leave the Garden Theatre one night and go and join the Rolling Stones at the Garden itself for "Like A Rolling Stone". Although it is believed Dylan got to the side of the stage in time, he was never called on. Unfortunately for lovers of the song everywhere, he was to play it with them later in the year; Dylan is hard enough to control on stage when he is totally in charge, far less when he has to interact with other "stars".

Given Dylan's recent high profile and the relative sales success of *Time Out Of Mind*, this was his first chance in years to fill arenas (as long as he had another big crowd-puller with him). Dylan would also continued to play smaller shows of his own, throughout the year, rebutting any claims that he was "selling out" the N.E.T..

After the Van Morrison dates, Dylan continued to tour, his appetite for the road seemingly as insatiable as ever. He even argued with the doctors over a decision to postpone one show due to influenza, though conceding in the end – accepting that it was unwise to push his luck too far. Notwithstanding this flu, January 27th found Bob in Poughkeepsie, starting on six dates that would take him through to February 2nd. Then, after a 12-day break, he picked up for another six shows before it was time for the Grammy Awards. Since Dylan's August 3rd return from illness, he had maintained a relentless pace.

The most exciting set list news for long-term fans was the frequent appearance of "Not Dark Yet", the integration of "Million Miles" into the standard numbers and the occasional duets (for curio hunters only!) with Van Morrison, such as "More and More" on January 18th. Van and Bob did produce one duet of intrinsic merit with their take (rehearsed even) on "Blue Suede Shoes" – a tribute to Carl Perkins, who had died, aged 65, on January 19th. The list of those close to Dylan who had passed away was growing at an alarming rate.

At Perkins' funeral, in what was becoming a regular occurrence, Dylan issued a stately tribute. Wynona Judd read it out:

"[Perkins] really stood for freedom. That whole sound stood for all the degrees of freedom. It would just jump right off the turntable. We wanted to go where that was happening,"

Days later, I'd catch my first 1998 glimpse of Dylan via a TV broadcast of the Grammy Awards where he played the song that had thrilled us so much back in October at Bournemouth, "Love Sick". One of Dylan's three nominations was for "Cold Irons Bound" so, being Dylan, you couldn't expect him to play that. The other nominations were for album of the year and "best contemporary folk album", both of which *Time Out Of Mind* won. (Incidentally, Dylan's son Jakob won two Grammies the same night, for "best rock vocal" and one for "best rock performance by a duo or a group with vocal".)

Despite the risible nature of some of the Grammy categories, the main award for Album of the Year is seen as a big thing. Certainly American record buyers take the award seriously; sales of the album subsequently increased fourfold and the album leapt almost 100 places back up the charts to number 27. The artistic merit of the awards might be somewhat more dubious given that when Dylan was putting out the likes of *Highway 61 Revisited* and *Blonde On Blonde* the winner was *Hello Dolly* or something like *The Tijuana Toastmasters Rock Cole Porter*. For all his ground-breaking albums, Dylan had never even been nominated for an Album of the Year Grammy before. (Excepting a one-of-the-crowd nomination for *A Concert For Bangladesh*).

If you could ignore the commercial setting, Dylan's performance itself was splendid, in spite of a rather bizarre distraction. In the middle of Bob's set, shirtless, self-styled "almost-vegetarian-multi-genre mastermind-artist" Michael Portnoy jumped on stage with the words "SOY BOMB" written in block letters on his body. Dylan and the band just kept playing, though the expression on

Dylan's face spoke volumes. Still, at least Portnoy's complaint injected some spontaneity into the Grammies.

"Soy is protein and life and energy, and bomb is explosive and propulsive," the stage invader explained to the press. "All art should be soy bombs."

One of the evening's highlights came when Dylan began his walk to the podium to collect one of his awards for *Time Out of Mind*. At that point, the TV shot of the audience captured high priestess of hip, Patti Smith, shouting "*Bob*" with all the intensity and demeanour of a teenage pop fan.

By April 4th, Dylan was back on the road for a rather strange little South American jaunt which took in two small venues and four dates as support to the Rolling Stones. The support slots brought the added trauma of the previously mooted Bob and Stones collaboration, with a joint performance of "Like A Rolling Stone" each night. It was even worse than expected. Dylan appeared not to know what to do on stage, and the Stones appeared not to know what to do with Dylan. The audiences, however, usually clapped wildly – it was being at the "event" that mattered, not the performances. In addition, some of the photographs from the shows let us see that Dylan and Jagger appeared to be having great fun, so maybe you just had to be there.

Next it was back to America to be reunited on the road with Van Morrison. However, Van pulled out and Joni Mitchell stepped in to fill his place. Van then did a U-turn, so the tour now comprised of three "singer-songwriter legends". Dylan and Van alternated as headliners, with Joni remaining in the middle slot on each of the seven nights. Having all three veterans on the same bill again led to acres of newsprint about "the old days". N.E.T. followers were less impressed, aware that when faced with a large audience many of whom are not there just to see him, Dylan normally plays safe. Dylan did indeed stick to conservative sets; breaking the habit only on May 26th when he performed "Restless Farewell" as a tribute to the recently deceased Frank Sinatra.

"I played at the Frank Sinatra Tribute show a few years back, and I played the next song," Dylan told the audience. "We had it all worked out and everything, but then they said they wanted to hear this one instead so ... I hadn't played it up till that time and I haven't played it since, I'll try my best to do it."

It was time for another on-the-mark obituary note from Dylan, and he provided the following:

"Right from the beginning, he was there with the truth of things in his voice. His music had an influence on me, whether I knew it or not. He was one of the very few singers who sang without a mask. It's a sad day".

With Dylan's energy levels apparently fully recovered from 1997's scare, he embarked on a long summer tour of Europe on May 30th. This leg took him all the way through to July 12th with hardly a night off. Unfortunately, Bob brought Van Morrison along for some of the dates, resulting, again, in fairly unadventurous set lists.

There was a change to the set structure in Leipzig on June 2nd, however, when the crowd refused to vacate the hall after the show. Dylan fans have often tried to win further encores with this tactic, but to no avail. I am not sure what was particularly special in Leipzig, but over 10 minutes after Bob's last encore, with the house lights on, the enthusiastically applauding crowd had still not dissipated at all. Dylan and the band returned to reward them with an extra encore of "Blowin' In The Wind". This extension of the encores obviously pleased Dylan because he retained this format for the forthcoming shows. However, the biggest change to the set lists's structure was to come after I saw him that summer.

In June '98 I was regularly travelling back and forth to Europe – both for work and the football world cup. I was also preparing to move house. The Dylan tour found me having to squeeze the shows into a frenetic itinerary. I did manage with the aid of yet another taxi dash from the airport to make Hamburg on the 12th June, once again at the Stadtpark. The venue was as lovely as ever but the Dylan I saw in 1998 was a travesty compared with what I had witnessed there before.

By the time Dylan elected to sing into his microphone, rather than away from it, one wished he hadn't – except that it let us know what a mood he was really in. To make matters worse, the band were lacklustre, the sound was appalling. I later heard various explanations for this, ranging from lack of accommodation the night before, to a broken sound system, and illness. Whichever the reason, I felt I had not yet really seen him at all.

Following the N.E.T. was immensely tricky that summer. The World Cup meant that every mode of transport to France, and every hotel in France, was fully booked. Somehow, with much manoeuvring, I managed to get to Rotterdam for the show on June 15th.

Hamburg had really hit me hard and the unexciting way the year had been going (plus, maybe even, the longevity of the N.E.T. itself) had reduced my customary over-the-top anticipation of seeing Dylan, to something more resembling curiosity. I played a couple of tracks from *Time Out Of Mind* as I left the flat to try and get in the mood. It kind of worked, but felt a little forced – a staged re-enactment of what once came naturally.

At this point I still didn't have a ticket. Despite all the years of going into concerts with enough tickets to cover an extended family and despite always seeing concert-goers (far less touts) selling spares, this situation always worries me. The nearer I got to the venue, the more worried I got. I took a taxi from Rotterdam Central to the arena, which was in a Godforsaken wasteland some distance away. Heavy machinery rather than touts greeted me.

As ever, I met up with people I knew. Both Carsten from Germany and Josh from America were following the tour around – as they always do – and both told me that Dylan played a much better show in Bremen than in Hamburg. I was relieved that they thought Hamburg was as bad as I had. If that show had been held up as typical of what was going on in the summer of 1998, the outlook would have been bleak.

Encouraged, I wandered around the tout-free zone looking for someone selling tickets. Finally, when I was just about to give up, a fan sold me one at face value! It was "up in the gods" but at least it was a ticket, and there was still some time to go before Van, far less Bob, was due on stage.

167

At this point I had no intention of watching Van's set but I wanted to go in and have a beer and a chat with Josh. So, after a couple of stewards refused to let us go in together as our tickets were for different parts of the venue, a series of sob stories coupled with my vehement – and frankly heartfelt – explanation that I'd leave the minute I thought Van was coming onstage, got me past security.

I had also had to promise not to steal anyone's seat – a promise I managed to keep rather easily as the snack bar offered a clear view of the stage. Once there I knew I was going to stay – even though it meant going back on my word, and worse, enduring Van's set – a glance up the steep sloped seats to the third tier where I was supposed to go was all the proof I needed that this little bar was the place for me. A seat for an absent toilet attendant completed my comfortable little perch. Sorted. It was all reminiscent of the show at the Tempodrom in Berlin in 1995 where my best view of the night came from a spot near a bar, where an upturned litter-bin provided an added height advantage.

Van was distant and disinterested; standing centre stage, moving one arm in time to the beat, but otherwise motionless. Even "Cleaning Windows" and "Tupelo Honey" were poor. I have seen a number of Van shows over the years, ranging from the so-so to the exhilarating, and this was the dullest of the lot!

Van's 90-minute set dragged on interminably. As Bob's set approached, I felt I had suffered so much that I needed a good Dylan performance to re-affirm my wavering commitment. When Bob finally appeared, I was just happy to see him rip into "Leopard-Skin Pill-Box Hat".

After a pretty neat "You Ain't Goin' Nowhere", a hard-rocking "Cold Irons Bound" was next, and it was clear already that Dylan was much more pumped up than he had been in Hamburg. It was just a shame for me that instead of, say, "Tears Of Rage" from the previous set-list I had to listen to this tedious, ham-fisted drivel.

In contrast, a dazzling, "Just Like A Woman" redeemed things before my pet hate, "Silvio". Maybe it was no longer the worst song of the set but this clumsy rock dirge was still totally dire. Worse, for the first time ever hearing it live I had no urge to go to the toilet. I was present for the whole song for the first time in years. That's what 90 minutes of Van-as-lounge-lizard can do to you!

I thought back over the last three songs and how the beauty of "Just Like A Woman"' was highlighted by the torpid thumped out hard rock on either side. Does Dylan not notice this contrast? I wondered to myself.

At least the audience here cheered "Just Like A Woman"; in other shows it had been "Cold Irons Bound" and "Silvio" that had drawn the most acclaim. "Silvio" received a football terrace-like reaction; exacerbated by the apt sight of a white-shirted Danny Baker[81] look-a-like stood on his seat, back to the stage, waving his arms to encourage people to clap in unison.

Like "Just Like A Woman", "Desolation Row" invoked a great cheer of recognition. As did "The Times They Are A-Changin'", particularly from the back and sides of the auditorium. As opposed to the front which was much more demonstrative for "Silvio".

The ovation for "Times" was oddly contradicted by the bar suddenly getting busy; so much so that for the first time my spot looked like a bad choice; luckily for me this was the only time during Dylan's set that this happened. A busy bar during "The Times They Are A-Changin'", after the rapt attention of the entire audience during "Silvio". Go figure.

It was also interesting from this somewhat-further-from-stage-than-normal position of mine to note what Dylan's songs mean to people – particularly the older songs, particularly around the sides of the auditorium and up where I should be sitting. These people were here to hear Dylan perform the classic songs they have listened to throughout their lives. Dylan sometimes views these as his audience, and at other times feels he is playing to people who always embrace his newest work. At this show I had a vantage point that allowed me to see almost two different audiences in the one hall.

Suddenly it was time for Dylan to mangle "Tangled Up In Blue". As Dylan ran through his 1998 desecration, I survived by casting my mind back to the original recording, a 1978 version, and a snatch of Barcelona 1984 – or was I thinking of Brussels? Never mind, he was nearly finished, it was time for me to pay attention again.

Except that the next song was the dull, unmelodic "Can't Wait". Appropriately large chunks of the audience agreed with the title's sentiment, and headed to the toilets in an exodus reminiscent of Earls Court in 1981 when Bob played a "religious" song.

Time Out Of Mind was mined again for the next song, "Make You Feel My Love". However well performed, this remains an over-blown ballad. Why could it not have been "Standing In The Doorway" or "Tryin' To Get To Heaven"? Not that the crowd seemed to be worried; they were showering the song and Dylan with acclaim. As for the coolest man the planet has seen – he was playing up to his front row groupies like the hammiest of hams. The grandeur of the arrangement for "Make You Feel My Love" had stretched his voice and "It Ain't Me, Babe" found his fractured vocals now sounding imbued with grace and even a hint of majesty – like a ruined cathedral, its beauty and magnificence still conjured by the shards that remain. I was finally moved, and once again in the palm of Bob's hand. "Highway 61 Revisited" found me down at the front bopping away and gaining a good viewing position for "Love Sick" which sounded as good as it had back in Bournemouth in 1997. Or perhaps this was just me fooling myself as I was desperately hoping that the trips to Hamburg and Rotterdam had been worthwhile. Maybe the lack of sleep was getting to me too, or maybe it actually was a good performance.

Dylan stood bathed in red light. Ah, those curls, that profile; what a powerful image it still presented. This visual side to a Dylan show is hugely important to many fans. Dylan standing clearly illuminated above the shadows of dark heads has a thrill all of its own.

The chorus of "Rainy Day Women # 12 and 35" was belted out by the occupants of the land of the "coffee shops" and it was all over. I faced a trek back to Amsterdam and a couple of hours sleep before heading off to see Scotland v. Norway in the warm embrace of the fabulous tartan army and the captivating hosts in Bordeaux. A great time was had by all and, sad to report, it seemed a more rewarding experience than watching Dylan.

Whilst admitting that the amount of time, energy and enthusiasm one has to put into touring as an audience member is influential, there were still a number of developments that made 1998 a low point of the N.E.T. for myself and for the majority of my long-term N.E.T.-going friends. As ever, there were many who loved the year, indeed many who liked every show.

In re-listening to the shows for the purpose of this book I began to see why; although I did not find any show I liked all the way through, I could see someone having a good night at the show in Stockholm, for example, where both "Desolation Row" and "Every Grain Of Sand" were performed with a mixture of dignity and vulnerability, and where the despairing chorus in "Forever Young" truly reflected the impossibility of the verses' altruistic pleas. "Love Sick" was as powerful as ever, and even "All Along The Watchtower" was given a different arrangement.

For me, though, Dylan had become quite distanced from his audience and detached from what had – until comparatively recently – driven the N.E.T.. Many disturbing elements seem to come to a head in 1998 – though they had begun to surface in previous years, combining to render a Dylan gig less of an event in the sense of something magical and special and more of an "event" in the sense of a deliberately calculated stage show.

The staged duck-walks and rock guitar hero poses that had initially seemed endearing were growing stale. Once you realised that it was all planned and prepared, like Bob's increasingly premeditated tease of picking up harmonicas and putting them down without playing them, the appeal rapidly diminished. It was as if Dylan was constantly checking his watch to see if it was time for another imitation of Chuck Berry in need of the toilet.

Worse by far was the increasing North American trend for carefully choreographed crowd invasions, keeping people back from the stage until a pre-set time or signal from the stage and then letting them flock forward; thus creating a false sense of sudden heightening of audience excitement. Then it developed further, in certain songs, (like "Rainy Day Women # 12 and 35", for example) people would get ready to invade the stage. If the time was right, security was given instructions to let them do so. Not all of them, though, just a select number of young, preferably good-looking women. It must be good fun for Bob to be surrounded by all these young Babes, jiggling their assets in front of his face and planting the occasional smacker on him, but since it is all pre-planned it has a tawdry look. Following on from Woodstock II Dylan's courting of a younger audience was threatening to run out of control. If you look at the hand-picked audiences at *MTV Unplugged* and the 1998 Grammies, you are faced with the stench of manipulation and false representation of what Dylan's audience actually looks like. These "spontaneous" crowd rushes were the same thing. How much of this was Dylan's idea, I don't know – but he must have agreed to it.

I know that this is a stage show, but does it have to be such a *staged* show? Dylan shows, and especially Dylan N.E.T. shows, were supposed to be something far more spontaneous and meaningful; to involve a more direct communication between artist and audience.

The band – and Dylan's own performances – all seemed too similar to me too. Each show sounded much like the one before. Naturally, he kept changing songs around but they were usually like for like ("Girl From The North Country" replacing "Boots of Spanish Leather" and "Maggie's Farm" replacing "Highway 61 Revisited" did not make for a different 1998 N.E.T. experience).

This was probably necessitated by the amount of double and triple headers that Dylan was playing, but again these are not what the N.E.T. was meant to be, or had been, in my eyes.

Dana Parsons, of *The Times Orange County Edition*, pointed out all the expensive cars in the car park at one Dylan show, and captured the appeal of the triple-header show to many of the audience:

"We've all come a long way, I guess, and these three superstars aged right along with us. They all wrote much of their best material while we were going to high school, graduating college, getting married, having first babies, signing for first mortgages, taking first jobs. It's a powerful bond many baby boomers have with the rock stars of our generation."

"He's representative of the culture I grew up with, he's inside me," fan Elizabeth Cumming told Parsons. "I love Van Morrison, too, he's exceptional in his own right. It's one of those things. If we don't do it now, when are we going to get the chance to see Van Morrison, Bob Dylan and Joni Mitchell together? It's an epic moment. How many more epic moments are we all going to get? So I want to take my epic moments when I can get them."

It's a viewpoint as different from mine as could be had between two people wanting to see Bob Dylan. I want to see a Dylan gig, not some travelling nostalgia show. Because, make no mistake about it, these shows were deliberately designed to cash in on the burgeoning economic power of a generation that was "born in the fifties".

Looking back on the period from mid-1997 to mid-1999, John Scher, president of New Jersey's Metropolitan Entertainment, explained to *The Philadelphia Inquirer* the change in the way concerts were being packaged and sold:

"There are a lot of baby-boomer artists seeing the end of their careers who are less sensitive to appearing greedy.... If you have to pay $200 for a pair of tickets ...you will if you feel a strong emotional connection to your favorite artist.... And the artists are saying, 'They're giving us so much money, how can we turn it down?' ... "

1988 and that opening one-hour rush of primal rock suddenly seemed far away. The other highly sellable qualities of these shows were the ages of the artists and Dylan's recent illness. Dana Parsons quoted another fan as saying: "With this kind of line-up, and with people dropping like flies...."

What is perhaps most remarkable is that these shows attracted fans, like those cited above, that Dylan specifically claimed to have finally freed himself from.

171

"I've found a different audience," Bob told *Guitar World*'s Murray Engleheart in 1998. "I'm not good at reading how old people are, but my audience seems to be livelier than they were 10 years ago. They react immediately to what I do, and they don't come with a lot of preconceived ideas about who they would like me to be, or who they think I am. Whereas a few years ago they couldn't react quickly...

"I was still kind of bogged down with a certain crowd of people. It has taken a long time to bust through that crowd. Even the last time I toured with Tom Petty, we were kind of facing that same old crowd. But that's changed. We seem to be attracting a new audience. Not just those who know me as some kind of figurehead from another age or a symbol for a generational thing. I don't really have to deal with that any more, if I ever did."

What Dylan is saying is true for the majority of the normal N.E.T. audience. He has toured so often now that the "tick-seeing-a-legend" masses have had chance after chance to see him. However with these big co-headliner shows (and the following year's double-headers with Paul Simon) Dylan was bringing back those very audiences, and to keep them happy he had to play in a different, more "professional" (for want of a better expression) way, which made him more detached from his material.

There is clearly a difficult balancing act needed between spontaneity and a premeditated show. In early 1991, I complained about the complete lack of professionalism, while in 1998 I complain of too much professionalism. In 1993 I objected to the sloppy, long drawn out endings, in 1998 I began to object to the band being too polished. But these complaints tell only part of the story; the elements I disliked in 1998 would still be present in the following two years, yet those years would see me return me to the "N.E.T. fold", and would renew my faith in Dylan's ability to still turn in killer gigs.

Back in 1998 Dylan was on his way, sans me for once, around the UK. Before the Newcastle show he made a change to the long standing set structure, extending the middle acoustic set from four songs to six. It was a most beneficial change and one that stayed in place for the remaining double headers with Van the Man.

Other than this, the UK gigs, interspersed with a quick return to the European mainland, were more of the same; mainly greatest hits sets plus *Time Out Of Mind* selections. There were some enjoyable enough shows, with certain standout individual song performances, but all in all generally very safe and predictable.

Most reviewers spent the time marvelling that the combined age of the two "old buzzards" was in three figures and compared their relative abilities to still perform at this stage of their lives. Like most critics, *Hot Press*'s Stuart Baillie placed Bob firmly on top.

"You want extraordinary?" Baillie asked his readers. "Look at Bob Dylan on the stage up yonder, blowing at his mouth harp, bucking at the knees, shaking those ancient hips. It's a wonderful testimony to the life-fizzing power of music, especially since old Bob was dangerously sick a while back.... tonight, he looks great in his western cut tuxedo and his white boots, the scratchplate of his battered Fender flashing in the sun, his voice rejuvenated....

"On tonight's evidence, it may be debatable whether Van is still 'the man'. But thankfully, Bob's yer uncle after all these years. In a harp-blowing, blues-wailing, gut-bucket, soul-believin' kind of a way."

The Guardian's Pat Kane was one of the minority of reviewers who begged to differ, praising Van as a "magnificent old bastard".

"The truth is that Dylan stands much, much closer to that mausoleum moment than Morrison," Kane opined. "Dylan was a man desperately fighting against what the passing years have done to his talent and ambition and only occasionally winning through....

"Mr Zimmerman's two-note guitar solos and gingerly executed rock poses suggest someone who's doing this music for therapy as much as artistic statement. And the trademark vocal drone – which once spoke truth and authenticity – has now permanently split between a frog-like gurgle and a thoroughly shattered falsetto scrambling the words of songs...."

One of the many rumours that has re-appeared virtually every year of the Never Ending Tour is that Bob Dylan would appear at the Glastonbury Festival. This rumour is about as frequent as the one that the Never Ending Tour is about to come to a close. I am not sure which of the two rumours worried fans more. The idea of having to go to Glastonbury because Dylan was there was all too much for some of us oldsters. However, 1998 was the fateful year Dylan did work on Michael Eavis's farm, and his short festival set was very well received by the massive Glastonbury crowd.

After a short break, guess what? It was time to tour again: beginning on August 19th in Melbourne, Australia, Dylan started a run of shows with Patti Smith supporting, (though unfortunately not singing duets this time), that ran until September 12th, finishing in Christchurch, New Zealand. On the second night of this leg, Bob made me a happy man by dropping "Silvio" from the set for the first time since September 27th, 1995. Not content with these Australian and New Zealand dates, Dylan returned to the States via Hawaii where he played on 17th and 18th September and then, starting on the 22nd, played six more dates in the United States.

On October 13th the world finally saw the official release of the most famous bootleg of all time, *Bob Dylan Live in 1966, "The Royal Albert Hall Concert"*. The most celebrated of gigs, where a defiantly electric Dylan responded with fury to a folk luddite's "Judas" accusation, was in keeping with Dylan's high media profile of the past 18 months. It also gave him an enormous amount to live up to; Dylan was then at the height of his powers, not only when playing with the Hawks but also in the stupendous acoustic set.

Two days after that release, Dylan hit the road again, touring Canada and the northern U.S. through to November 7th, and taking in a November 1st Madison Square Garden show with Joni Mitchell as support. To celebrate the occasion he unveiled a one-off gem, with a sublime rendition of Charles Aznavour's, "The Times We've Known" ("Les Bon Moments").

"I want to try something here from a guy playing off the streets that I've always liked, Charles Aznavour," Dylan told the crowd. "I usually play these things all by myself, but I feel I am all by myself now."

In a poignant performance, Dylan invested the words with his whole being. A mere two days later, at Rochester, New York, "I Believe In You" returned for the first time since I saw it in Cottbus, Germany, July 14th, 1996. It was joined in the set list by "Across The Borderline", which had not been played since the wonderful interpretation at Ames, Iowa, eight years and one day before.

After one hundred and ten shows, the year's touring ended on November 7th in Atlanta, Georgia. It was a prodigious number of shows for Dylan, but my lowest-equal attendance rate – other than in 1988 when he never crossed the ocean and I sure could not make it to the States. Yet, due to the wonders of modern technology, I kept in constant touch with what was going on. Not just Bill Pagel's Web site, not just the fanzines, the tapes, the CD-Rs and so forth; but also the official Sony Bob Dylan Web site, www.bobdylan.com.

From August 1997 onward, the official Bob Dylan web-site developed into a goldmine for fans. Apart from its many other attributes (including an impressive on-line lyric service) it features live recordings of Dylan performances old and new. As Dylan was playing his early 1998 shows the Web site was featuring songs from his recent performances, as well as some of the Supper Club songs, for example, and superb recordings from the 1997 December club tour. It was an act of immense largesse, at odds with the tradition of live Dylan material being hard to come by without resorting to the bootleg market.

In January, when Dylan was running through a standard set in a huge arena before Van Morrison took the stage, I was sitting at home listening to things like the 16th of December 1997's "The Lonesome Death of Hattie Carroll".

Listening to this you felt that his voice was still so needed. Dylan's history is behind this song by now, as much as Hattie Carroll's painful story. The fact that you are at a show in the N.E.T. hearing this song sung by its author, as only he can, and that you listen to it knowing that, sadly, its relevance has scarcely diminished makes it all the more moving. By being at the show or listening to the song via this marvellous new service from the official Bob Dylan Web site, you were, as Jack Nicholson had said at Live Aid, being presented with "one of America's great voices of freedom".

Here Nicholson's words rang true and suited so much better than at that sad performance, where a befuddled, bloated and sweaty Dylan figure seemed far removed from any purpose in life. The Never Ending Tour has given him back this purpose and relevance and has given Dylan back to us, his lucky audience.

This largesse included many highlights from the current year. From the 17th January show we were presented with "Tears of Rage". This is such a special song – such a magical, majestic, gut-wrenching meld of melody, lyric and vocal delivery – and to have a live performance available in perfect quality from a line recording seemed almost too good to be true. It reawakened in me a feeling of how precious and powerful Dylan's presence is in this world. How lucky one is to be alive and have the opportunity to go and witness something like this.

Imagine you had lived in the early 17th century and could have made it to a public oration by John Donne, you'd go, wouldn't you? You might have hankered for an inspired author's reading of "The Sun Rising", a poem that had so moved you when you were growing up – or some other masterpiece that had changed your views on life and love. Yet you may have been offered a gloomy treatise based on "The First Anniversary" instead. Then again you just might have got the best, most passionate exploration of Donne's thoughts and emotions you could ever have imagined. You might also get an entirely new work of insight and imagination, fused from the experience of a life that had soured the earlier optimism and grand vision into a fatalism bolstered by dark cynicism, and yet still shot through with wit and insight. You might, with Dylan, get all three in a row with "Tears Of Rage", "In The Garden" and "Not Dark Yet". In either artist's case, if you don't take your chances to go and hear a master at work, it's your loss.

"Girl From The North Country" from January 20th came with a wonderful Mexican flourish in the guitar playing. "To Make You Feel My Love" from Los Angeles on May 21st proved that, for all I have said about Bob's ravaged voice in the later years of the Never Ending Tour, he could still bring out a vocal that tore the stars out of the very sky. *"You ain't seen nothing like me yet,"* Bob growled.

"I could make you happy, make your dreams come true
Nothing that I wouldn't do
Go to the ends of the earth for you
To make you feel my love."

These words neatly summed up what he does for his fans year in, year out with the Never Ending Tour.

From Leipzig, Germany (June 2nd) we were given a magnificent "A Hard Rain's A Gonna Fall". Another stand out was "Mama, You Been on My Mind" from Brussels, June 17th; a great vocal performance of a song that gets me every time. I may, in general terms, feel that 1998 was a poor year, but vocals like this and "Tomorrow Is A Long Time" (not featured on www.bobdylan.com) at Glasgow in June are exemplary. Glasgow was present on the site, however, in the form of "Boots of Spanish Leather" – the extended acoustic sets giving Dan Levy, who runs the Web site, a plethora of riches to select from. Levy has an almost impossible task – though a hugely enviable and enjoyable one!

Best of all though, was an outstanding rendition of Gordon Lightfoot's "I'm Not Supposed To Care". This was Dylan as "Uncle Bobby" rather than the cool Big Brother of the mid-sixties. We now know for ourselves what the world is like, we do not need him, "to sit behind our eyes and tell us how we see". What we have instead is a travelling musician, singing his heart out in this song of a hopeless romantic (with a small "r"). This most affecting of performances

ended with what could almost be taken as a message to those dedicated followers of the N.E.T.

"If you need somebody, somewhere
You know I'll always be there
I'll do it, although –
I'm not supposed to care."

All these covers transformed by Dylan's interpretative powers year after year
in the N.E.T. – somebody should gather them altogether and put them out as a
multi-CD box set. What Dylan has always known is that there is the strength
in, what we might roughly refer to as "popular music" to move men's hearts,
to shift mountains, to open up the better side of ourselves that we keep hidden
away.

In a way this sums up why the cover versions in the N.E.T. have had such a
prominent place in this book. Despite my love of, and admiration for, Dylan's
magnificent lyrics, he never had to write a single one of all his phenomenal
words to be the most influential artist in my life. His voice reaches higher and
speaks even more deeply than all those linguistic triumphs.

Yet, for all my praise of the covers, most fans feel a special bond when
seeing Dylan sing songs he has authored, especially recent ones. It was clear
from the very first playing that "Not Dark Yet" – sadly not available through
the Web site – was not only one of the best songs on *Time Out Of Mind*, but
also a bona fide masterpiece. Bob's vocals on this live version were, as on the
album, exemplary; the perfection of the way he sings "gay *Paree*" is one of the
reasons we all get so excited by new Dylan material, and by his singing. The
epic grandeur in this one song would later ensure that my relative estrangement
from the N.E.T. was just a passing phase, though I did not realise this at the
time.

1998 had ended with me having only caught a paltry two shows – the same
as in 1989. However, while back in '89 I was starving for more, this year I was
sated, I didn't need any more live shows. There were many reasons for this: the
amount of times and the regularity with which I'd seen him, the predictability
of it all in 1998, the ready access to top-quality recordings just in case anything
great did go down. All of this notwithstanding, 1998 marked the lowest point
of my interest in the N.E.T.. I was on a downer; the only way to go now, Bob
willing, was up again!

Chapter Fifteen: 1999

Right now, I'm enjoying it.

"Touring is something you either love or hate doing. I've experienced both. I try to keep an open mind about it. Right now, I'm enjoying it. The crowds make the show. Going onstage, seeing different people every night in a combustible way, that's a thrill. There's nothing in ordinary life that even comes close to that."

Bob Dylan, *USA Today* [82]

I could have realized as early as January that 1999's shows had great potential, but I failed to listen to the testimony of my friend Nigel Simms, who reported back from the opening Florida dates with news of a great performance, including a fascinating (Daytona Beach, 29th January) debut of Lefty Frizzel's, "You're Too Late". Cynical old me just thought "yeah, yeah" – and made no effort to track down the tapes so I did not hear Bob's Florida performance until later in the year. My loss, Nigel was spot on! The Frizell number saw Bob's voice erupt into a country-tinged melody like a damaged but beautiful diamond, sending shafts of emotion through the ether into one's very soul. Thus, did another year of great covers begin.

Due to my tardy awakening to what was going down, my N.E.T. year was not at all the same as Dylan's. I heard far more from the spring European tour than from the January to March US ones. I remember the double set at Atlantic City on February 27th causing a bit of a stir but before I was really fully "on board" listening-wise, Bob was swinging into the April shows.

Before that, though, I did pick up on a number of individual performances. I was really glad to hear "Blue-Eyed Jane" in February and enjoyed his rather strained attempt at it here, despite the crowd's incessant chatter. As the background intrusion receded, Dylan's just-about-to-go-but-just-hanging-in-there vocals guided us through this pop-country treat of a love song. There was also that great song, "Honky Tonk Blues" – enough to make you think that touring with rockabilly band BR-549 in 1993 wasn't a complete waste of time after all! Of course, Hank Williams was a big favourite of Bob long before BR-549 started their excellent covers. I do so wish they had joined him on stage and backed him on this, when they toured with him, but, hey, for now this would do just fine.

In addition to the great covers, early highlights included a rare outing for "Ring Them Bells", and Brian Setzer's horn section on "Ballad Of A Thin Man" on the 13th February. The horns were great, and their presence seemed to make Dylan try that bit harder.

My early 1999 NET consisted of sporadic bursts from the Web site www.bobdylan.com, and tour compilations. "I Don't Believe You" from one such compilation convinced me it was time to start listening harder, and plan my return to the concert trail.

Meanwhile, there was yet another triumph of new technology for this Dylan watcher. Bob was one of many who contributed a song to a Johnny Cash tribute broadcast on TV. Dylan sang "Train Of Love" while rehearsing in Spain and his contribution (taped April 6th) was beamed to the event and therefore broadcast on April 18th. When I got up the next morning there was a video of this in my E-mail inbox; it was good to see it so soon after it had taken place.

Even better would have been being in Spain for the April shows. I was by now getting into the year, but not yet really listening to entire performances. Time constraints meant that I was still on compilations in the main. So the European tour – indeed the majority of the year – came to me in compilation form. One of the tracks I rushed to play – as did all Dylan fans, I am sure – was "Fourth Time Around".

A surprise choice, this: an N.E.T. debut and a very agreeable one at that. The music here was much more understated than the original's delicious pop and blues confection but it had an appealing swing to it. Dylan growled gorgeously enough for one not to feel overly wistful for past glories.

"Not Dark Yet" just seemed to get better and better, the acoustic standards were unfailingly well sung. By the time I heard Malaga and Granada – two of a number of standout Spanish shows – I was no longer declining the kind offers of full shows on CD-r. The long awaited change of set structure had made a dramatic impact on the NET. The long dominant: 5-6 electric songs, 3-4 acoustic, 2-3 electric and then encores had become 5-6 acoustic songs followed by up to 6 electric songs and then the encores.

Now we had classic Dylan acoustic songs and covers followed by electric rockers, paced so as to build, and then subside into a more please-pay-attention-to-this *Time Out Of Mind* selection or a one-off, a rarity or a new arrangement. The sets would then build up to full on rave out encores.

Once again, I couldn't get enough of them, and so you find me scurrying across Europe in late April, once again caught up in the excitement and whirl of following Dylan on tour. As war and atrocities raged in nearby Yugoslavia, there was something profoundly moving in Dylan singing songs like "Masters Of War", "Blowin' In The Wind" and "A Hard Rain's A-Gonna Fall", especially as he was singing them with a passion, clarity and engagement I had feared was lost forever.

Dylan was really up for these shows and after the reflective brilliance of the acoustic sets was looking for a party atmosphere to propel him to ever greater rock outs in the electric sets. Now there are many Dylan fans, especially among the older ones, who do not like this side of the modern Dylan shows. They prefer the idea of the audience sitting in rapt attention and only moving and clapping in-between the songs. While this would certainly make for better tapes it is undoubtedly not what Dylan usually wants. Having had the pleasure of hearing his carefully presented and perfectly delivered acoustic sets, if Dylan wants an all out rocking second half to the nights that was fine by me. It was like getting two concerts in one.

There was one problem: arena security guards. After a spell-binding opening set in Vienna, Dylan lit into "Cold Irons Bound" and a heartfelt "Make You Feel My Love". At the end of each of these songs, he peered below the front of the stage to see how everyone was reacting and his disappointment was palpable when he saw no-one there. His "thank you kind folks" comment after the latter was a mixture of the routine and the ironic.

The problem was that the security guards at Vienna's Stadthalle were stopping anyone moving forwards. Dylan enticed the fans to come to the front by extending the beginning and endings to songs that normally found the front-stage area full, but the guards wouldn't let anyone move down to the front section (which was inhabited by less demonstrative members of the audience). I was sitting to the side watching a cat and mouse game develop as Dylan kept trying to pull people towards him with extended guitar playing. Vienna, unsurprisingly, became the longest Dylan concert I had been at for many a long year. Something had to give, and give it did during the damn-the subtlety-get-up-and-party noise of "Stuck Inside Of Mobile With The Memphis Blues Again" which brought a forward crowd surge from behind the front section.

Then a big guy, who had already been removed from the front a few times, had finally had enough. He defiantly walked straight down the centre aisle with arms extended above his head, clapping along all the way, and planted himself in front of Bob. He was dragged away on more than one occasion, but kept returning; exhorting as he went those at the front to sit up and cheer. They did not. A few others were also playing cat and mouse with the security guards trying to get down first one aisle, then another. They had moved forward again when this incident diverted the attention of the guards. Both they and our now retreating hero were wildly cheered by the rest of the crowd so kept going back down one aisle after another; the cheers increased, and the song just kept going on. A couple of other people tried to get down the front, then a few more, then the trickle became a flood that the guards could no longer repel and the cheering got even louder.

Not being too shy at coming forward at times like this, I joined the "front of the stage" storm troops. For all the world it was like the 1970s at football games in the UK all over again. I used people who were being held by guards as my decoys and gained remarkable speed for one of my advancing years – all down to the motivation factor. The first two guards were dead easy; as they seized another fan I ducked around them. I was close to the stage now and

I could have stayed put as others filled in behind me but the magical barrier was only a stride or so away so I tried the same trick one more time. This last guard was up to it. Holding one fresh captive with one arm, he caught me with the other; impressively, if distressingly, enough, he held us both while shouting something in German. But, through no fault of his own he was on a loser; hundreds had caught up with us and I could feel them pressing me forward and him backward. I made a break for it and the crowd heaved forward, allowing me to squeeze under his arm and onwards.

I hit the barrier just to the left of Dylan's centre microphone position. The delay had been costly but not disastrous and the extra few places away would make me less self-conscious about using my binoculars from so close to the stage. I should say that the last I saw of our erstwhile captor was him being helped over into the moat by all his comrades who had given up what was, after all, an unwinnable situation.

During all this the auditorium rang to the crashing sound of the guitar driven "Mobile" and huge cheers from the crowd who had made it to the front. Some of the audience further back didn't make it all the way but were clearly there in spirit.

Meanwhile Bob's sudden realisation that the vast majority of the crowd were loving his performance and wanted to share the joy of the night with him brought out the showman in him. The exaggerated dancing, facial expressions and guitar flourishes that had gone before seemed pale now.

Rather than a hooligan pitch invasion it suddenly seemed like our team had just won the cup and we had streamed onto the pitch to be thanked by our captain for helping cheer him to victory. It was a great moment; but the whole thing was by now so cranked up that it was as though we were at the last two songs of the encore aiready. So what's a man to do? Simple: quieten things down for a bit with "Trying To Get To Heaven" and stare right into my face when you get to the "Baltimore" verse, Bob.

After a shout for "Sugartown" this was exactly what he did and my cynical 1998 persona was completely shed and shredded as I stood, once again, all misty-eyed at the feet of the maestro.

As for the song itself; Dylan was putting a lot into the vocals. The way the second half of the show was arranged left the audience in no doubt which songs they were to party to and which to pay attention to. Unfortunately, Dylan became miffed by some of the band's playing and Bucky got "the look", the like of which I hadn't seen since John Jackson's or Tony Garnier's early days. It happened after two verses at the same musical moment and both the unplanned discordant note, and Dylan's expression of anger with it, caused me to fear that he may not have continued to play the song live (certainly, it boded ill for Bucky's future in the band). Dropping the song would have been a cause of great regret, it was very atmospheric: dark, smoky and yearning – and it sure sat well in the same set list as "Not Dark Yet".

The song ended with a mumbled apology explaining this was something they had been wanting to try out, and when the song re-appeared in Munich two days later, it was back in the acoustic set.

In between the Europe shows and the summer tour of the States, Bucky Baxter (over 700 shows behind him) left the band. He was replaced by Charlie Sexton, a guitarist held in high regard and one who could bring, amongst many other benefits, a cutting edge to the increasingly blues-dominated sound. With Sexton on board the band could Roll as well as Rock; swinging from a plaintive country sound to a howling blues at the flick of a switch. However, it would take a while before Sexton bedded in.

As a critic of Bob's double headers with Van Morrison et al, the summer brought depressing news of a extortionately priced joint arena tour with Paul Simon. Art was losing out to Mammon as the promoters chased baby boomer bucks.

After recent big money tours by the Eagles, Fleetwood Mac and the Rolling Stones, Bruce Springsteen was also touring that summer. Meanwhile, Crosby, Stills, Nash & Young ; Tom Petty, Steely Dan, John Mellencamp, Rod Stewart and James Taylor were amongst others chasing older rock fans' dollars.

Gary Bongiovanni, editor of *Pollstar* was quoted as saying: "The baby boomers typically don't go out to more than a couple of shows a season...to appeal to that audience, you have to do things that reach 'event' status, in their minds at least."

"It's the summer of the outrageously priced concert ticket," *The Philadelphia Inquirer's* Dan DeLuca bemoaned. "Nationwide, prices for premium seats are going through the amphitheatre roof, particularly for superstar acts favored by baby boomers... Bob Dylan and Paul Simon are getting $100 for tickets to their July concert at Camden's Waterfront Entertainment Centre... Industry buzz has it that Dylan and Simon will split $525,000 a night"

However, Once In A Lifetime Event or not, it seemed a hundred bucks for a ticket might be too much.

"A study in contrasts, Dylan and Simon have indelibly shaped and broadened pop's musical landscape", George Varga reflected in *The Union Tribune*. "[They] had never performed together before... making their unlikely-to-ever-be-repeated tour even more special, as does the on stage duets... So why are the ticket sales lagging for this historic tour? In a word: money.... For those fans who can afford it, hearing them together may be worthwhile at any price. But for many more, this tour may be remembered more for its prohibitive cost to attend than for its music"

Dylan, as you would expect, played the line of "I'm just a travelling musician, I'll play for anybody, I'll do what it takes to get on stage". More shocking were Bob's comments that implied he considered Simon to be on an artistic par with himself.

"I consider him one of the pre-eminent songwriters of the times", Bob commented. "Every song he does has got a vitality you don't find everywhere."[83]

Robert Hilburn, a writer convinced of Dylan's pre-eminence in the songwriting field, concurred. Elevating Simon above such celebrated Dylan concert partners as The Band, Joni Mitchell and Van Morrison, Hillburn concluded, "Simon deserves a place alongside Dylan on the list of the half-dozen most enduring songwriters of the modern pop era."

As it turned out, my fears re the Paul Simon double headers were not fully realized; Dylan turned in high level performances despite relatively unchanging set-lists. He was in better voice in many of the joint shows than in the much lauded "Tramps" New York show on July 26th. This show quickly passed into legend among Dylan fans because of its appealing set list (including "Every Grain Of Sand", "Visions Of Johanna" and an extra encore with special guest Elvis Costello), the more intimate venue and, most of all, its lack of Paul Simon. Hardly reasons I'd disagree with; but, on hearing the show, I was disappointed. Dylan's voice was thin and reedy; he was straining for effect. Naturally, I'd love to report that a Dylan-only show with an inspired set list showed up the money-making Simon shows for the rip off they were, but I just don't hear it.

I should also point out that all those at the "Tramps" show found it to be amongst the best they had ever witnessed. Given most who were there would be faced with Madison Square Gardens the next night, I can understand their enthusiasm for the location. For the record they were treated to a "Visions Of Johanna" that repeatedly spoke of "visions of Madonna" for some reason known only to the man himself.

Despite the Simon shows sounding better than I had feared, I did not want to listen to all of them. As a long term Dylan listener I had heard too many of the songs in their current guise too often. "Tangled Up In Blue", "The Times They Are A-Changin'", "Silvio", "Seeing The Real You At Last", "Ballad Of A Thin Man", "Tombstone Blues", "Maggie's Farm", "Highway 61 Revisited", "Like A Rolling Stone", "It Ain't Me, Babe", "Not Fade Away", "Blowin' In The Wind" and "All Along The Watchtower" could no longer hold my interest in these incarnations.

One of the "selling points" of this tour (of which there was another leg in September) was the nightly, cringe-making, duets of "The Sound Of Silence", "I Walk The Line"/"Blue Moon Of Kentucky" (medley), and "Knockin' On Heaven's Door".

The whole idea of these duets was silly in the extreme but the contrast between the two singers was illuminating. It was instructive for us Dylan fans bemoaning the rigidity of the set lists night after night that Dylan was praised for the variations in his performance over Simon's bland professionalism. Where we see predictability by Bob's standards, the standard reviewer sees a wealth of creative exploration in Dylan's attitude to performance compared with the "professional" approach of someone like Paul Simon.

These particular duets were "fairly nice" in a very bland way; amusing too, for their very awkwardness but not too obnoxious. Or at least not until the reggae-lite "Knockin' On Heaven's Door" was jarred by the monstrous perversion of incorporating some absurd lines from a Simon song into the Dylan original. This nearly cost me a CD player and a replacement window.

If I'd made it to the shows themselves I'd have avoided Simon's solo set completely, I'd have been uninterested in most of Dylan's set and I'd have been torn asunder by an aesthetic dilemma ("Should I Stay Or Should I Go?" Indeed!) at the duets. On CD I could listen to the bits of the shows I was interested in at my leisure and, in any case, the shows were not aimed to please the likes of me.

Nonetheless, as I say, I liked them more than I thought I would. Especially the only one I listened to repeatedly (and certainly the only one I listened to all of) which was from June 16th at Sacramento.

That night's opener, "Cocaine Blues", is a song he always does well, but I particularly loved the Sacramento version. Another song that regularly fully engages Dylan is the superlative "My Back Pages" and the Sacramento show was no let down here. The "younger than that now" phrase here became a howl of independence and the band's playing was splendid, as was Bob's harmonica.

Sacramento also featured a very fine "Don't Think Twice, It's Alright". Here was a song he performed as well as when he was much younger. This serves as a reminder that I (and 'we all', I suspect) take great versions of songs like "Don't Think Twice, It's Alright" / "Girl From The North Country" / "Boots Of Spanish Leather" etc. for granted when often, despite being 'not exciting' in terms of set list appearance, they are amongst the best performed songs in a show. "Masters Of War" followed it and was equally impressive.

In fact, throughout 1999 this song was brilliantly played time after time. Dylan's somewhat aged and ragged voice perhaps perfectly expressed the appalling never-ending relevance of the blunt unforgiving words. When I heard it again, live, that year in Europe with the bombs, bullets and torturers at close quarters, it was chilling. As Robert Hilburn wrote of the performance he witnessed four days later at Arrowhead Pond in Anaheim: "This version of 1963's "Masters of War" carried the urgency of a news bulletin."

"Tangled Up In Blue" was next (it was ever present, again, in 1999, be it a "greatest hits" night like this or even in other, more adventurous, sets). Dylan was struggling to overcome a hoarse voice as the run of acoustic songs reached its climax with a performance of this magnificent song that added absolutely nothing to the transcendent versions of yore. It was as close to boring as such a masterly song sung by the master could ever be. The crowd loved it, naturally.

Then, "All Along The Watchtower" appeared, or "old number 3" as I think of it, with a reasonably understated opening. The unmistakable melody is still a foot-tapper and still an audience favourite. "Positively 4th Street" was taken slowly, Dylan sang it with a warm rasp, sounding more understanding than vindictive. "Stuck Inside Of Mobile With The Memphis Blues Again" was OK, but the vocals became a bit whiney by the end. "Not Dark Yet" on the other hand was a flawless reading of a song that was nailed more than once in 1999.

After the introduction of the band it was into the slam-bam-rock encore of "Highway 61 Revisited" which sounded fresher than it often had been. "Love Sick" was still as it sounded in its debut back in Bournemouth, UK '97; still sounding atmospheric and film noir-ish, still marred, though not for much longer, by the calamitous "thunder/plunder/wonder" triplet.

Then it was time to please the audience with that greatest of greatest hits: "Like A Rolling Stone". I must admit to preferring "Love Sick" in these kind of performances. Although it is an immeasurably slighter piece of work it was consistently performed with a commitment missing from the done-a-thousand-times-and-more other electric encores.

As had become common, the best of all encore performances was to be found in the penultimate slot, reserved for the last acoustic song of the night. In Sacramento, it was "It Ain't Me, Babe" that reminded us of Dylan's power and glory with words and music before he and the band attempted to destroy any similar memories of Buddy Holly's gifts by trashing the life out of "Not Fade Away".

Considering I was not representative of the target audience (Dylan's altruistic interview comments that it would be the same show as he'd normally play can be easily disproved by comparing these shows with those in the upcoming November), I found it had much of merit and I got a great deal of enjoyment from a number of plays. You may well wonder, given my antipathy to this leg why I ended up playing it at all, far less repeatedly. It was all down to luck.

I was sent Sacramento by one of those lovely people who like to send on rarities the minute they get them. In this case the rarities were to be found as "bonus tracks" at the end of the Sacramento shows. As one of these tracks was much sought after I would be copying the discs for many friends. Out of curiosity I listened to the show as well as the extra tracks and found myself drawn to it from the first listen.

These delightful surprise songs and covers included, for example, "Down Along The Cove". This was from July 10th at Maryland Heights, Missouri. Sadly, hearing about it being played was much more exhilarating than actually hearing it.

"Somebody Touched Me" was also on my double disc. I know it is a bit of a trifling piece but I thoroughly enjoyed it. This made you want to "slap your thighs", get out that banjo and join in the shindig. It was a joyful, religious celebration of a hands on experience from the Lord Himself.

However, the greatest of summer buzzes, and one in which the headiest of anticipations were met in full, was the stunning live debut of "Highlands" on 25th June. This was why I was repeatedly copying the CDs for friends. It is hard to describe the excitement amongst Dylan fans when we heard he'd done this song, though this excitement, it must be said, was tinged with a fear that he'd not do it justice. Many of us have never recovered from hearing that he had sung "Brownsville Girl" in 1986 only to discover on playing it that although he had indeed sung "Brownsville Girl' a few more of the words would not have gone amiss!

There were no such problems with "Highlands" on 25th June. Anchored to a steady beat Dylan sang it with panache and, praise be, he remembered the lyrics!

The song is a bit jauntier than that on the album, the humour and the fun elements more stressed. The "Neil Young" verse and the superb waitress interlude were very effective (well they are on the studio track too but they stood out even more here). All in all it was fabulous – "worth all of 1998 on its own" was my immediate, perhaps exaggerated, reaction.

After a break, September saw Dylan continuing to tour with Simon for another 10 dates. It was more of the same with the most surprising song selection being a one-off cover of Dwight Yoakam's, "The Heart That You Own" on September 2nd, at West Palm Beach, Florida.

Dylan was far from finished yet with 1999. After another short break he resumed touring in October sharing the bill with Phil Lesh. Yes, the world famous Phil Lesh, if you are wondering who he is, think ex-Grateful Dead bassist. Think then on Lesh being so much more popular than Dylan that he would end up headlining the shows. It speaks volumes for the pulling power of the Dead's surviving members, and of the diminished appeal Dylan's non-stop touring had led to. *The Worcester Phoenix*'s concert previewer was gob-smacked. "Hey, we like Bob Dylan just as much as the next lopheaded freak, right on up to on *Time Out Of Mind*. But lately we're starting to wonder about the crowd he's hanging with. First there was his cameo on *Dharma & Greg*. C'mon – 30 years of reclusiveness and the guy comes out of his shell for these retards? And now he shows up on tour with that dreaded spectre of post Grate-ful death, Phil Lesh. And Friends. Wooga. Choke us with an ankh, but we'll wait for the VH1 Special."

Notwithstanding the validity of these catty remarks, the shows themselves blew any depression out the water. We were in N.E.T. wonderland; you could pick almost any of them and remain impressed. The quality was as consistent as the set lists were full of surprises. Dylan, freed from the restraint of perform-ing greatest hits for the baby boomers, shook things up with ever changing set-lists and arrangements. It was a rewarding time for those who follow the tour night after night.

For example, on the 8th November at Baltimore the set included: (acous-tically) "I Am The Man, Thomas", "Mr. Tambourine Man", "Visions Of Johanna", "Ring Them Bells", (electrically) "Big River", "Joey", "Down Along The Cove", "Man In The Long Black Coat" and "Tombstone Blues" amongst others. The following night had none of these but did boast (as well as an extended encore) (acoustically) "Hallelujah, I'm Ready To Go", "The Lone-some Death Of Hattie Carroll", "Boots Of Spanish Leather", "A Satisfied Mind", "Mama, You Been On My Mind", (electrically) "Folsom Prison Blues", "Man Of Peace", "I'll Be Your Baby Tonight" and "Shooting Star" amongst others.

On 26th October Dylan played another small club gig at Atlantic City; two shortened sets in the one night, announced only a few days prior to the event. The two sets augured well for the upcoming leg with Phil Lesh. Even songs like "Tombstone Blues" and a differently paced "Like A Rolling Stone" ben-efited from a freshness and renewal of energy. You know when a throwaway song like "Everything Is Broken" is enjoyable that Bob is really on song. After the October Atlantic City shows, the next I heard was 13th November, East Rutherford. I played these tapes repeatedly. Half a dozen of East Rutherford's finest tracks were put on the official web-site in the year 2000 (and remain there at the time of writing). Both shows featured warm, avuncular stabs at "Visions Of Johanna". You could tell when he drew out the line endings it was to please the crowd; this was not the incandescent "wild mercury" perform-ance of *Blonde On Blonde*, after all it would be odd if he still sang lines like "the ghost of electricity howls in the bones of her face" exactly as he did then.

In the month or so following, we had a run of consistently high standard affairs. As ever during good spells of the N.E.T., there were interesting covers and oddities, including five cover debuts ("A Satisfied Mind", "Hoochie Coochie Man", "Money Honey", "Duncan and Brady" and "This World Can't Stand Too Long") and a stellar outing for Johnny Cash's "Big River". This last was on the 8th at Baltimore where Bob paid his dues near Miss Mary's house with a notable performance. This was a show I quickly fell in love with. All the good elements of this run were in place for a night that found Dylan and the band in top form from beginning to end. Then more shows came in from November, and I was listening to whole shows again. The Baltimore show remained my favourite but listening to the 3rd of November I had to question whether my preference was swayed by the intrusive crowd noise on the tape of the 3rd. Dylan's heartfelt singing in the opening acoustic numbers had to com-pete with loud shouts, talking and, of all things, repeated attempts by someone to cry "Woof! Woof"". In an attempt to draw attention to what he was laying down, Dylan addressed he crowd: "We're gonna slow it down just a little a bit...". Unfortunately his attempt to make them pay attention was fruitless. So the Baltimore show remained my most played but the important point was the non-stop, high standard of these shows; the seventh and ninth that surrounded my Baltimore choice could make loud and long claims for being the best... and so it could go on.

The band and lead singer pulled out all the stops night after night, and not just on the covers and "oddities". Dylan songs from throughout his career were showcased to great effect. Stand-out performances included; "Ring Them Bells", "My Back Pages" (repeatedly), "Highlands" (at Worcester on the 14th), "Senor", "To Be Alone With You" and so on. The band sounded better than they had in goodness knows how long too, especially with Sexton's presence really beginning to tell. Effective harmony singing on "Tears Of Rage" spoke of a team working in, well in, harmony.

For all the splendours of earlier in the year, this last leg was the most consist-ently triumphant. By the time he brought the year's touring to an end with an extended set on November the 20th, he had played 121 shows – the most in his entire career.

It had been a very good year, the best since '95. While it never reached the heights of the best of that year's Spring shows, it was also more consistent, in that it did not include as embarrassingly a poor leg as the one on which '95 sadly ended.

Chapter Sixteen: Millennium

It's As Natural To Me As Breathing.

"A lot of people don't like the road, but it's as natural to me as breathing. I do it because I'm driven to do it, and I either hate it or love it. I'm mortified to be on the stage, but then again, it's the only place where I'm happy. It's the only place you can be who you want to be."

Bob Dylan, 1997

When I began this book the plan was to draw it to a close at the end of the Millennium. However, with the Never Ending Tour, the road goes ever on and on. I asked myself, why stop at the end of one particular year? Perhaps I was worried that 2000 would be a disappointment after 1999's many highs, and that the book would end in anti-climax.

After all, good years are often followed by dodgy ones. Oh, me of little faith!

The start of post-Millennial touring involved two sets in Anaheim. The first, on March 10th, included lots of surprising song selections, a tight band and Dylan in great and authoritative voice, willing to radically experiment (the re-worked "Dignity", for example) and – once again – reinventing his back pages.

The biggest surprise was the first live performance of "Tell Me That It Isn't True" since it appeared on *Nashville Skyline* at the end of the 1960s. Brilliantly sung, it was the standout song in a remarkably strong set. The following show at the same venue featured the almost equally unexpected "We Better Talk This Over". However, unlike "Tell Me That It Isn't True" this was not an entirely successful version and has not been played again.

This awesome opening show kicked off a spring tour packed with highlights. Overall, however, the shows could not maintain the consistent high standards of Anaheim. As the weeks passed, I found myself drifting back to compilations rather than complete shows. The further the year progressed the more this was the case.

I mentioned in the chapter on 1997 that Dylan had to develop a way of performing that allowed him to put on around one hundred shows a year without ruining his voice and (following his illness) his lungs. One way to do this was to pace himself; to hold back from giving his all on every song, every night. He didn't stop trying, but he came to rely on an increasingly polished band to help him put on a good show even when he was not entirely on top of his own game. Rather than the more extreme variance of the earlier N.E.T. years, when Dylan's performance seemed to be a mirror of his mood of the moment, we have now had years of consistently "fine" shows. I say consistently fine because that is how the press and most fans I talk to see it. Other than at certain times (especially in parts of 1999), I am not so convinced.

To me Dylan is often coasting, "fine" though he sounds. He achieves this by over-burring his "r"s for a strong, masculine tone and extending the "i" sounds for a light, feminine touch. He drags out vowel line endings in a parody of his Blonde On Blonde vocals, with inevitable crowd pleasing results. All the other switches he flicks to get Pavlovian responses from the aisles – as mentioned in the chapter on 1998 – are still present too.

When he is fully engaged all the above devices sound and *feel* genuine – because they *are*; because he has entered into the song and, until he brings it to a close and snaps back out of it, he projects the song out to the lucky recipients.

Shows have come to seem to me either "good" or "bad" (I am judging by Dylan's own high standards here) depending on how much "coasting" they have in them. Obviously the ones like Anaheim on the 10th where I feel he is totally switched on throughout the night, his vocals fully engaged, are my very favourites. Other nights range from me liking most of the songs to only liking a few; on the occasional bad night I feel he never gets into it at all.

A lot of these feelings were clarified for me as I wrote this book and listened and re-listened to so many shows. They came to a head just before I finished it, in the Autumn of 2000 during yet another European tour. Earlier in the year Dylan had once again toured Germany and I had originally intended to close this book with a review of the show I first attended in 2000, in Cologne.

Cologne, May 11, 2000
Kölnarena, Cologne, Germany

1.   Roving Gambler (acoustic)
2.   The Times They Are A-Changin' (acoustic)
3.   It's Alright, Ma (I'm Only Bleeding) (acoustic)
4.   Mr. Tambourine Man (acoustic)
5.   Tangled Up In Blue (acoustic)
6.   Gates Of Eden (acoustic)
7.   Country Pie
8.   Things Have Changed
9.   Down Along The Cove
10.   Every Grain Of Sand
11.   Cold Irons Bound
12.   Leopard-Skin Pill-Box Hat

13.   Love Sick
        *
14.   Like A Rolling Stone
15.   Forever Young (acoustic)
16.   Not Fade Away
17.   Don't Think Twice, It's All Right (acoustic)
18.   Rainy Day Women #12 & #35

Bob opened with a so-so "Roving Gambler", though he looked fabulous. "The Times They Are A-Changin'" was next and to begin with, the lyrics were all over the place. I suddenly saw Dylan with extreme clarity. He was sweating heavily and all of a sudden, he looked terribly frail. Nonetheless, he sorted the song out, and his voice began opening up. We even got the right words for the second half of the song. It was quite affecting.

Most noticeable to me was the crystal clear sound. It was years since I had heard Dylan's singing so clearly via the sound system. The difference this makes is startling; and it also puts him under a much more intense spotlight in that you know for sure now when he's fluffing because you can hear everything. You also know when it is a beautifully modulated aside rather than a fluff. With the harmonica solos you know almost instantly whether it's the real thing or just "silly old Bob on stage, hamming it up for the fans".

Another huge change was that Dylan was restricting his guitar playing to the odd stab. This was great for two reasons. Firstly, it allowed the band to play and marked the end of long pointless Dead-like jams. Instead, we got real music played by craftsmen taking pride in their jobs. Sexton was exceptional and Kemper, Campbell and yes, even Tony, were more than satisfactory. Secondly, it allowed Dylan to concentrate on his singing, as evidenced by a riveting "It's Alright, Ma (I'm Only Bleeding)". Things were looking up for a good show when a fine "Mr. Tambourine Man" found Dylan's soaring voice move me to tears.

The highlight of the whole night was then presented in the form of an extraordinary "Gates Of Eden". After a brief wrestle with his guitar, Dylan stopped playing, making way for a Prague '95-type delivery. This time there was an added piquant twist: as Bob crooned a delicious and involved reading into the mic, he kept hold of the guitar neck with his right hand and used it to punctuate his delivery. It was magical. A bit like the crossed arms at the wrists delivery of "Isis" in Rolling Thunder days. I was in Heaven, far less Eden.

"Country Pie" was fun, if limited, while "Things Have Changed" was streets ahead of the studio version, he really sang it so well. An enjoyable "Down Along The Cove" poured over the audience in wave after wave of sound, building and building to a climax that seemed never to come. Then the mood changed again for the other highlight of the night, a passionate, crafted "Every Grain Of Sand".

After that, my interest faded: a female fan (Lola) was onstage with an *acoustic* guitar, not that you could hear her at all, playing on a dire "Like A Rolling

Stone". The rest of the electric songs were just party animals but "Forever Young" was moving and "Don't Think Twice, It's Alright" was magnificent.

This would have been an ideal stopping place for this book; with me on a high after the Cologne show. Yet it would not have been a fair representation. The next night at Hanover was not nearly as good – it was a terrible hall acoustically and Dylan kept forgetting lyrics and mumbling half lines to disguise the fact. On the other hand, it had a very lovely "Tomorrow's A Long Time" and a pretty fine "Ring Them Bells". Plus, "Like A Rolling Stone" was much better than in Cologne and – of all things – there was a driving "Leopard-Skin Pill-Box Hat" with tour-de-force harmonica playing. Most songs other than these were only partial successes; "It Ain't Me, Babe", for example, had one great verse, and "Tombstone Blues" started horribly but ended well.

If the concerts had happened the other way round, it would have been the excitement of Cologne that lingered in my mind, rather than the disappointment of Hanover. Of the concerts I had personally attended, Hanover was probably better than any I was at from 1996 to 1998. It was because Cologne was so special that Hanover seemed a bit of a letdown.

As it transpired, Cologne was partially a fluke – benefiting from technical problems with Dylan's guitar. Guitar playing was not his forte this year, whereas his singing and harmonica playing were great. For reasons quintessentially Dylanic, as the year advanced, he played more and more guitar – more and more eccentrically. Larry Campbell and Charlie Sexton would stand around idly while Dylan took the leads.

With US and European tours already behind him, Dylan was not for slowing up. Back to the States he went to tour with Phil Lesh again, before returning for another European jaunt, this time taking in a number of gigs in the UK that were rapturously received by the majority of fans and press. To me they were a mixture of the detached Dylan putting on a show and the genuine spine-tingling excitement of Dylan really getting into it. Most (like the Portsmouth shows) were a fairly even mixture; others tended to one extreme. Sheffield was an example of Dylan at his most detached while the following show at Cardiff found him at his most engaged. Not that the reception Dylan received varied with the quality. He gets the same reception in the UK whatever he does. I was very disappointed after the Sheffield show but found, on leaving the arena, that most people were enthusing wildly about it. I began to wonder if I'd been at the same show as everyone else. I did eventually hear some comments that were more in line with my own views, Michael Gray being as deflated by the show as I was, and Clinton Heylin dismissing it as the worst Dylan show he'd ever seen. The much travelled, many hundred show man, Andrew Goldstein, concluded simply that "it sucked". Still many others saw it as a triumph.

In stark contrast, at the next show in Cardiff Dylan was fully engaged throughout. The overall consistency of the show was remarkable. The "Ballad of Frankie Lee and Judas Priest" was just brilliant: that knowing voice, with no backing, drew us in until we were completely mesmerised.

This is what ensures the N.E.T. remains an engrossing and exhilarating experience. Dylan, the great live experimenter performing one of his most loved songs with a completely different arrangement. All my disappointments at Dylan's "coasting" are made irrelevant by moments like these. Though much derided by casual fans, and certain critics, this constant recreation is his strength rather than a weakness.

As *The Herald*'s Ian Bell put it:

"Had he been a jazz musician no-one would think twice that he takes old songs and breathes new, startling life into them...

"...there is an aspect to all this that appears to elude most commentators on Dylan's work. The idea of him as a poet of the page was never plausible. Listen to him shape the phrasing of something like 'Rolling Stone' or 'It Ain't Me, Babe', however, and you realise that a performance is never the same twice, never final and perfected – is the very point. the end in itself. Is any production of a play ever definitive? Is there only one way to perform Brahms? Dylan, playing in the same league, appears to think not."

This acute insight stands in stark contrast to an e-mail sent to www.bobdylan.com after Dylan's Santa Cruz shows in 2000. This correspondent asked for a refund on the basis that Dylan had not played enough "hits" and that when he had performed familiar material, the arrangements had been so altered from the original that this poor audience member could not "recognize and sing along to the songs of his youth". Ian Bell, in the same piece, had anticipated and rebutted such nonsense with these words:

"...the ever-changing arrangements, long his habit in any case, are also part of the argument over ownership... Dylan was challenging the audience even to attempt to 'sing along' with songs they thought they knew. As a believer in corporal punishment for lachrymose community singing, this writer, for one, owes him a debt."

This writer makes it two. Dylan is well aware of the problem his performing style has for a portion of his audience. In the Hilburn interview quoted in earlier chapters (post Madison show, November 1991 – published 1992) it is a problem he views as being mainly consigned to the past:

"Older people – my age – don't come out anymore," he says. "A lot of the shows over the years was people coming out of curiosity and their curiosity wasn't fulfilled. They weren't transported back to the '60s. Lightning didn't strike. The shows didn't make sense for them, and they didn't make sense for me. That had to stop, and it took a long time to stop it. A lot of people were coming out to see The Legend, and I was trying to just get on stage and play music."

Cardiff was also one of many shows to feature the new arrangement of "Trying To Get To Heaven". Another song from *Time Out Of Mind*, the much lesser "Cold Irons Bound" was given just as experimental a reworking. In this case, the reworking involved replacing its near non-existent melody with something Lou Reed would have cavilled at including on *Metal Machine Music*. If the magical spell of "Trying To Get To Heaven" had to be broken for the show to continue, this dissonant blare and Dylan's swaggering vocals sure broke it. It was good to see him still experimenting with the *Time Out Of Mind* songs.

There were too many highlights to recount; but special mention should be made of two distinctly different (but both triumphant) outings for "Fourth Time Around". After an exhilarating electric interpretation at Portsmouth (the first time that both it and "Visions Of Johanna" had been played in the UK since the legendary 1966 shows) it appeared in acoustic guise at Wembley. There it was sung with tenderness that evinced a different kind of life-knowledge than that which infused the gorgeous, incomparable *Blonde on Blonde* version.

On a less elevated level, the nutty side of Dylan's onstage remarks also was well represented by a rambling speech at Wembley about Churchill and Britain standing alone during WWII. Doubtless prompted by the backstage gift of a book about London's East End during the Blitz, this one is worth filing alongside previous statements that "Hitler was not a German" and "I'm descended from Vikings" from Hamburg and Oslo respectively.

Meanwhile, set lists continued to change and included more than a few surprises. Anything seemed possible. Dylan writer John Stokes even mused, on our way to Portsmouth, that maybe he'd get to hear his all time number one concert wish – "If Dogs Run Free". This completely untypical song (from *New Morning* some 30 years previously) replete with scat singing no less, seemed to me to be just about the most unlikely performance choice imaginable. I confidently stated on September 24th that "If we live to be a million, he'll never play that song." No-one was likely to disagree – except Dylan. It debuted a week later in Munster, Germany. I saw it at Paris on October 3rd. The last live show, so far, on my own Never Ending Tour. It was a splendid show and a good night out. It was mostly high energy with Sexton's guitar more prominent than it had been earlier in this European leg – but also laced with impressive readings of "Standing In The Doorway" and "Trying To Get To Heaven". As fitting a place as any to draw breath and some conclusions on the wall in an attempt to answer the most commonly posed question of the N.E.T.. Namely *"Why does he do it?"*

***

Earlier in these pages Gregory Peck said of Dylan, "He is surprises and disguises; he is a searcher with his songs. In him we hear the echo of old American voices: Whitman and Mark Twain, blues singers, fiddlers and balladeers. Bob Dylan's voice reaches just as high and will linger just as long."

These well chosen lines encapsulate the twin Romantic views of Dylan on the N.E.T. He is seen as a physical and artistic embodiment of one of the main strands of the American Literary tradition – still out "on the road", restlessly searching for some higher truth. Alternatively – or simultaneously – N.E.T. Dylan is the troubadour, in the great oral tradition of Woody Guthrie, Hank Williams, Robert Johnson and the cast of Greil Marcus's *Invisible Republic*.[84]

It is an enticing image, bolstered by the fact that Dylan keeps on travelling and touring and by Dylan's repeated comments on how much he enjoys playing on stage, as well as his avowed insights into what the covers he is playing mean to him:

"I love that whole pantheon. To me there's no difference between Muddy Waters and Bill Monro... Those old songs are my lexicon and my prayer book.

"All my beliefs come out of those old songs, literally, anything from 'Let Me Rest on That Peaceful Mountain' to 'Keep On The Sunny Side.' You can find all my philosophy in those old songs. I believe in a God of time and space, but if people ask me about that, my impulse is to point them back toward those songs. I believe in Hank Williams singing 'I Saw The Light.' I've seen the light, too." [85]

Occasionally, Dylan seems attracted to a romantic view of touring; in one of his many responses to the question "why do you keep touring?", he declared how appealing it was to see the sunrise over a new road every morning.

Combining the two Romantic views of Dylan on tour, the entire N.E.T. experience can be seen as a vehicle akin to Mark Twain's Mississippi raft – on which Huck Finn and Jim drifted downstream, uncompromised by the "civilising" effects of settled society on the land either side. Or you can see the N.E.T. convoy as Herman Melville's Pequod, with Dylan at the helm, separated from home and family; though the white whale Dylan is determined to chase and slay is his own myth.

Many years before the N.E.T., Dylan had alluded to both Twain and Melville at different times. Interestingly, this was at a time when he returned to touring after a lengthy absence. Certainly he saw the N.E.T. as a way of dispensing with his own myth: "It was important for me to come to the bottom of this legend thing, which has no reality at all," he said in 1992. "What's important isn't the legend but the art, the work."

Yet one cannot help but recall the amount of times Dylan himself has kept that myth going in the N.E.T. through crazy publicity stunts and stadium appearances with other "icons".

Yet the view of Bob as Ahab or Ethan on a never ending Quest, year after year without respite, does not really add up. For most of the N.E.T., Dylan has spent more time off the road than on it.

Dylan has a more restrained schedule than the travelling bluesmen he is often compared to. "I do about 125 shows a year," he has commented. "It may sound a lot to people who aren't working that much, but it isn't. B.B. King is working 350 nights a year." Dylan may overestimate B.B. King's gigs per year here but his overall contrast is valid. King usually plays at least twice as many shows a year as Dylan does.

As he acknowledged in the notes to *Planet Waves*, like Huck Finn, the younger Dylan "lit out for parts unknown"[sic]. Now Dylan retraces his steps year after year. Yet Bob's adherence to touring doesn't make him a Romantic Kerouac figure. After 1966 he stopped touring to be with his family. In 1974 he toured again after the lay-off. The Rolling Thunder Revue tours of 1975 and 1976 were specifically an attempt to root his psyche in the Romantic Artist/Genius/Travelling Minstrel carrier of the American Dream locale. It ended up in divorce and born again Christianity.

Dylan knows such traditions inside out in both a personal and artistic sense. He lived it and progressed to the next stage of his life a generation ago. He got to a stage when he could see Sara and continue to be a father to his children. He even finally got to the stage where he toured precisely as he wanted to – the N.E.T...

Obviously, the N.E.T. as a stirring, mythic quest would be a wonderfully uplifting note on which to end my book but it would also be a cop out, as it offers only a partial truth. It is only one of the many categories critics try and force the whole concept into, at the other extreme we have the cynical view.

The cynics portray Dylan as a different kind of fictional character, a far-less attractive Huck Finn, who rather than being admirably unsullied by civilisation, simply doesn't want to grow up. Instead of a Romantic hero we have a grown man playing at "Peter Pan", using the N.E.T to avoid responsibility and as a substitute for lasting relationships.

In fact, closer examination shows Dylan's life is actually far more balanced than this theory suggests. Away from the N.E.T. for half the year, Dylan can spend his time in any way he wants. The children he had with Sara are all grown up, he is not avoiding them. As far as I know he spends much of the Thanksgiving to January holiday periods with as many of them as as possible (often with Sara). Dylan has a private life; he has a family. Dylan "grew up" and accepted his responsibilities a long, long time ago. He takes his responsibilities as a father more seriously than anything else; it's one of the reasons he has toured so much more after his children had grown up.

Another charge levelled at Dylan's N.E.T. is that he does it because he has nothing else; he is "trapped" on the road because he hasn't a clue what to do if he stops. Occasionally Dylan himself will give this theory a boost as, unsurprisingly, given that he views the N.E.T. as his "trade", his "job", he sometimes tires of it. At worst he feels that his "job" – as perhaps we all do ours from time to time – to be nothing more than the mundane routine. Some even take the rather inelegant lines (in the otherwise assured) "Highlands" from *Time Out Of Mind* autobiographically:

> *"Woke up this morning and I looked at the same old page,*
> *Same ol' rat race, life in the same ol' cage".*

Dylan himself may wistfully dream of an alternate life – "I would prefer to start my life anew over and over again. Learn a new trade, marry another girl, live in another place." (1997)[86] – yet these are just natural sentiments. To make out of them a case for Dylan being chained to a life he hates is to ignore a whole swathe of countering points. Undoubtedly the N.E.T. pays Dylan well, allegedly commanding some $50,000 per show and playing over a hundred of them a year plus festivals, he makes a fortune from it, but Dylan doesn't need the money. He could stop whenever he wanted. (Apart from all his other income he could make money by the occasional show – like the three-song mega-grossing Pope bash, by releasing old or new songs, by putting out a book, doing a movie cameo, etc. etc. (I haven't even mentioned selling a few copyrights to advertisers).

So, if the N.E.T. was *only* a grind why would he keep doing it? The point is that it is much more than that. Yes, Dylan views it as his "trade" but as he has pointed out many times, it's a trade he still loves carrying out:

"There's a certain part of you that becomes addicted to a live audience. I wouldn't keep doing it if I was tired of it." (1997)

The final "charge" against the N.E.T. by those who seem determined to find a sinister explanation for it, is that Dylan is only performing so much because he can no longer write songs and produce albums.

Certainly Dylan has written little in the many years of the N.E.T. compared to the prolific days of his youth. (It may be worth remembering that *Oh Mercy*, *under the red sky* and *Time Out Of Mind*, along with the second Travelling Wilburys album, have come out, however.) Dylan has mentioned in interviews that writing has become more difficult for him, that the flow of songs has been reduced to (comparatively) a trickle.

He has also intimated that he no longer feels motivated to finish many of the songs he starts. It is not something that he sees as particularly important any more; in 1991 he told *Song Talk*:

"The world don't need any more songs. They've got enough. They've got way too many. As a matter of fact, if nobody wrote any songs from this day on, the world ain't gonna suffer for it....The world don't need any more poems, it's got Shakespeare."

It is also surely normal for a creative artist to produce less in his 50s than in his 20s and 30s. I know there are one or two exceptions to this rule – but that's exactly what they are, exceptions. The miracle is the amount Dylan has produced rather than the relative lack of new material in later life. In addition we are not in a position to know how many songs he has written. He intimated in 1998 that he had written "a bunch of songs" since *Time Out Of Mind* (with a similar sparseness of tone, apparently) and implied they'd be coming out. We still await them but this may not be due to Dylan "drying up", it could just be the fact that his long held antipathy to recording studios has increased the more digitized they have become.

"Yeah. The recording process is very difficult for me. I lose my inspiration in the studio real easy, and it's very difficult for me to think that I'm going to eclipse anything I've ever done before. I get bored easily, and my mission, which starts out wide, becomes very dim after a few failed takes and this and that." [87]

Dylan often contrasts the falseness of trying to create in the studio with the natural feeling of conceiving new art on stage. This seems more like an artist knowing exactly what he wants rather than someone being 'forced' into touring because he cannot do anything else.

I am not claiming that all the theories above hold no validity whatsoever – though at best they are very partial views, propounded by people who are only pretending that they know Dylan's mind – and they will hold more truth than at others. Even if one acknowledges that Dylan seems no longer capable (or interested) in writing as many new songs as he used to, there is no need to jump to the conclusion that therefore he must tour. He could do anything he wanted; luckily for us he wants to perform.

I am not claiming that I can read his mind any more than any other commentator, but some straightforward points can be made and Dylan's own comments taken into account. For starters, I do not think it is reasonable to expect that Dylan's motivations for, and feelings towards, the N.E.T. are going to have remained the same day in day out since 1988. Some fluctuation is surely inevitable; in addition there's nothing to stop contradictory reasons being at work simultaneously. In Dylan's art and career, contradictory states often hold the greatest truths.

When introducing Dylan at the 1991 Grammy Awards, Jack Nicholson said that he had searched the dictionary for the 'fairest word' to describe Dylan. He chose acutely, deciding on "paradox" because it meant: "A statement seemingly self-contradictory but in reality possibly expressing a truth". More prosaically Dylan sees himself as "inconsistent":

"That's just the nature of my personality," he says. "I can be jubilant one moment and pensive the next, and a cloud could go by and make that happen. I'm inconsistent, even to myself."[88] Notwithstanding paradox and inconsistency, it is easy to propose a more balanced view than the extreme Romantic and Cynic positions discussed above. A view based on Dylan's own comments and the facts we can be sure of rather than on speculation about Dylan's personal life and current mindset.

From the first year of the Never Ending Tour onwards, Dylan has equated his touring with day-to-day work rather than the Romantic, beat-style existence. Speaking near the beginning of the N.E.T. he said,

"There's just something instinctive that tells me that a man must support his family, no matter what. As it is, I'm doing what I do because I've been given to do it, but most of the people who work 9 to 5 have got to support families, and I've a tremendous regard for that. You don't see much of that being heralded with heroic words and fancy awards. But that's what makes the world either rise or fall, that commitment to family." [89]

It is a theme he has returned to; he sees himself as doing his job, his trade, his craft. It is, simply, what he does. This was the same interview in which he succinctly answered all these questions about touring by saying, "*We want to play because we want to play.*"

Paradoxes become resolved in the Dylan experience. What seems complicated comes down to those simple oft-repeated but just as oft-ignored, truths. He has even told us how this happens:

"A lot of people don't like the road, but it's as natural to me as breathing. I do it because I'm driven to do it, and I either hate it or love it. I'm mortified to be on the stage, but then again, it's the only place where I'm happy. It's the only place you can be who you want to be. You can't be who you want to be in daily life. I don't care who you are, you're going to be disappointed in daily life. But the cure-all for all that is to get on the stage, and that's why performers do it. But in saying that, I don't want to put on the mask of celebrity. I'd rather just do my work and see it as a trade."[90]

In a nutshell, as he wrote in *Blood On the Tracks'* "Buckets Of Rain":

"Life is sad
Life is a bust
All ya can do is do what you must
You do what you must do and ya do it well. "

Finally, – to turn the question around – why shouldn't Dylan be touring? What is so surprising about him practising his particular trade? Out of which we get the munificent bounty that is the N.E.T.; we get the greatest artist of his time going out year after year recreating his magic in front of our very eyes and ears. Far from the ceaseless re-working of his old songs being a sign of loss of artistic creativity, it is the very centre and expression of his art. The refusal to take the easy option and just sing the songs the same way time after time is borne out of his inherent understanding that the core of his art is the never ending challenge of the new performance, the nightly ritual where:

"Well I'm living in a foreign country, but I'm bound to cross the line
Beauty walks a razor's edge, someday I'll make it mine. "

***

As I have been typing this book, Dylan followed his European 2000 leg with another Fall Tour in the States. By the time this reaches the shops he'll have started the fourteenth year of the N.E.T.; starting in Japan and expected to continue on to Australia and America. I just happen to have in my possession a flight ticket to any British Airways destination in the world. Wonder if he'll play anything new?

Appendix

Statistics From The Never-Ending Tour

by Olöf Björner

Introduction

1. Tour Overview
The Never-Ending Tour so far consists of no less than 1277 shows during 13 years!

Year	Leg	Name	# of shows	Time
1988	1	Interstate 88	71	June-October
1989	1	Summer Tour of Europe	21	May-June
	2	US Summer Tour	51	July-September
	3	US Fall Tour	27	October-November
1990	1	The Fastbreak Tour	15	January, February
	2	Spring Tour Of North America	16	May-June
	3	The Summer Festival Tour of Europe	9	June-July
	4	Late Summer Tour of North America	23	August-September
	5	US Fall Tour	30	October-November
1991	1	The Second Fastbreak Tour	21	January-March
	2	US Spring Tour	17	April-May
	3	Summer Tour Of Europe	18	June
	4	Summer Tour Of North America	15	July
	5	South America Tour	9	August
	6	US Fall Tour	21	October-November
1992	1	Tour Of Australia	20	March-April
	2	West Coast Spring Tour	21	April-May
	3	Summer Festival Tour Of Europe	11	June-July
	4	Late Summer Tour Of North America	20	August-September
	5	US Fall Tour	20	October-November
1993	1	Winter Tour Of Europe	15	February
	2	US Spring Tour	9	April
	3	Mediterranean Tour	21	June-July
	4	US Fall Tour With Santana	31	August-October
	5	Supper Club Dates	4	November
1994	1	Far East Tour	14	February
	2	US Spring Tour	25	April-May
	3	Summer Tour of Europe	17	July
	4	US Summer Tour	15	August
	5	US Fall Tour	33	October- November
1995	1	Winter Tour of Europe	26	March-April
	2	US Spring Tour	29	May-June
	3	Summer Tour of Europe	19	June-July

	4	Fall Classics Tour	32	September-November
	5	Paradise Lost Tour	10	December
1996	0	Private Gig	1	February
	1	Spring Tour of North America	27	April-May
	2	Summer Tour of Europe	28	June-July
	3	The Olympic Games Shows	2	August
	4	US Fall Tour	28	October-November
1997	1	Tour of Japan	11	February
	2	Spring Tour of North America	25	March-May
	3	US Summer Tour	22	August
1998	1	US Winter Tour	21	January - February
	2	South America Tour w/The Rolling Stones	8	March - April
	3	US and Canada West Coast Tour		
		w/ Joni Mitchell and Van Morrison	8	May
	4	Europe Summer Tour	33	May - July
	5	Tour Of Australia And New Zealand	15	August - September
	6	US West Coast Tour With Van Morrison	8	September
	7	US And Canada Fall Tour	17	October - November
1999	1	US Winter Tour	28	January - March
	2	Europe Spring Tour	21	April - May
	3	US Summer Tour with Paul Simon	38	June - July
	4	US Fall Tour with Paul Simon	10	September
	5	US Fall Tour with Phil Lesh	22	October - November
2000	1	US Spring Tour	25	March - April
	2	Europe Spring Tour	19	May - June
	3	US Summer Tour with Phil Lesh & Friends	33	June - July
	4	Europe Fall Tour with Paul Simon	18	September - October
	5	US Fall Tour with Phil Lesh	17	October - November

The statistics presented here include all shows on the NET. The following shows are not considered to be part of the tour:

1988	New York City	January 20	Hotel Waldorf-Astoria,	Rock And Roll Hall Of Fame Induction Ceremony
	New York City	May 29	Lone Star Café	Guest appearance at a Levon Helm concert.
	Oakland	December 4	Oakland Coliseum	Second Bridge School Benefit Concert.
1989	Los Angeles	February 12	The Forum, Inglewood	Guest appearance at a Grateful Dead concert.
	Los Angeles	September 24	L'Chaim To Life	Telethon '89
1990	Los Angeles	February 24	Universal Amphitheater,	Roy Orbison Tribute
	Los Angeles	March 1	The Forum, Inglewood	Guest appearance at a Tom Petty concert
1991	New York City	February 20	Radio City Music Hall	Grammy Awards Ceremony
	Milan	June 9	Arena di Milano	Guest at Van Morrison's opening concert.
	Los Angeles	September 15	Chabad TV Studio	L'Chaim To Life, Telethon '91
	Seville	17 October	Auditorio de la Cartuja	Leyendas de la Guitarra
1992	New York City	January 18	Radio City Music Hall	Letterman 10th Year Show Taping
	New York City	October 16	Madison Square Garden,	30th Anniversary Concert
1993	Washington	January 17	Lincoln Memorial	Bill Clinton Inaugural Concert
	Washington	January 17	Blue Jean Club	Blue Jeans Bash
	Dublin	February 6	The Point Depot	Guesting Van Morrison
	Austin	April 28	Austin City TV Studio	Willie Nelson's 60th Birthday Bash: Big Six-O
	New York City	November 19	CBS TV Studio	David Letterman
1994	Los Angeles	March 23	Universal Amphitheater	The Rhythm Country & Blues Concert
	Nara	May 20-22	Todaiji Temple	The Great Music Experience
	New York City	October 17	Madison Square Garden	Guesting a Grateful Dead concert.
	New York City	November 17-18	Sony Music Studios	MTV Unplugged taping sessions
1995	Montpelier	July 27	Espace Grammont	Guesting The Rolling Stones
	Cleveland	2 September	Cleveland Stadium	Opening of the Rock & Roll Hall Of Fame Museum
	Los Angeles	November 19	Shrine Auditorium	Frank Sinatra 80th Year Tribute concert.
1997	Los Angeles	May 22	Beverly Hilton Hotel	Simon Wiesenthal Center benefit dinner.
	Bologna	27 September		World Eucharistic Congress
1998	New York City	25 February	Radio City Music Hall	40th Annual Grammy Awards
1999	New York City	30 June 1999	Madison Square Garden	Eric Clapton & Friends Benefit, Crossroads Centre

The following concerts are included:

1990	New Haven	12 January	The legendary four set gig at Toad's Place
1993	New York City	16-17 November	The Supper Club, 4 shows
1996	Phoenix	2 February	The Pavilion, Biltmore Hotel, Private event sponsored by Nomura Securities

Atlanta	3-4 August	The Olympic Games shows
1999	Summer	All duets with Paul Simon & his band

Sound checks and rehearsals are not included.

2 Show summary 1988-2000

	Σ	88	89	90	91	92	93	94	95	96	97	98	99	00
Shows:														
Total	1277	71	99	93	101	92	80	104	116	86	94	110	119	112
Circulating	1254	71	99	93	85	91	80	100	116	84	94	110	119	112
Circulating & comp.	1249	71	98	93	82	91	80	99	116	84	94	110	119	112
Unique	1271	71	98	92	99	91	80	103	116	86	94	110	119	112
Different	1271	71	98	92	99	91	80	103	116	86	94	110	119	112
Songs:														
Different	419	92	136	163	129	123	86	78	101	99	103	104	125	126
Unique	318	86	122	134	110	104	78	77	100	94	101	102	124	126
Performed, total	20516	1118	1614	1809	1796	1641	1210	1472	1684	1256	1417	1678	1827	1994
Performed, mean	16	15	16	19	18	17	15	14	14	14	15	15	15	17
Variation		5.8	8.3	8.4	7.3	6.9	5.7	5.5	7.0	6.8	6.9	6.9	8.1	7.1

Notes
1 a show is unique if no other show has the same songs in the same order.
2 a show is different from another show if the set of songs are different, regardless of order
3 electric and acoustic versions are counted as different songs
4 a song is counted as unique regardless of how it is performed
5 variation is computed as the quote between number of different songs and mean number of performed songs

3 Song statistics
3.1 Alphabetical song listing

Types

AB	acoustic with the band
AC	acoustic, solo or with one other guitarist
AE	starts acoustic ends electric
IN	instrumental
6	Vocal by Doug Sahm.

Song		88	89	90	91	92	93	94	95	96	97	98	99	00	S
(Sittin' On) The Dock Of The Bay				1											1
10,000 Men														1	1
2 x 2						4									4
20/20 Vision					1										1
Absolutely Sweet Marie	AB						1								1
Absolutely Sweet Marie		21	6	12		27				5	40	29	1		141
Acoustic Jam	AC				1										1
Across The Borderline		1		3	1							1			6
Alabama Getaway									29	43	7	1	3		83
All Along The Watchtower		39	63	82	89	86	76	104	115	86	38	8	52	40	878
And It Stoned Me			2												2
Answer Me	AB				6										6
Answer Me					1										1
Around And Around						1									1
Baby Let Me Follow Me Down	AC	1	3												4
Ballad Of A Thin Man		27	34	27	47	38	27	47	22	12	7	7	6	12	313
The Ballad Of Frankie Lee And Judas Priest	AB													11	11
The Ballad Of Frankie Lee And Judas Priest		3													3
Ballad Of Hollis Brown	AB			8	3	2		1		7	1	2			24
Ballad Of Hollis Brown	AC	1			1	2									4
Ballad Of Hollis Brown			24	3											27
Barbara Allen	AE		1												1
Barbara Allen	AB			2	2										4
Barbara Allen	AC	24	19	2	7										52
Big River		1											1	1	3
Black Muddy River						3									3
Blackjack Davey	AB					18									18
Blind Willie McTell											17	13	9	7	46

200

Song		88	89	90	91	92	93	94	95	96	97	98	99	00	S
Blood In My Eyes	AB						2								2
Blowin' In The Wind	AB			57	36		1	6		2		66	63	89	320
Blowin' In The Wind	AC	15	16	3	2	51									87
Blue Bonnet Girl	AB													1	1
Blue Moon Of Kentucky	AB												11		11
Blue Moon Of Kentucky													10		10
Bob Dylan's 115th Dream			6												6
Bob Dylan's Dream	AB				28										28
Bob Dylan's Dream	AC				18										18
Boots Of Spanish Leather	AB			16	11	2	21	11	28	10	3	5	9	7	123
Boots Of Spanish Leather	AC	18	20	3		36									77
Born In Time							17	11	6	2	8	9		2	55
The Boxer	AB												5		5
The Boxer													5		5
B-Thang	IN		1												1
Buckets Of Rain				1											1
Can't Wait											31	64	29	11	135
Cat's In The Well						53	37	3	5	3	1		2	6	110
Chimes Of Freedom	AB													3	3
Clean-Cut Kid			1		1										2
Cocaine Blues	AB										29	24	15		68
Cold Irons Bound											32	82	6	22	142
Confidential	AB								1						1
Confidential				3	1	7									11
Congratulations				2	1										3
Country Pie														104	104
Crash On The Levee (Down In The Flood)									88	40	24			11	163
Crazy Love				1											1
Dancing In The Dark				1											1
Dark As A Dungeon	AB			1								1		2	4
Dark As A Dungeon	AC		2	1											3
Dark Eyes	AB								7						7
Dead Man, Dead Man				4											4
Dear Landlord							3							1	4
Delia	AB							1						4	5
Delia							2								2
Desolation Row	AB			28	13	13	9	6	9	7	1	15	19	42	162
Desolation Row	AC					1									1
Detroit City				1											1
Dignity									10					10	20
Disease Of Conceit	AB						2								2
Disease Of Conceit				11	2		2	2	8	4	1				30
Dixie	IN			6	1										7
Dolly Dagger							1								1
Don't Let Your Deal Go Down							6								6
Don't Pity Me				1											1
Don't Think Twice, It's All Right	AB			31	44	27	36	42	35	27	33	33	51	40	399
Don't Think Twice, It's All Right	AC	21	30	3	5	7									66
Don't Think Twice, It's All Right				1											1
Down Along The Cove													4	2	6
Drifter's Escape						12			25	20				38	95
Driftin' Too Far From Shore			13	1											14
Duncan And Brady	AB													47	47
Duncan And Brady													1		1
Dust My Broom					1										1
Early Morning Rain				4	2	2									8
Eileen Aroon	AC	8	3												11
El Paso	IN		2												2
Emotionally Yours							2								2
E-Thang	IN		4												4
Every Grain Of Sand	AC		1												1
Every Grain Of Sand			4	1	9	2	6	3	9	5	1	3	4	5	2	54
Everybody's Movin'			2	2	1										5
Everything Is Broken				27	48	92	39	28	4	2	9	7	2	10	2	270

201

Song		88	89	90	91	92	93	94	95	96	97	98	99	00	S
Farewell To The Gold						1									1
Female Rambling Sailor	AC					6									6
Folsom Prison Blues					11	1	4						2		18
Forever Young	AE	1	1	6											8
Forever Young	AB							4		5	21	51	9	27	117
Forever Young	AC	1													1
Forever Young		2	8	1					1				1		13
Fourth Time Around	AB												5	7	12
Friend Of The Devil	AB									21	19	4	30		74
Friend Of The Devil				5	8	4			1				1		19
Gates Of Eden	AB			28	20	10	16	14	14	3				8	113
Gates Of Eden	AC	5	27	5	1	9									47
Gates Of Eden		8													8
Girl From The North Country	AB			12	21	2	8	4	11	16	5	5	21	24	129
Girl From The North Country	AC	26	16	2	1	8			1						54
The Girl On The Green Briar Shore	AC					2									2
Give My Love To Rose	AE		1												1
Give My Love To Rose	AC	2													2
God Knows					17		18	64	32	11	10		1	2	155
Golden Vanity	AC				3	4									7
Gotta Serve Somebody		7	11	65	88							31	25	7	234
G-Thang	IN		1												1
Had A Dream About You, Baby		4													4
Hallelujah		2													2
Hallelujah, I'm Ready To Go	AB												10	14	24
Happy Birthday	AB											1			1
A Hard Rain's A-Gonna Fall	AB			5	3	7		3	4	3	2	8	11	4	50
A Hard Rain's A-Gonna Fall	AC	22	12	3	1	2									40
Hard Times	AB						30								30
The Harder They Come			4												4
A Hazy Shade Of Winter						2									2
Heart Of Mine			1			1									2
The Heart That You Own													1		1
Help Me Make It Through The Night				1											1
Hey Joe						1									1
Hey La La (My True La La)			3												3
Hey, Good Lookin'				1											1
Highlands													4	2	6
Highway 61 Revisited		49	46	68	72	67	22	20	38	32	56	92	102	81	745
Homeward Bound	AB				1										1
Homeward Bound					2										2
Honky Tonk Blues												8			8
Hootchie Cootchie Man												2	1		3
House Of Gold				2											2
House Of The Risin' Sun													1		1
I Am The Man, Thomas	AB												21	12	33
I And I							13	53	24	6	5	4	1	1	107
I Believe In You			6	23	29	4	1	6	9	1		1			80
I Can't Be Satisfied						9									9
I Don't Believe You	AC	1													1
I Don't Believe You		2	9	2	11	16	8	18	13	10	5	3	5	8	110
I Dreamed I Saw St. Augustine		1	1	1		4									7
I Shall Be Released	AB							1			1			14	16
I Shall Be Released		49	60	59	35		2	12	16	7	9	10	4	1	264
I Threw It All Away												2		2	4
I Walk The Line	AB												12		12
I Walk The Line													14		14
I Want You	AB				1		3								4
I Want You		4	30	11		3			18	11	12	11	4		104
Idiot Wind						40									40
If Dogs Run Free	AB													21	21
If Dogs Run Free													1		1
If Not For You						10	6	11	16	8	8	6	2	8	75
If You See Her, Say Hello								15	11	10	2	5	2		45

Song		88	89	90	91	92	93	94	95	96	97	98	99	00	S
I'll Be Your Baby Tonight	AB						2								2
I'll Be Your Baby Tonight		7	12	12	36	20	1	22	16	17	13	9	5	8	178
I'll Not Be a Stranger											2				2
I'll Remember You			18	22	21	19	11	5	15	12	8	5	14	2	152
I'm A Rovin' Gambler	AB										24	4			28
I'm A Rovin' Gambler	AC				1										1
I'm Glad I Got To See You Once Again	AC	1													1
I'm In The Mood For Love	AC	1	1												2
I'm In The Mood For Love				2											2
I'm Moving On							3								3
I'm Not Supposed To Care												3			3
In The Garden		24	23	22	10			24	9	1					113
In The Pines	AC		1												1
In The Pines					1										1
Instrumental Jam	IN		1												1
It Ain't Me, Babe	AB			27	46	5	59	86	36	25	19	38	33	25	399
It Ain't Me, Babe	AC	34	25	6	1	38									104
It Takes A Lot To Laugh, It Takes A Train To Cry		2	22	15	6	12	12	6	18	16	13	8	6	3	139
It's All Over Now, Baby Blue	AB			23	17	12	16	24	24	11	10	12	28	18	195
It's All Over Now, Baby Blue	AC		25	4	1	3									33
It's All Over Now, Baby Blue		13	4												17
It's Alright, Ma (I'm Only Bleeding)	AB			38		2							17	37	94
It's Alright, Ma (I'm Only Bleeding)	AC	3	27	2	1	4									37
It's Too Late					1				2						3
I've Been All Around This World	AB			2											2
I've Been All Around This World				8		2									10
Jack-A-Roe	AB						2								2
Jim Jones	AB					31									31
Joey		4		27	2	2		7	6	3	3	1	3	1	59
John Brown	AB			11	3	5		4	6	4	3	2		1	39
John Brown	AC					2				1					3
John Brown		9	13	2		1									25
Jokerman								103	15	8	1	1			128
Just Like A Woman		11	20	14	11	54	29	22	38	15	12	29	36	12	303
Just Like Tom Thumb's Blues		3	2	1		3	2	1	10	11	4	3	6	7	53
Key To The Highway				1						1					2
Knockin' On Heaven's Door	AE	6	33	1			1	2		1					44
Knockin' On Heaven's Door	AB			1	1				1	2	4	9	23	2	43
Knockin' On Heaven's Door	AC	5	2												7
Knockin' On Heaven's Door		6	2	5	11			4	3	16		2	20		69
Lady Came From Baltimore	AB							3							3
The Lady Of Carlisle	AC					1									1
Lakes Of Pontchartrain	AB			1											1
Lakes Of Pontchartrain	AC	7	8	1	1										17
Lay Lady Lay	AB						3								3
Lay Lady Lay			5	18	62	9	4	23	14	8	12	10	9	3	177
Legend In My Time			3												3
Lenny Bruce			2	3	19	5	2	4	9	2	1		1	1	49
Leopard-Skin Pill-Box Hat			2	18	10	11	3	1	9	13	21	24	24	79	215
Let's Learn To Live And Love Again				2											2
License To Kill		1					1		6			3			11
Like A Rolling Stone		69	99	93	46	12	1	13	41	26	69	6	73	105	653
Little Maggie						1									1
Little Moses	AB						28								28
Little Moses	AC					68									68
Lonely Is A Man Without Love	IN		1												1
The Lonesome Death Of Hattie Carroll	AB			13	10	10	10	11	3	8	5	6	5	4	85
The Lonesome Death Of Hattie Carroll	AC	16	13	4	3	2									38
Lonesome Town			3												3
Lonesome Whistle Blues				2											2

Song		88	89	90	91	92	93	94	95	96	97	98	99	00	S
Long Black Veil	AB													4	4
Long Black Veil											1				1
Love Minus Zero/No Limit	AB			12	8	1		21	16	10	6	6	12	20	112
Love Minus Zero/No Limit	AC	5	19	2	4	48									78
Love Sick											36	103	75	43	257
Maggie's Farm			51	54	36	49	66	63	101	32	39	42	13	22	24	592
Maggie's Farm	IN								1						1
Make You Feel My Love											1	34	33	8	76
Making Believe			1												1
Mama, You Been On My Mind	AB			1				46	11	7		11	14	12	102
Mama, You Been On My Mind	AC	6	10	2		14				1					33
Man Gave Names To All The Animals			3	1	4										8
The Man In Me		6	8	1	41		11	8	5	2	2	8	1	2	95
Man In The Long Black Coat			15	22	52	22	16	30	18	10	8	10	3	1	207
Man Of Constant Sorrow	AB			5											5
Man Of Constant Sorrow	AC	2	4	1											7
Man Of Peace			11	10	1					1			3	1	27
Marine Hymn	IN			17											17
Masters Of War	AB							64	56	36	15	49	60	24	304
Masters Of War		30	28	61	8										127
Matchbox								1				1			2
Million Miles												25	19		44
Money Honey													1		1
Moon River				1											1
Moondance						1									1
More And More				1											1
Most Likely You Go Your Way (And I'll Go Mine)			42	16	17	3		7	14	8	3		4	4	118
Most Of The Time			23	2		11									36
The Mountains of Mourne	IN				1										1
Mr. Tambourine Man	AB			40	45	21	36	41	86	37	36	18	61	27	448
Mr. Tambourine Man	AC	19	64	8	5	9				1					106
My Back Pages	AB						3	3	17	21	11	13	21	19	108
My Back Pages		5	6	9			1								21
My Blue Eyed Jane	AB												3		3
My Head's In Mississippi				3											3
Nadine		1													1
Never Gonna Be The Same Again									8	4	3		1		16
The New Minglewood Blues										2					2
New Morning					62	3									65
No More One More Time				4											4
Not Dark Yet											1	4	56	29	90
Not Fade Away											1	1	84	38	124
Nothing But You			3												3
Nowhere Man				1											1
Obviously Five Believers									31	8	1				40
Oh Baby It Ain't No Lie	AB										16	2	11	7	36
Oh Baby It Ain't No Lie				1											1
Ol' Mac Donald	IN			5											5
Old Rock & Roller				1											1
One Irish Rover			14		3		1								18
One More Cup Of Coffee (Valley Below)	AB						1								1
One More Cup Of Coffee (Valley Below)		1		3	1		2								7
One More Night	AB								1						1
One More Night				1											1
One Of Us Must Know (Sooner Or Later)											2				2
One Too Many Mornings	AB			12	7		1	6	16	13	13	10	14	10	102
One Too Many Mornings	AC	16	20	3											39
Oxford Town	AB			1											1
Pancho And Lefty			2		3										5

Song		88	89	90	91	92	93	94	95	96	97	98	99	00	S
Pass Me Not, O Gentle Saviour	AB												2	3	5
Paid The Price				1											1
Peace In The Valley			1												1
People Get Ready						1									1
People Puttin' People Down						2									2
Pledging My Time			2	3					8	3	1		1		18
Political World				29	1										30
Positively 4th Street			22	11	15	19	10	19	14	20	6	11	11	14	172
Precious Memories			2	1											3
Pretty Peggy-O		1	6	3		21	3	2		4	7	3			50
Queen Jane Approximately	AB						4								4
Queen Jane Approximately			9	6	2	3		4	6	3	1	5	2	2	43
Ragged And Dirty	AB						3								3
Ragtime Annie											1				1
Rainy Day Women # 12 & 35	AB								3	2					5
Rainy Day Women # 12 & 35			13	27	23	39	11	9	71	75	84	102	25	53	532
Rainy Day Women # 12 & 35	IN					4									4
Ramblin' Man									1						1
Rank Strangers To Me	AE		10												10
Rank Strangers To Me	AB										1	3	2	3	9
Rank Strangers To Me	AC	3	3												6
Real Real Gone									3	1					4
Red Hot						1									1
Restless Farewell	AB											1			1
Ring Them Bells	AB				2		4						2	4	12
Ring Them Bells			1					1	4	1					7
Rock Of Ages	AB												3	7	10
The Roving Blade	AB											1		1	2
The Roving Blade	AC					1									1
Roving Gambler	AB											2	6	23	31
Sally Sue Brown						2									2
San Francisco Bay Blues	AC	2													2
A Satisfied Mind	AB											1			1
Searching For A Soldier's Grave	AB													52	52
Seeing The Real You At Last		3	14	10	27	8			36	17	15	1	3	5	139
Señor (Tales Of Yankee Power)					3	2		22	17	8	12	15	7	4	90
Series Of Dreams							1	9							10
Seven Days										13					13
Shake Sugaree										7	1				8
She Belongs To Me	AB			5	2							1			8
She Belongs To Me	AC	3	4	1											8
She Belongs To Me						29	15	20	18	12	4	8	4	7	117
Shelter From The Storm		18	23	13	40	14	9	14	12	7	6	4	5	2	167
Shenandoah	IN			3											3
She's About A Mover		1												1	2
Shooting Star				20	17	7	6	3	8	1	8	2	1	2	75
Shot Of Love			6												6
Silvio		61	49	22	4	35	9	1	84	85	94	99	38	1	582
Simple Twist Of Fate		24	22	21	22	33	24	20	15	10	11	14	8	9	233
So Long, Good Luck And Goodbye				1											1
Somebody Touched Me	AB												10	9	19
Song To Woody	AB			9	1								3	18	31
Song To Woody	AC	2	5	1											8
The Sounds Of Silence	AB											17			17
The Sounds Of Silence												17			17
Stand By Me				1											1
Standing In The Doorway														12	12
Stone Walls And Steel Bars	AB										12	13	7	4	36
Stuck Inside Of Mobile With															
The Memphis Blues Again		32	33	48	11	21	72	8	18	15	23	18	62	29	390
Subterranean Homesick Blues		71	14	15	1										101
T.V. Talkin' Song				20											20
Tangled Up In Blue	AB								30	40	76	109	114	111	480
Tangled Up In Blue	AC		1												1

205

Song		88	89	90	91	92	93	94	95	96	97	98	99	00	S
Tangled Up In Blue		13	1	12	4	48	57	103	14						252
Tears Of Rage			8	10	2	1		6	9	7	5	7	2	3	60
Tell Me That It Isn't True													16		16
That Lucky Old Sun	AB					1			1					1	3
That Lucky Old Sun						1									1
That'll Be The Day	AB												11		11
That'll Be The Day													7		7
Things Have Changed														70	70
This Wheel's On Fire	AB											1			1
This Wheel's On Fire										16	24	10	2	3	55
This World Can't Stand Long	AB												1	15	16
Tight Connection To My Heart	AB						2								2
Tight Connection To My Heart				12											12
Til I Fell In Love With You											32	67	11	1	111
The Times They Are A-Changin'	AB			13	11	69	7	7	29	11	6	17	17	24	211
The Times They Are A-Changin'	AC	32	13	2	5										52
The Times They Are A-Changin'			3			3									6
The Times We've Known												1			1
To Be Alone With You			4	9	7	9		1	1	11		6	6	2	56
To Ramona	AB		4		1	4		6	14	10	7	5	10	33	94
To Ramona	AC	22	15	1	2	4									44
Tombstone Blues									19	6	1		7	21	54
Tomorrow Is A Long Time	AB			1	1						1	6	7	11	27
Tomorrow Is A Long Time			1	2	5										8
Tomorrow Night	AB						42	15				1			58
Tonight I'll Be Staying Here With You				2		1		1	8	18	22	19		4	75
Tough Mama											26	3	1	1	31
Trail Of The Buffalo	AB			5	2										7
Trail Of The Buffalo	AC	7	1		23	3									34
Trail Of The Buffalo			2												2
Trouble			7												7
Trouble No More				1											1
Tryin' To Get To Heaven													7	17	24
Tupelo Honey - Why Must I Always Explain					1										1
Two Soldiers	AB			4	3			1							8
Two Soldiers	AC	3	6		6	1									16
Unbelievable						25			2						27
Under The Red Sky				18	14	15	6	15	7	4	6	7	1	2	95
Union Sundown						24									24
Viola Lee Blues	AB										1				1
Visions Of Johanna	AB			1	2	8			1	2			8	6	28
Visions Of Johanna	AC		1	1	2										4
Visions Of Johanna		1	2												3
Wagoner's Lad	AB			1											1
Wagoner's Lad	AC	5	2												7
Walk A Mile In My Shoes				1											1
The Wanderer	AB												12		12
The Wanderer													11		11
Watching The River Flow		3	3	8	18	13	41	20	16	25	17	5	17	20	206
The Water Is Wide	AB			1											1
The Water Is Wide			2												2
We Better Talk This Over													1		1
We Three (My Echo, My Shadow And Me)	AC	1													1
Weeping Willow	AB						1								1
West L.A. Fadeaway	AB					1									1
West L.A. Fadeaway						2			6				1		9
What Good Am I?			18	21	29	25	23	20	9	4	2	3	2		156
What Was It You Wanted				20	1				1						22
When Did You Leave Heaven?	AC		2												2
When Did You Leave Heaven?			5	1	2										8
When First Unto This Country	AC				1										1
When First Unto This Country			1												1

Song		88	89	90	91	92	93	94	95	96	97	98	99	00	S
When I Paint My Masterpiece					19	5			3	8	5		1	1	42
When You Gonna Wake Up			1												1
Where Teardrops Fall				6					2	1					9
The White Dove	AB											3		1	4
The White Dove											6				6
The Wicked Messenger											1			20	21
Wiggle Wiggle				26	76	3									105
Wild Mountain Thyme	AC	1													1
Willing	AB								1						1
Willing					6	1	1								8
With God On Our Side	AB								1						1
With God On Our Side	AC	6													6
Yesterday	AB										1				1
You Ain't Goin' Nowhere											28	5	3	1	37
You Angel You				2											2
You Don't Know Me			5			6									11
You're A Big Girl Now		26	25	16	2	4	17	19	10	7	8	10	4	2	150
You're Gonna Quit Me	AB						28						3		31
You're Too Late													1		1

3.2 Twenty most played songs

1.	All Along The Watchtower	878
2.	Highway 61 Revisited	745
3.	Tangled Up In Blue	733
4.	Like A Rolling Stone	653
5.	Maggie's Farm	593
6.	Silvio	582
7.	Mr. Tambourine Man	554
8.	Rainy Day Women # 12 & 35	541
9.	It Ain't Me, Babe	503
10.	Don't Think Twice, It's All Right	466
11.	Masters Of War	431
12.	Blowin' In The Wind	407
13.	Stuck Inside of Mobile with the Memphis Blues Again	390
14.	Ballad Of A Thin Man	313
15.	Just Like A Woman	303
16.	I Shall Be Released	280
17.	Everything Is Broken	270
18.	The Times They Are A-Changin'	269
19.	Love Sick	257
20.	It's All Over Now, Baby Blue	245

3.3 Ten most played acoustic songs

1.	Mr. Tambourine Man	554
2.	It Ain't Me, Babe	503
3.	Tangled Up In Blue	481
4.	Don't Think Twice, It's All Right	465
5.	Blowin' In The Wind	407
6.	Masters Of War	304
7.	The Times They Are A-Changin'	263
8.	It's All Over Now, Baby Blue	228
9.	Boots Of Spanish Leather	200
10.	Love Minus Zero/No Limit	200

3.4 Ten most played covers

1.	Not Fade Away	124
2.	Little Moses	96
3.	Friend Of The Devil	93
4.	Alabama Getaway	83
5.	Cocaine Blues	68
6.	Tomorrow Night	58
7.	Barbara Allen	57
8.	Searching For A Soldier's Grave	52

9.	Pretty Peggy-O	50
10.	Duncan And Brady	48

3.5 Favourites

The following songs have been played at least once every year during the Never-Ending Tour:

All Along The Watchtower
Ballad Of A Thin Man
Boots Of Spanish Leather
Don't Think Twice, It's All Right
Every Grain Of Sand
Girl From The North Country
Highway 61 Revisited
I Don't Believe You
I'll Be Your Baby Tonight
It Ain't Me, Babe
It Takes A Lot To Laugh, It Takes A Train To Cry
It's All Over Now, Baby Blue
Just Like A Woman
Like A Rolling Stone
The Lonesome Death Of Hattie Carroll
Maggie's Farm
Maggie's Farm
Mr. Tambourine Man
She Belongs To Me
Shelter From The Storm
Silvio
Simple Twist Of Fate
Stuck Inside Of Mobile With The Memphis Blues Again
Tangled Up In Blue
The Times They Are A-Changin'
To Ramona
Watching The River Flow
You're A Big Girl Now

3.6 Live debuts of Dylan songs
3.6.1 Old songs

Song	First performed	Venue
Blind Willie McTell	5 August 1997	Montreal, Quebec, Canada
Bob Dylan's 115th Dream	13 October 1988	Upper Darby, Pennsylvania
Bob Dylan's Dream	28 January 1991	Zürich, Switzerland
Buckets Of Rain	18 November1990	Detroit, Michigan
Country Pie.	10 March 2000	Anaheim, California, Late show
Down Along The Cove	14 June 1999	Eugene, Oregon
Drifter's Escape	30 April 1992	Eugene, Oregon
Driftin' Too Far From Shore	7 June 1988	Concord, California
Had A Dream About You, Baby	9 June 1988	Sacramento, California
If Dogs Run Free.	1 October 2000	Münster, Germany
My Back Pages	11 June 1988	Mountain View, California
New Morning	19 April 1991	New Orleans, Louisiana
Obviously Five Believers	15 May 1995	Palm Desert, California
One More Night	6 June 1990	Toronto, Ontario, Canada
Oxford Town	25 October 1990	Oxford, Mississippi
Silvio	21 June 1988	Cuyahoga Falls, Ohio
Subterranean Homesick Blues	7 June 1988	Concord, California
Tears Of Rage	26 June 1990	Patras, Greece
Tell Me That It Isn't True	10 March 2000	Anaheim, California, Early show
Things Have Changed	10 March 2000	Anaheim, California, Early show
This Wheel's On Fire	13 April 1996	Madison, New Jersey
Tight Connection To My Heart	12 January 1990	Toad's Place, New Haven, Connecticut
To Be Alone With You	15 October 1990	Upper Darby, Pennsylvania

Trouble	21 July 1989	Holmdel, New Jersey
You Ain't Goin' Nowhere	10 April 1997	Portland, Maine
You Angel You	17 January 1990	Penn State, State College, Penn.

3.6.2 Songs from OH MERCY

Song	First performed	Venue
Disease Of Conceit	27 October 1989	Troy, New York
Everything Is Broken	10 October 1989	New York City, New York
Man In The Long Black Coat	13 October 1989	New York City, New York
Most Of The Time	10 October 1989	New York City, New York
Political World	12 January 1990	Toad's Place, New Haven, Connecticut
Ring Them Bells	20 October 1990	Poughkeepsie, New York
Series Of Dreams	8 September 1993	Vienna, Virginia
Shooting Star	9 June 1990	East Troy, Wisconsin
What Good Am I?	10 October 1989	New York City, New York
What Was It You Wanted	12 January 1990	Toad's Place, New Haven, Connecticut
Where Teardrops Fall	12 January 1990	Toad's Place, New Haven, Connecticut
Dignity	16 March 1995	Bielefeld, Germany

3.6.3 Songs from UNDER THE RED SKY

Song	First performed	Venue
10,000 Men	12 November 2000	South Kingston, Rhode Island
2 x 2	5 July 1992	Correggio, Italy
Born In Time	25 February 1993	Belfast, Northern Ireland
Cat's In The Well	18 March 1992	Perth, Western Australia, Australia
God Knows	28 January 1991	Zürich, Switzerland
TV Talkin' Song	11 October 1990	Brookville, New York
Unbelievable	22 August 1992	Ottawa, Ontario, Canada
Under The Red Sky	11 October 1990	Brookville, New York
Wiggle Wiggle	12 January 1990	Toad's Place, New Haven, Connecticut

3.6.4 Songs from TIME OUT OF MIND

Song	First performed	Venue
'Til I Fell In Love With You	24 October 1997	Starkville, Mississippi
Can't Wait	24 October 1997	Starkville, Mississippi
Cold Irons Bound	24 October 1997	Starkville, Mississippi
Highlands.	25 June 1999	Chula Vista, California
Love Sick	1 October 1997	Bournemouth, England
Make You Feel My Love	2 November 1997	Columbia, South Carolina
Million Miles	14 January 1998	New London, Connecticut
Not Dark Yet	30 October 1997	Columbus, Georgia
Standing In The Doorway	15 June 2000	Portland, Oregon
Tryin' To Get To Heaven	7 April 1999	Lisbon, Portugal

3.6.5 One off covers

Song	Performed	Venue
20/20 Vision	25 October 1991	Austin, Texas
Around And Around	10 July 1992	Leysin, Switzerland
Blue Bonnet Girl	1 November 2000	Bloomington, Indiana
B-Thang	1 September 1989	Salt Lake City, Utah
Crazy Love	28 June 1989	Athens, Greece
Dancing In The Dark	12 January 1990	Toad's Place, New Haven, Connecticut
Detroit City	12 November 1990	East Lansing, Michigan
Dolly Dagger	18 March 1992	Perth, Western Australia, Australia
Don't Pity Me	31 July 1989	Joliette, Quebec, Canada
Dust My Broom	12 November 1991	Detroit, Michigan
Farewell To The Gold	2 November 1992	Youngstown, Ohio
G-Thang	5 September 1989	Santa Barbara, California
The Heart That You Own	2 September 1999	West Palm Beach, Florida
Help Me Make It Through The Night	12 January 1990	Toad's Place, New Haven, Connecticut
Hey Joe	12 July 1992	Juan-les-Pins, France
Hey, Good Lookin'	26 October 1990	Tuscaloosa, Alabama
House Of The Risin' Sun	17 June 2000	George, Washington
I'm Glad I Got To See You Once Again	4 August 1988	Los Angeles, California

The Lady Of Carlisle	14 April 1992	Sydney, New South Wales, Australia
Little Maggie	18 March 1992	Perth, Western Australia, Australia
Lonely Is A Man Without Love	3 September 1989	Berkeley, California
Making Believe	24 June 1989	Istanbul, Turkey
Money Honey	15 November 1999	Ithaca, New York
Moon River	27 August 1990	Merrillville, Indiana
Moondance	19 November 1991	Erie, Pennsylvania
More And More	26 August 1989	Houston, Texas
The Mountains of Mourne	3 February 1991	Glasgow, Scotland
Nadine	17 June 1988	St Louis, Missouri
Nowhere Man	12 August 1990	Edmonton, Alberta, Canada
Old Rock & Roller	3 July 1990	Hamburg, Germany
Pay The Price	12 January 1990	Toad's Place, New Haven, Connecticut
Peace In The Valley	13 June 1989	Frejus, France
People Get Ready	8 August 1991	Buenos Aires, Argentina
Ragtime Annie	14 December 1997	Chicago, Illinois
Ramblin' Man	30 November 1995	Tampa, Florida
Red Hot	8 November 1992	Little Rock, Arkansas
Restless Farewell	21 May 1998	Los Angeles, California
A Satisfied Mind	9 November 1999	Philadelphia, Pennsylvania
Sitting On) The Dock Of The Bay	18 August 1990	George, Washington
So Long, Good Luck And Goodbye	12 January 1990	Toad's Place, New Haven, Connecticut
Stand By Me	28 August 1990	Merrillville, Indiana
The Times We've Known	1 November 1998	New York City, New York
Trouble No More	12 January 1990	Toad's Place, New Haven, Connecticut
Tupelo Honey	6 February 1991	Belfast, Northern Ireland
Viola Lee Blues	24 February 1997	Sapporo, Japan
Walk A Mile In My Shoes	12 January 1990	Toad's Place, New Haven, Connecticut
We Three (My Echo, My Shadow And Me)	6 August 1988	Carlsbad, California
Weeping Willow	17 November 1993	New York City, New York
Wild Mountain Thyme	22 June 1988	Riverbend, Ohio
Yesterday	26 June 1996	Liverpool, England
You're Too Late	29 January 1999	Daytona Beach, Florida

4 Album statistics 1988-2000

Electric and acoustic variants of a song are counted as the same song in the following table:

Album	Number of songs	% of total	number of performances	% of total
Bob Dylan	2	1.2%	89	0.5%
Freewheelin'	7	4.1%	1624	8.6%
The Times They Are A-Changin'	7	4.1%	796	4.2%
Another Side	5	3.0%	884	4.7%
Bringing It All Back Home	9	5.3%	2122	11.3%
Highway 61 Revisited	8	4.7%	2167	11.5%
Blonde On Blonde	12	7.1%	1923	10.2%
Basement Tapes	4	2.4%	314	1.7%
John Wesley Harding	9	5.3%	1207	6.4%
Nashville Skyline	7	4.1%	437	2.3%
Self Portrait	1	0.6%	8	0%
New Morning	4	2.4%	258	1.4%
Greatest Hits Vol 2	4	2.4%	562	3.0%
Pat Garrett	1	0.6%	143	0.8%
Planet Waves	3	1.8%	170	0.9%
Blood On The Tracks	7	4.1%	1370	7.3%
Desire	2	1.2%	67	0.4%
Street-Legal	2	1.2%	91	0.5%
Slow Train Coming	4	2.4%	323	1.7%
Saved	2	1.2%	114	0.6%
Shot Of Love	6	3.6%	123	0.7%
Infidels	5	3.0%	297	1.6%
Empire Burlesque	7	4.1%	332	1.8%
Knocked-Out Loaded	2	1.2%	17	0.1%
Hearts Of Fire	0	0.0%	0	0.0%
Down In The Groove	6	3.6%	626	3.3%

Traveling Wilburys Vol 1	1	0.6%	3	0%
Oh Mercy	12	7.1%	939	5.0%
Under The Red Sky	5	3.0%	485	2.6%
Traveling Wilburys Vol 3	0	0.0%	0	0.0%
Bootleg Series Vol 1	1	0.6%	135	0.7%
Bootleg Series Vol 2	1	0.6%	13	0.1%
Bootleg Series Vol 3	2	1.2%	56	0.3%
Biograph	0	0.0%	0	0.0%
Good As I Been To You	5	3.0%	168	0.9%
World Gone Wrong	4	2.4%	14	0.1%
Greatest Hits Vol 3	1	0.6%	20	0.1%
MTV Unplugged	1	0.6%	67	0.4%
Time Out Of Mind	10	5.9%	897	4.8%

5 Musicians
5.1 The Never-Ending Tour Bands

Line-up	Band members	first show	last show	# of shows
1	G.E. Smith (guitar), Kenny Aaronson (bass), Christopher Parker (drums).	Concord 7 June 1988	London, 8 June 1989	78
2	G.E. Smith (guitar), Tony Garnier (bass), Christopher Parker (drums).	Dublin 3 June 1989	New York City 19 October 1990	163
3	John Staehely (guitar), Cesar Diaz (guitar), Tony Garnier (bass), Christopher Parker (drums).	Richmond, 21 October 1990	Detroit , 18 November 1990	22
4	John Jackson (guitar), Cesar Diaz (guitar), Tony Garnier (bass), Ian Wallace (drums).	Zürich, 28 January 1991	Mexico City, 2 March 1991	22
5	John Jackson (guitar), Tony Garnier (bass), Ian Wallace (drums).	New Orleans, 19 April 1991	Charlottesville, 20 November 1991	80
6	John Jackson (guitar), Bucky Baxter (steel guitar a.o.), Tony Garnier (bass), Ian Wallace (drums).	Perth, 18 March 1992	Waikiki, 24 April 1992	22
7	John Jackson (guitar), Bucky Baxter (steel guitar a.o.), Tony Garnier (bass), Charlie Quintana (drums), Ian Wallace (drums).	Seattle, 27 April 1992	Omaha 5 September 1992	44
8	John Jackson (guitar), Bucky Baxter (steel guitar a.o.), Tony Garnier (bass), Winston Watson (drums), Ian Wallace (drums).	Kansas City, 6 September 1992	West Palm Beach 15 November 1992	25
9	John Jackson (guitar), Bucky Baxter (steel guitar a.o.), Tony Garnier (bass), Winston Watson (drums).	Dublin 5 February 1993	Atlanta 4 August 1996	358
10	John Jackson (guitar),	San Luis Obispo,	Sapporo,	39

	Bucky Baxter (steel guitar a.o.), Tony Garnier (bass), David Kemper (drums).	17 October 1996	24 February 1997	
11	Larry Campbell (guitar), Bucky Baxter (steel guitar a.o.), Tony Garnier (bass), David Kemper (drums).	St. John's, 31 March 1997	München, 2 May 1999	242
12	Charlie Sexton (guitar), Larry Campbell (steel guitar a.o.), Tony Garnier (bass), David Kemper (drums).	Denver, 5 June 1999	Towson, 19 November 2000	182

Artist	First show	Last show	# of shows
Kenny Aaronson	7 June 1988	7 June 1989	78
Bucky Baxter	18 March 1992	2 May 1999	730
Larry Campbell	31 March 1997	19 November 2000	424
Cesar Diaz	21 October 1990	30 April 1991	44
Tony Garnier	3 June 1989	19 November 2000	1199
John Jackson	28 January 1991	24 February 1997	590
David Kemper	17 October 1996	19 November 2000	463
Christopher Parker	7 June 1988	18 November 1990	263
Charlie Quintana	27 April 1992	5 September 1992	44
Charlie Sexton	5 June 1999	19 November 2000	182
G.E. Smith	7 June 1988	19 October 1990	241
John Staehely	21 October 1990	18 November 1990	22
Ian Wallace	28 January 1991	15 November 1992	193
Winston Watson	6 September 1992	4 August 1996	383

5.2 Guests

Name	Show	Date
Kenny Aaronson	Long Island	23 July 1989
	Canandaigua	25 July 1989
Bucky Baxter	Springfield	19 August 1989
	New Orleans	25 August 1989
	Houston	26 August 1989
	Dallas	27 August 1989
	Las Cruces	29 August 1989
Ray Benson	Austin	27 October 1996
	Reno	17 March 2000
	Bozeman	24 March 2000
	Denver	6 April 2000
Dickey Betts	Sarasota	9 November 1991
	New Orleans	23 April 1993
	Tampa	30 September 1995
David Bromberg	Chicago	14 December 1997
Stephen Bruton	Victoria	19 August 1990
	Vancouver	20 August 1990
	Portland	21 August 1990
	Pueblo	24 August 1990
	Des Moines	26 August 1990
	Merrillville	27 August 1990
	Merrillville	28 August 1990
	Falcon Heights	29 August 1990
	Brookville	11 October 1990
	Springfield	12 October 1990
T-bone J. Henry Burnett	San José	9 May 1992
James Burton	Shreveport	30 October 1996
Tracy Chapman	Vancouver	21 August 1988
	Calgary	23 August 1988
Elvis Costello	London	30 March 1995
	London	31 March 1995
	Dublin	11 April 1995
	New York City	26 July 1999

Sheryl Crow	Los Angeles	19 May 1995
	New Orleans	16 October 1995
	Los Angeles	19 December 1997
Jimmy Dale	Austin	25 October 1991
Rick Danko	Wallingford	18 August 1997
Carl Denson	New York City	18-19 October 1990
Cesar Diaz	Allentown	12 July 1989
	Santa Fé	11 September 1990
	Mesa	12 September 1990
	Springfield	12 October 1990
	West Point	13 October 1990
	New York City	15-19 October 1990
	Wilkes-Barre	15 November 1991
	Gothenburg	28 June 1992
	Dunkerque	30 June 1992
	Juan-Les-Pins	12 July 1992
	London	7 February 1993
	Cascais	13 July 1993
	Philadelphia	17 December 1995
Steve Earle	Springfield	19 August 1989
Jerry Garcia	San Francisco	5 May 1992
	Washington	25 June 1995
Martin Gross	Detroit	12 November 1991
Ronnie Hawkins	Toronto	6 June 1990
Henry Hirsch	New York City	19 October 1990
Chrissie Hynde	London	31 March 1995
	Dublin	11 April 1995
Paul James	Toronto	28 April 1996
	London	12 May 1996
	Buffalo	23 February 1999
Flaco Jiminez	Montreux	9 July 1990
Miles Joseph	Lincoln	31 August 1990
	Lampe	1 September 1990
	Hannibal	2 September 1990
Jewel Kilcher	Burlington	17 April 1996
	Providence	18 April 1996
Carole King	London	31 March 1995
	Dublin	11 April 1995
Al Kooper	Liverpool	26 June 1996
	Liverpool	27 June 1996
	London	29 June 1996
Alison Krauss	Fort Lauderdale	29 September 1995
Lenny Kravitz	New York City	19 October 1990
Nils Lofgren	Mesa	20 October 1996
Aimee Mann	Burgettstown	18 May 1996
Dave Matthews	Konstanz	3 July 1996
Eddie McDonald	Santa Barbara	7 August 1988
Roger McGuinn	Tampa	14-15 November 1989
	Cleveland	17 May 1996
Joni Mitchell	George	16 May 1998
Ian Moore	Austin	November 4-5 1995
Leroi Moore	Konstanz	July 3 1996
Van Morrison	Aten	28 June 1989
	Belfast	6 February 1991
	London	12 June 1993
	Dublin	11 April 1995
	Molde	19 July 1996
	Boston	24 February 1998
	George	16 May 1998
Stevie Nicks	Phoenix	9 November 1995
Carl Perkins	Jackson	10 November 1994
Mike Peters	Los Angeles	4 August 1988
	Santa Barbara	7 August 1988
Billy Lee Riley	Little Rock	8 September 1992
Steve Ripley	Tulsa	4 September 1990

	Oklahoma City	5 September 1990
	Dallas	6 September 1990
	San Antonio	8 September 1990
	Austin	9 September 1990
	Tulsa	30 October 1991
Jason Roberts	Reno	17 March 2000
Doug Sahm	Edmonton	24 August 1988
	Austin	5 November 1995
Brian Setzer	Normal	13 February 1999
	Grand Rapids	15 February 1999
Charlie Sexton	Austin	25 October 1991
	Austin	4 November 1995
	Austin	26 October 1996
	Austin	27 October 1996
Dave Sharp	Los Angeles	4 August 1988
	Santa Barbara	7 August 1988
G.E. Smith	New York City	14 December 1995
Patti Smith	Boston	10 December 1995
	New York City	11 December 1995
	Bethlehem	13 December 1995
	New York City	14 December 1995
	Philadelphia	December 15-17 1995
Jo-El Sonnier	New Orleans	19 April 1991
Liz Souissi	Eindhoven	17 February 1993
Bruce Springsteen	New York City	20 October 1994
John Staehely	New York City	16-19 October 1990
Ringo Starr	Frejus	13 June 1989
Dave Stewart	Juan-Les-Pins	12 July 1992
	London	9 February 1993
	London	13 February 1993
Marty Stuart	Antioch	8 September 1999
Boyd Tinsley	Konstanz	3 July 1996
Derek Trucks	Clearwater	11 November 1992
Nigel Twist	Los Angeles	4 August 1988
	Santa Barbara	7 August 1988
Joe Walsh	Memphis	26 July 1988
Adam Widoff	New York City	19 October 1990
Ron Wood	London	16 February 1991
	London	29 June 1996
Bono Vox	Dublin	4 June 1989
Neil Young	Concord	7 June 1988
	Berkeley	10 June 1988
	Mountain	June 11 View 1988
	Mountain View	9 October 1993
	New York City	20 October 1994
Steve van Zandt	Zürich	25 April 1999

Notes and Sources

Introduction

1 And here we have the reasons why the N.E.T. is so called by the fans – the stripped down garage band backing and the plethora of small venues stand in direct contrast to the big band/supergroup/backing singers in large arena tours of previous years

Prologue

2 From the *Hunky Dory* album, the lyrics that come with the (otherwise superb) remastered CD manage to get this, as well as most other lines, incorrect. Apt, I suppose, given Dylan's own published, error strewn, lyrics

3 A term Dylan was still dismissing vehemently – idols, he remarked, were little wooden carved things.

Chapter One

4 Not a term Dylan himself accepts, despite the specific references to being "Born Again" in many lyrics.

5 "Actually, if you wonder why all these things are happening nowadays, Joshua, you know, he went into, I believe it was, uh, Canaan land, and God told him that in certain times He would destroy all the people, every man, woman, children there. You see, that's bad. Certainly he hated to leave the children, but they was all just defiled. And there was some cities. God said, 'don't go in their yet', so Joshua wondered why, and God said 'because their iniquity is not yet full'. So now, you look around today, when we started out this tour we started out in San Francisco. It's a kind of unique town and these days, I think it's either one-third of two-thirds of the population that are homosexuals in San Francisco. I heard it said. Now, I guess they are working up to a hundred percent. I don't know. But anyway, it's a growing place for homosexuals, and I read they have homo-sexual politics, and a political party. I don't mean it's going on in somebody's closet, I mean its political! Alright, you know what I'm talking about? Anyway, I would just think, well, I guess the iniquity is not yet full. And I don't wanna be around when it is!" Hartford 8th May, 1980.

6 "Russia will come down and attack in the Middle East. China's got an Army of two million people. They're gonna come down in the Middle East. There's gonna be a war called the Battle of Armageddon which is like something you never even dreamed about. And Christ will set up His Kingdom and He'll rule it from Jerusalem. I know, far out as that may seem this is what the Bible says..."

"Anyway, "The Lamb of God which taketh away the sin of the world" -- I wonder how many of you people understand that. I'm curious to know how many of you understand. (by the minmum response he gets – seemingly very few – A.M.) It's like the Shah of Iran. He's been out of hospital now. Who knows what he's doin'? Been walking around, looking out of the window. Meantime, 50 or 60 American hostages are being held somewhere out in the desert. This man plundered the country, murdered a lot of people, escaped."

7 Dylan's first "Christian" single and a Grammy Award winner for Best Male Vocal.

8 1980 radio interview

9 A very real plight, and I am all for Dylan drawing attention to it and something been done to publicize and hopefully alleviate their problems – but just not then!

10 Bob Geldof, *Is That It?* Sidgwick & Jackson 1986

11 Since I wrote this, further tapes have been unearthed showing that on another occasion they were treating the forthcoming event with more respect. It includes the totally surprising news that Dylan was intending to play "Dark Eyes" at the event. That could have been a very triumphant move, in other circumstances. As it turned out it would be over eleven years before he sang "Dark Eyes" on stage.

12 This is what Dylan gets for setting such high standards of performance where inspiration and innovation seemed always available to him even on long gruelling world tours. Dylan fans do not turn up at shows hoping for meticulously professional copies of album tracks (if that's what you want why not just stay at home and play the albums?). Rather they crave transcendently moving experiences and the miracle that they have had this so often simply means the demands and expectations never diminish,... at least not until NET and ageing Dylan..... Like songwriting, performing is a mixture of inspiration and hard working craftsmanship; a combination of planning and tightrope walking.

13 I still do credit them with this though I am no longer clear to what degree the Dead influenced Dylan's song selection and how much came from Dylan himself. Via Susan Ross's testimony and the songs rehearsed it appears now that Dylan himself was in an even more experimental mood than the shows originally revealed.

14 Interviewed by Kathryn Baker, Associated Press.

15 I amd recreating my own personal listening experience.

16 Repeated in *NME* interview with Gavin Martin, 1995

17 Do you think he actually listened to "You're a big Girl Now"?

18 Going by the audio evidence alone.

Chapter Two

19 Considering Mr Ronson was referring to the Rolling Thunder Tour he could not have been more wrong at the time – but there have certainly been times in the N.E.T. when the remark has been recalled.

20 Dylan began his 1984 European tour by using the opening show as an on-stage rehearsal.

21 If you want to know how Dylan performs this song consult the witty, insightful and exuberant liner notes to 1993's *World Gone Wrong*

22 Bob Dylan, Roy Orbison, George Harrison, Tom Petty and Jeff Lynne

23 If you are into detail, you may wish to note that the 1988 performance was acoustic whereas the 1989 versions were all electric performances, which leads me to think the 1988 one was played specially due to the circumstances.

24 1966, *Playboy* interview by Nat Hentoff

25 *The Guardian* newspaper fulminated against Dylan's delivery of "Blowin' In The Wind" at the Fleadh festival one year. It was not on the set-list. This kind of thing makes you wonder when the reviewers actually write their reviews and if they even attend the shows.

26 A footnote to the year's touring was Dylan and GE Smith performing an acoustic set at Neil Young's annual Bridge School Benefit; where along with four of his own songs Dylan sang "San Francisco Bay Blues" and "Pretty Boy Floyd".

Chapter Three

27 Talking to Edna Gundersen, *USA Today*

28 This seems to be a favourite song for many women – meanwhile men tie themselves in knots over its "sexism". For me the "sexist" argument – which is overwhelming if one reads the lyrics – is made specious by the way he performs the song.

29 Two years later his cry of "long live Scotland" as he ended a chaotic gig (aimed perhaps at boosting the "Just Say No" campaign?) would seem a less real acknowledgement somehow.

30 David Belcher, a fine man really, though he does enjoy winding up Dylan fans!

31 This review prompted Dylan writer and friend Robert Forryan to return to the obsession that is Bob.

32 You're right, I don't know how an arm does this, but it seemed to, and to be angry with the air for being empty.

33 Years later the rehearsals to this tour were to emerge and "Peace In The Valley" was there as were Buddy Holly and Gram Parson songs and Robert Johnson's "Queen Of Spades". Not on this circulating tape but also run through were a huge number of covers including the Who's "I Can See For Miles" and the Beach Boys' "God Only Knows" among the more mind-boggling. (Christopher Parker, interview, *The Telegraph* #36.)

34 Robert Forryan: "Queen Jane – An Incomplete History". *Dignity* issue 8 : Jan/Feb 1997

35 Dylan drops verses 2 and 4; but it is truncated in terms of words only not in feeling imparted.

Chapter Four

36 A.k.a. "I've Been All Around The World" a.k.a "The Blue Ridge Mountains"

37 E.Waugh, *Brideshead Revisited*, Penguin Books, 1951, p.40

38 *Oh Mercy* became at this point only the third album ever, from which all songs had been played in concert

39 The next song was "Desolation Row"

40 John Bauldie tragically died in helicopter crash in 1996 so I cannot ask him. Prior to this John's editorial – I would speculate – partly reflects the weariness of the hard working editor and indeed the weariness of the never ending tour that comes and goes in many fans.

41 "Pot", "kettle" and "black" spring to mind, I know

42 Stevie Ray Vaughan had played on *under the red sky*. He died in a helicopter crash near East Troy, Wisconsin, after having appeared as a guest at an Eric Clapton concert in Alpine Valley. Dylan was quoted in *USA Today,* "He was a

sweet guy. Something else was coming through him besides his guitar playing and singin..."It's almost like having to play the night that Kennedy died. He'll probably be revered as much as and in the same way as Hank Williams".

43 Dylan is viewed by many as a Finn like character; a correspondence he alluded to in his notes to *Planet Waves* "I lit out for parts unknown"

Chapter Five

44 Published February 1992, *The Los Angeles Times (Magazine)*

45 Michael Gray, *The Guardian*

46 Had it been going when Dylan announced his joint tour of 1999 with Paul Simon I'd probably be in jail by now.

47 On the newsgroup rec.music.dylan; of which more later.

48 By attributing the words to his father, Dylan is following a long tradition of attribution in Judaism. He can be said to be using "father(s) in a wider sense, meaning his heritage." Martin Grossman, *Expecting Rain* Web site

49 *Record Collector*, May 1991

50 I think my favourite quote to the crowd came in Ljubljana: "Thank you everybody! Well, English is my only language. Sometimes not even that." (after "All Along The Watchtower").

Chapter Six

51 Which Dylan has identified (along with the sublime "The Wind Cries Mary") as his favourite Hendrix track(s).

52 Clinton Heylin (*Behind The Shades: Take Two* speculates that Dylan was moved by the memory of a longstanding ex-girlfriend of his, Carol Lopez, who had taken her own life' and 'apparently named Dylan in her suicide note'. Mr Heylin concludes from this that:

Though Dylan never admitted that he had received her suicide note, one night in April, 1992, when playing in Carol's adopted hometown of Sydney, he performed a rare acoustic performance of 'Desolation Row' and, most uncharacteristically, when he came to the verse about Ophelia – for whom "death is quite romantic" – visibly became moved to tears...

53 This is the same drummer that appeared with Dylan in the Letterman show in 1984 with The Plugz

54 I am thinking of others such as "House Carpenter", "Golden Vanity", "Like A Ship On The Sea".

55 In the most recent years of the N.E.T. this has ceased to be the case

56 This event was intended to celebrate the thirty years since its release. That the album was released on March 19th 1962 and it was now October 16th was yet another unexplained oddity about the entire affair

Chapter Seven

57 By no means all of us; many fans thought the shows excellent and the reviews were mixed – all the way from hatchet jobs to stellar praise.

58 Ironically enough, the 'bootleg centre' of the city.

Chapter Eight

59 Mike Sutton has been going to Dylan shows around the world for over 30 years. Known for his dedication in queuing for hours before the door opens so he can be as near Dylan as possible. He usually spends days in Camden High Street near Compendium Bookshop. On this particular day he went to a local

supermarket instead and missed everything. I always point out how amusingly ironic this was. He has not laughed yet, no matter how wittily I put it.

60 Compendium Bookshop sadly closed in the year 2000.

61 Flukes Cradle featured heavily in the "Blood In My Eyes Video". It had paintings on the walls for sale, and Bob is sitting beneath one such on the cover of *World Gone Wrong*. Alas Flukes Cradle is no more. Shortly after my Dylan experience it was sold, redecorated and renamed. The new venture subsequently closed and when last I passed it, was all boarded up.

62 At least I think I called him "Bob" from here on in but I cannot be sure.

63 Why did I say that? How should I know? Maybe I thought he had read a nasty comment. More likely that it was just another blurted out answer. You may think I was handling this very badly – and you'd be correct – but wait till you try it. I contend that the wittiest, most informed mind ever would gibber in the Presence. So what chance did I have? Anyway at least I hadn't fainted or vomited, both of which were ever distinct possibilities.

Chapter Ten

64 We were to feel the same initial excitement then longing for change in relation to "Down In The Flood" in 1995.

65 Matt Damsker Interview; September 15, 1978 at the Senatro Hotel, Augusta, Maine.

66 I knew it was too long since I had listened to tapes from this period!

67 A new interview with Dylan is published in *St. Louis Post-Dispatch*. By: Ellen Futterman, Post-Dispatch Entertainment Editor Date: 7th April 1994 Section: G1, 7

68 With the exception of The Supper Club performances – then again, they too were in an out-of-the-ordinary setting both physically and musically.

69 Q: Was playing at Woodstock a special moment?
A: Nah, it was just another show, really. We just blew in and blew out of there. You do wonder if you're coming across, because you feel so small on a stage like that. Edna Gundersen 5th May 1995 *USA Today*;

70 Showing yet again how much expectations affect the impression we get of a show.

Chapter Eleven

71 Excepting Dylan's guest appearance at The Band's New Year's Concert at the Academy Of Music (New York) Concert 31st December 1971

72 Actually, it extended beyond the spring, but it peaked here and in the UK where Glasgow, Manchester and Dublin especially had performances to die for.

73 These past glories being the reason he is still cheered to the rafters just for picking a harmonica up and putting it to his lips.

74 Down In The Flood/ Just Like Tom Thumb's Blues/ All Along The Watchtower/ What Good Am I ?/ Tombstone Blues/ Tears Of Rage (Dylan/Manuel)/ Mr. Tambourine Man/ Desolation Row/ To Ramona/ Highway 61 Revisited/ Jokerman/ Lenny Bruce/ Like A Rolling Stone/ It Ain't Me, Babe

75 Fort-Lauderdale, *Sun Sentinel* 29th September 1995
"A Midnight Chat With Bob Dylan" by John Dolen

Chapter Twelve

76 Partly as it had become so idiosyncratic that the non-Dylan items on it were more fun than the Dylan ones (it was that kind of year) and partly as the rise of the Internet seemed to make such telephone services pretty cumbersome and out-of-date.

77 *The Independent*, Section 2, Monday 1st July, 1996

78 I later found the following piece of information from the Dave Matthews Band Web Site:

"Boyd Tinsley: (violin, vocals) finds it strange sometimes that he abandoned the reserved precision of classical violin for the spontaneity of contemporary musical performance. 'This was an area I hadn't explored before,' says Tinsley, who has been playing popular music since 1985. 'When I'm really into the music, my whole body, my whole soul is into it.' In fact, one of his trademarks are his 'jams' with Dave Matthews. The best thing, though, he says, is how much it matters to the audience, and to the players. 'People are drawn to it,' he says. 'There's a passion here'."

79 There were two nights at the House of the Blues but I have only seen the video from one.

Chapter Fourteen

80 Not published until March 1999.

81 A self-styled football pundit in England.

Chapter Fifteen

82 "Two titans on tour Dylan and Simon mix and match" *USA Today*; Arlington; Apr 5, 1999; Edna Gundersen

83 "Two titans on tour Dylan and Simon mix and match" *USA Today*; Arlington; Apr 5, 1999; Edna Gundersen

Chapter Sixteen

84 Greil Marcus – *Invisible Republic* Henry Holt & Co., New York, 1997

85 Jon Pareles c. 1997 *N.Y. Times* News Service

86 *Der Spiegel* 16-10-1997.

87 *Guitar World* Interview, published March 1999

88 Jon Pareles c. 1997 *N.Y. Times* News Service

89 Interviewed by Kathryn Baker for *Associated Press*,1988

90 Jon Pareles c. 1997 *N.Y. Times* News Service

Thanks and Acknowledgements

Derek Barker, Clive Barrett, Olöf Björner, Sean Body, Jim Brady, David Bristow, Mark Carter, Dangerous Daniel, John Denley, Peter Doggett, Larry Eden (Lambchop), Stephan & Chris Fehlau, Robert & Elaine Forryan, Alan Fraser, Michael Gray, John Green, Jim Heppell, Clinton Heylin, Alex and Olive Hill, Duncan Hume, Jailhouse John, Raymond Landry, Rod MacBeath, Joe McShane, Olive Muir, Josh Nelson, Pia Parviainen, John Perry, Chris Ramsey, Stephen Scobie, Nigel Simms, Lucas Stensland, John Stokes, Manny & Philly Vardavas (you know why), Peter Vincent , Roy Whiteaker, Paul Williams, Ian Woodward, Keith Wooton, Andy Wright, The Cambridge Society, Freewheelers, Friends of Homer (you know who you are),Tracy & Mike.
Many thanks for comments on drafts to David Bristow, Robert Forryan, Clinton Heylin, and Peter Vincent .
Special thanks to Peter Vincent for proof-reading; all remaining grammatical infelicities must have been re-introduced at a later date by the author or the editor.

During the writing of this book two major studies of Dylan have appeared; one of his Art and the other of his life. *Song and Dance Man Vol III* by Michael Gray and *Behind The Shades: Take Two* by Clinton Heylin may not have directly impacted on the text herein, however the author is lucky enough to be in regular communication with both authors and, therefore, the indirect influence is likely to be extensive – as is the effect of their previous editions.
Paul Williams, not only for his ground-breaking studies of Dylan As Performing Artist; but also for e-mail conversations, interviews for *Homer, the slut* and the occasional visit, is another whose effect is obvious.

Mark Carter's cartoon history of Bob Dylan's life includes reminders of what fans were thinking at the time as the N.E.T. developed and he runs a comprehensive news cuttings service. This involves him collecting, collating and distributing stories about Dylan from the press around the world. Mark can be contacted at:

Mark Carter, 25 Marlborough Road, Norwich, Norfolk, NR3 4PH, UK

The Fiddler Now Upspoke (vols 1-5) by Desolation Row Promotions is an invaluable collection of Bob Dylan interviews, as is the internet archives of many newspapers, in particular, *USA Today* (http://www.usatoday.com/) and *LA Times* (http://www.latimes.com).

Official Dylan Site
http://www.bobdylan.com/

Tour info
http://www.execpc.com/~billp61/dates.html
http://www.users.wineasy.se/olof.bjorner/Chronologies.htm

General Dylan sites
http://www.expectingrain.com/
http://www.punkhart.com/dylan/dylan.html
http://www.edlis.org

Bob Links
http://www.execpc.com/~billp61/boblink.html

Current Dylan Fanzines

Dignity
Desolation Row Productions, 57 Tempsford,
Welwyn Garden City, Herts, AL7 2 PA

Isis
http://www.bobdylanisis.com/

On The Tracks
http://www.b-dylan.com/

The Bridge
http://users.powernet.co.uk/barrett/
The Bridge, PO Box 198, Gateshead, Tyne and Wear, NE10 8WE, England
Email: the.bridge@virgin.net

Freewheelin '
Freewheelin ', Woodstock,
St Ives Road, Hemingford Grey, Cambridgeshire PE28 9DX. United Kingdom
mace44@dial.pipex.com   http://www.freewheelinmagazine.com/

Dedicated Dylan Net Resources
As I work all day on computers I use Olof's Dylan Chronology pages at:
http://www.users.wineasy.se/olof.bjorner/Chronologies.htm

and a Dylan database program, "Dylanbase", details of which can be found at
http://www.keme.co.uk/~nye/dylanbase.htm#.

For a published reference to Dylan's touring records, I turn to Glen Dundas's
"Tangled Up In Tapes" (go to http://www.baynet.net/~gdundas/tuit/ for details)

Titles available from Helter Skelter Publishing

Helter Skelter have a wide range of music-related titles which are
all available by mail order from the world famous
Helter Skelter bookshop.

Either consult the websites below, or phone, fax or write (enclosing sae) to
Helter Skelter to request the latest catalogue.

You can phone or fax Helter Skelter on the following numbers:

Telephone: +44 (0)20 7836 1151 or Fax: +44 (0)20 7240 9880
Office hours: Mon-Fri 10:00am – 7:00pm, Sat: 10:00am – 6:00pm,
Sun: closed.

**Helter Skelter Bookshop,
4 Denmark Street,
London, WC2H 8LL,
United Kingdom.**

If you are in London come and visit us, and browse the titles in person!!

Email: helter@skelter.demon.co.uk

www.skelter.demon.co.uk

About the Author

Andrew Muir is a Dylan commentator of long standing and founder and editor of the celebrated and much missed fanzine, *Homer the slut*, of which Bob himself said, "This is eh, uh, really interesting…" He lives in Cambridge. This is his first book.

[